When We Arrive

When We Arrive

A New Literary History
of Mexican America

José F. Aranda Jr.

The University of Arizona Press   Tucson

The University of Arizona Press
© 2003 Arizona Board of Regents
All rights reserved
⊛ This book is printed on acid-free, archival-quality paper.
Manufactured in the United States of America
First Printing
08 07 06 05 04 03   6 5 4 3 2 1
Library of Congress Cataloging-in-Publication Data
Aranda, José F., 1961–
When we arrive : a new literary history of Mexican America /
José F. Aranda, Jr.
p. cm.
Includes bibliographical references and index.
ISBN 0–8165–2141–7 (acid-free paper)
1. American literature–Mexican American authors–History and
criticism. 2. Mexican Americans–Intellectual life. 3. Mexican
Americans in literature. I. Title.
PS153.M4 A73 2002
810.9′86872–dc21
2002006412
British Library Cataloguing-in-Publication Data
A catalogue record for this book is available from the British Library.

Para K. C. por todo

Contents

Foreword ix
Acknowledgments xi
Introduction xv

PART I
Foundational Histories: The Future of Chicano/a Literary Studies   1

1.   Making the Case for New Chicano/a Studies: *Recovering Our Alienated Selves*   3
     The Chicano/a Political Imaginary   8
     Chicano/a Marxism and the Foundations of Chicano/a Studies   13
     The Difference Mestizaje Makes   24
     The Future of Chicano/a Studies   36

2.   Literary Origins in an Age of Multiculturalism   43
     The Puritan Legacy of Self-Invention   48
     A Pledge of Literary Allegiance   51
     What's Puritan about Chicano/a Literature?   58
     Calls for Change in American Literary History: Two Views   62
     Opportunities for Comparative Approaches   70

PART II
Nuestra Literatura Americana: Toward an Integrated Literary History   81

3.   All Strangers in a Strange Land: *When Anglo and Mexican Histories Collide*   83

A Short Biography of María Amparo Ruiz de Burton   88

Questionable Differences: Mexicanos y Anglos in Baja California, 1848   98

Civil War and the Absence of Thanksgiving in *Who Would Have*
    Thought It?   107

Recognized at Last   117

4.   One Nation under New England: *Immigration, Citizenship, and*
     Representation   121

     Land of Dreams, Land of Nativism, 1880–1920   124

     Constructing the Ideal Immigrant Community, 1920–1940   131

     A Community of Scholars, Harvard 1946   134

     The Immigrant Dilemma: Mexican American Literature, 1900–1960   139

     Immigration and Xenophobia: María Cristina Mena (1893–1965)   145

     Greenhorn Immigrants and the Debunking of America: Daniel Venegas
         (Dates Unknown)   147

     Immigration and the Crisis of Identity: Américo Paredes (1915–1999)   150

     Immigration and the Pursuit of Civil Rights: Jovita González
         (1904–1987)   153

     The Fulfilled Immigrant: America, Land of Education: Luis Perez
         (1904–1962)   156

     Exodus and the Birth of the Pocho: José Antonio Villarreal (b. 1924)   158

5.   From Camelot to Barrio on a Hill: *Contemporary Chicano/a Literature and*
     the Puritan Crucible   161

     Common Ground on Different Borders: A Comparative Approach   167

     Cotton Mather and Pat Mora: The People of the New World   169

     Michael Wigglesworth and Lorna Dee Cervantes: Jeremiads Then and
         Now   178

     Edward Taylor and Gary Soto: Shaping Masculinity through
         Community   191

     Afterword   205

     Notes   207

     Bibliography   229

     Credits   247

     Index   249

Foreword

Tiofilio Duarte, the protagonist of Tony Diaz's first novel, *The Aztec Love God* (1998), begins his tale by admitting readers into his past. In those years, Tiofilio confides, he was "a young, good Brown man." That phrase has haunted me ever since I first came across it. I once asked Tony Diaz if the phrase had anything to do with Nathaniel Hawthorne's short story "Young Goodman Brown." But Tony shrugged off the question. I smiled. Tony is going to make it, I thought to myself.

Now as my own book has taken its final shape, I see myself in that phrase. When I was fourteen and in ninth grade, I was completely engrossed with Hawthorne. Raised a Catholic, I understood the moral dilemma of choosing not to be evil, since, I was taught, we are all born with sin. I understood that being the firstborn son of a Mexican immigrant family had its privileges, but, as a child, I lived in a time and place that made me feel very vulnerable. I wanted and needed a moral compass that would guide me around the confusions of my young life: the Bomb, Vietnam, assassinations, marches and riots, and the occasional gunshot in the night as my family and I huddled down to our middle-class dreams in the Houston barrio of Magnolia. I looked for direction wherever I could, and found one surprising, heroic example in Hester Prynne, another character created by Hawthorne. I wanted to make her story my own, to know how to become a young, good Brown man in a culture that consistently hailed me as immigrant but refused me a history.

Like Tiofilio Duarte, I have admitted you into my past so that you might be better able to navigate what is to come. While this study is a serious attempt to offer what I call an "integrated" narrative that begins to explain the literature and experiences of people of Mexican descent since 1848 in the United States, it is hardly complete. Instead, I try to put in motion, carefully and methodically, a dialogue between Chicano/a studies and American literary history that will clarify the interrelationships between Chicano/a literature and mainstream literary discourses. This is not a book that rehearses explicitly the origins of Chicano/a literature in indigenous, Spanish, and Mexican oral and literary traditions. There are plenty of studies that do so to their authors' credit and the benefit of Chicano/a studies. Rather, I have gone down the road less traveled toward Anglo America mainly because Mexican American writers since 1848 have done so in ample numbers. To follow their footsteps in the making of a new literature, I traverse the domains of many fields, from Chicano/a studies, Puritan studies, and American studies to Chicano/a history, New Western History, and immigration history. Those intellectual travels are visible in my detailed meditations on how best to integrate Chicano/a literature with mainstream writers in a single but complex and fluid narrative. For all of the above, I envision a diverse readership, with diverse needs and expectations.

I have written this book with the hope it might dignify the work of writers who are the subject of this study, and thereby honor the significance of the last one hundred and fifty years for all Mexican Americans and their allies. Because of its historical range, I conceived this book as a synthesis of a variety of materials, from novels and poetry to biography and history. My goal has been to bring together diverse materials, to provide a kind of sourcebook of historic figures, texts, and ideas normally found in a multitude of separate journals, periods, and fields. Lastly, I have tried, by my style, to create a different relationship between readers of literature, readers of history, readers of criticism, and students in the classroom. I fancifully imagined this book to move like an accordion in a *conjunto* band—you'll recognize the sound, acknowledge the beat, but something internal to the brassiness of the accordion encourages you to try your own variation. I say the more the merrier.

Acknowledgments

At a communal level this book has been in the making for decades. This is not the first literary history of Mexican American literature, nor will it be the last. It builds on the reality of Chicano/a criticism and history as well as the reality of countless writers of Mexican descent who committed themselves to leave a record of their thoughts and aspirations, their struggles and joys. Through all their efforts as writers, they have bequeathed a profound belief in literature and its transformative potential in the world. All this has been going on clearly since 1848. This book is therefore a study in gratitude.

Closer to home, this book owes its beginning and end to *familia*. My mother and father, Edelmira and José Francisco (Paco) Aranda, most certainly breathed into me life, spirit, and perseverance. Together they ushered me to the challenges of late–twentieth–century life in the United States, gave me the tools of education, and expected me to handle my future in the most ethical way possible. They have been in my corner rooting for me ever since I left home for school out East. They also gave me siblings, my brothers Jorge and Carlos, and adorable sister Laura. With them I learned to play and see the world through others' eyes, and they graciously suffered me as their big brother.

Closer still is the world Krista Comer and I have fashioned together. Krista has given me herself, her intellect, and her indomitable belief in this project. Her support and wisdom are found throughout this book. Our children, Benito and Jesse, are here too. Benito was only weeks old, sitting on my lap and gurgling his editorial advice, when I finished my dissertation. Jesse came later, teaching me the fine art of setting priorities between work and parenting.

Elsewhere enter my beautiful nieces Samantha and Sophia, my gorgeous nephew Quinn, my loving sisters–in–law, Corrine, Jeannie, Lee, Jamie, and Veronica, and brothers–in–law, Mike and David. Every boy should grow up to have a mother–in–law like Jean Houston Comer. No thanks comes close to fathoming the depth of my regard for her financial and personal support over the years. Jean, I always will owe you.

Like many Chicanos and Chicanas, my sense of family is large. I have been fortunate to learn, to travel, and to meet so many people who have played a role in my life. They are schoolmates, teachers, mentors, housemates, colleagues, readers, and just plain friends. They are here in no particular order: Joe Calvillo, Ernest Lizcano, Larry Perez, Armando Sanchez, John Del Campo, Ray Melchor, Johnny Lazo, Mrs. Franklin, Ms. Caesar, Sister Nicolás, Sister Jean, Pam Grier, Scott Vogel, Ray Purser, Pat Bell, Joe Pont, Mark Vitelli, David Golden, Alex Vargas, Father Smith, Father Schneider, Louis Swilley, Mr. Z, N. E. Venza, Dorothy Murphey, Mutlu Blasing, Walter Davis, Jim Egan, Lorraine Mazza, Mark Gaipa, John Lowney, Jim Kilfoyle, Greg Pingree, Randy Bass, Gail Solomon, Martha Cutter, Ashley Cross, Yuko Masukawa, Bernard Bruce, Sacvan Bercovitch, José Limón, José David Saldívar, Ramón Saldívar, María Gonzalez, Nicolás Kanellos, María Herrera-Sobek, Juan Bruce-Novoa, Cathy Davidson, Carla Mulford, John–Michael Rivera, Amelia de la Luz Montes, Jesse Alemán, Anne Goldman, and Andrea Tinnemeyer.

Shannon Leonard, my former student, has seen me through thick and thin with earlier drafts of this book. She has been a stalwart companion in helping me research, revise, edit, and photocopy the final product. *Mil gracias.* You're the best.

My editor, Patti Hartmann, her assistants, and the staff of the University of Arizona Press have been wonderful with me from start to finish. Truly, this book would not have been possible without their unflagging support. John Mulvihill, my copy editor, has been "a prince among princes."

Portions of chapters 1 and 3 have appeared as "Recovering Our Alienated Selves: Making the Case for New Chicano/a Studies," *Arizona Quarterly* 58, 1 (spring 2002); as "Contradictory Impulses: María Amparo Ruiz de Burton, Resistance Theory, and the Politics of Chicano/a Studies," *American Literature*, 70, 3 (September 1998); as "María Amparo Ruiz de Burton," in

Dictionary of Literary Biography: American Women Prose Writers, 1870–1920, vol. 221, ed. Sharon M. Harris (Detroit: Gale Group, 2000); and as "Questionable Differences: Mexicanos and Anglos in Baja California 1848," translated into Spanish for the journal *Historias,* ed. Antonio Saborit (Mexico, D.F., 2001).

Introduction

> Little by little the crickets ceased their chirping. It seemed as though they were becoming tired and the dawn gradually affirmed the presence of objects, ever so carefully and very slowly, so that no one would take notice of what was happening. And the people were becoming people. They began getting out of the trailer and they huddled around and commenced to talk about what they would do when they arrived.
>
> —Tomás Rivera,
> *... Y no se lo tragó la tierra/And the Earth Did Not Devour Him*

In Tomás Rivera's classic tale about Mexican American migrant workers of the 1940s and 1950s, the episode "When We Arrive" articulates the mythical and economic ground of Mexican American experience prior to the Chicano/a Movement.[1] "When We Arrive" unsettlingly dramatizes the movements of an ethnic people who inhabit familiar and unfamiliar landscapes in Thomas Jefferson's country of yeomen farmers. In streams of consciousness, Rivera tells the stories of a migrant community shaped by one hundred years of cultural displacement, neglect, discrimination, and loathing. And yet, the beauty of Rivera's narrative is that these people also shape themselves. Trapped as they are by economic dependency on migrant labor, individuals and families nevertheless see themselves as having a future. This future, as the bulk of *... Y no se lo tragó la tierra/And the Earth Did Not Devour Him* demonstrates, is not without its painful compromises, but it is full of promise, a promise that comes from a spirituality that Rivera would later identify as the basis for all migrant narratives in the Americas. *When We Arrive* forecasts a bright future for people of Mexican descent by first imagining a new literature. For through a new literature, readers might transcend a tragic past and reimagine their place in the Americas.[2]

This book takes its name from Rivera's short story in order to launch a renarration of American literary history as told from the vantage point of Chicano/a studies. I try to make sense of how a people so identified with twentieth-century migration to the United States are yet so far afield from the cultural, social, and political institutions that have enfranchised other immigrant groups. This paradoxical distance derives in part from the complicated roles played by origins myths in the evolution of both Chicano/a and Anglo American cultural and literary histories. This project thus historicizes a dialogue that began in the nineteenth century between Mexican American writers and Puritan culture and colonialism, and that continues within curriculums of American literature and history from kindergarten to graduate school. I emphasize the cultural privileging of Puritan history, its role in nation-building during the nineteenth century, its primacy in the formation of canonical American literary history at mid-twentieth century, and its persistent centrality to contemporary cultural life in the United States. Despite the discourse of multiculturalism, this privileged Puritan history is the guiding force and mechanism for every nationalist celebration from Thanksgiving to the country's symbolic reinvention every Fourth of July.

Donald Pease's reconceptualization of American studies as "postnational" is thoroughly present in this study, especially in reimagining key field imaginaries important to the analysis of Mexican American literature, whether they be Chicano/a studies, Early American studies, or that much larger script of what counts as American literature.[3] Even so, the critical aim of this book is not to deconstruct Anglo American Puritanism as much as it is to integrate Early American studies with Chicano/a studies. Only by revising the symbolic content of American literary history can one hope to present questions of authorship, canon formation, and nationalism within multiethnic, multihistorical contexts. With this type of revision, I seek to further José David Saldívar's argument (in *Border Matters*) to respatialize the field of American studies by way of a knowledge base that is Mexican and Mexican American, and acutely conscious of the significance of the U.S./Mexican border to American culture, history, and politics since 1848.

Like its namesake, Tomás Rivera's episode, my project imagines not a utopia for Chicano/a writers, but a better place in American literary history, and consequently a much different literary future. The American literary history conceptualized here recognizes that people of Mexican

descent are descendants of alternative but powerfully influential colonial narratives, namely Spanish and Mexican colonial histories, and that
these same people have a played a major role in shaping U.S. national
and literary discourses since 1848. If American literary history cannot
be accurately understood apart from its Mexican American influences,
by the same token, Chicano/a literary history cannot be fully understood if taken out of the context of *dominant* literary discourses. In the
end, this book aims for a more subtle understanding of "center" and
"margin." It avoids assiduously the romanticizing of mythologies that pit
the unjustly persecuted against the unholy persecutor but still adheres
to calls for social justice from storytellers rarely heard–whether the re-
ligiously tormented, like the sixteenth–century Puritans, or the racially
and politically oppressed, like illegal "aliens" targeted in California's
anti–immigrant Propositions 187 and 209 of the mid-1990s.

Despite the multiple, non–Anglo Saxon, colonial enterprises that
also laid claim on the North American continent from the 1500s on, the
field of Early American literature has been consistently constructed to
promote a singular cultural vision of United States history and literature.
Viewing early American literature as the foundation of a national literary history, scholars of the period have directed the politics and shaped
the aesthetic values that have defined American literature in the twentieth century. Of course, the field's promotion of a national literature
based on a New England past has not gone uncritiqued or unrevised by
women and/or people of color in the twentieth century. But what has
gone unnoticed are the diverse and dynamic interactions of ethnic writers with a Puritan past–especially the deployment of alternative colonial
histories by ethnic writers, one strategy for dealing with an origins myth
that profoundly excludes ethnic cultural production.

This study explores the influence of a nationalized Puritan ethos
on nineteenth- and twentieth–century writers of Mexican descent–
particularly upon constructions of ethnic identity and aesthetic values. I
frame the rise of Chicano/a literature within a larger institutional history, produced during the 1930s, 1940s, and 1950s, that conflates a Puritan myth of origins with a literary history in which American literature
is heralded as the product and producer of social and political dissent.
The canon debates of the 1960s revive this discussion, not invent it,
although debate is now waged over precisely which traditions of dissent
will best represent the nation as a whole. One of the many positive

results of the so-called culture wars has been the recovery not only of forgotten authors and texts but lost literary histories. Unfortunately, an incomplete understanding of the discourse of literary origins persists. Attempts to rewrite national literary history have often lagged behind specific revisions of the canon by scholars of ethnic literature and/or feminists. Questions of canonicity continue to plague educators, scholars, and students because of inadequate attention to the relationship between a Puritan past and "other" national identities.

Among literary historians of the 1930s, New England assumed its canonical stature because it was already the beneficiary of a nineteenth-century discourse that converted Puritan theocracy and history into the global, economic mandate known as Manifest Destiny.[4] In turn, twentieth-century scholars read in the Puritan past a blueprint for a national future, and they constructed their literary histories from what they saw as an enduring Puritan influence upon United States culture and history.[5] As the Great Depression hit and fascism in Europe unfolded, American writers of the colonial period and the nineteenth century gained a new preeminence among scholars as scholars merged modernist values with contemporary political resolve. F. O. Matthiessen's *American Renaissance* solidified the alignment of American writers with political rebellion, and did so through a more socialist definition of democratic values. The canon that emerged after World War II portrayed American writers as champions of literary, social, and political progressivism.

By the 1970s, it was clear that the canon had emphasized a tradition of dissent in American letters that nevertheless left many women and minority writers unrepresented. For Chicanos/as, the explosion of protest poetry in the late 1960s announced a separatist aesthetic politic, in spite of the fact that the protest aesthetic was itself influenced by the dissent tradition of the mainstream canon. As Chicano/a scholars fashioned a literary history faithful to a broad Chicano/a social politic, they made aesthetic choices that represented what I see as a "double conflict" in their resistance to the mainstream canon. They had to walk the line between claiming Chicano/a authors as either Mexican descendants or American writers, and never both without some awkwardness. Precisely because so many aimed to be cultural nationalists, they had to carve out an alternative to the Anglo Puritan model of citizenry in order to recover a historically marginalized identity in the Southwest. Yet, this identity also had to function within the models of political and literary resistance intelligible in United States history, or risk further political erasure as "foreign."

Mindful of the mainstream canon, Chicano/a writers and scholars developed a literary history that seemed to mirror the social realities of people of Mexican descent living in the United States. Because this literary history required a special narrative to compete with the Puritan model of individual and communal identity, Aztlán was resurrected as the mythical homeland of Chicanos/as. Paradoxically, while Chicano/a writers and scholars constructed a non–Puritan myth of origins, they simultaneously enacted categories of national identification that invariably reproduced the Puritan ethos of writing oneself and/or one's community into American history. That is, they substituted Aztlán for New England. For Chicano/a writers, this paradox was/is the crux of their binational identity.

In "Letting Go Our Grand Obsessions: Notes Towards a New Literary History of the American Frontiers," Annette Kolodny makes clear that "theories of continuity" that dominate literary history make it impossible to offer alternative histories of origins. In other words, the insistence upon one origin myth, the Puritan myth, frustrates and embattles the presentation of "other" literary histories that also have origins in America.[6] Today, Early Americanists, who have a long tradition of embracing contemporary politics and cultural issues, must again reexamine their field's relationship to the canon, and thereby help expand our knowledge of alternative literary origins. Similarly, Chicano/a scholars must move beyond the boundaries of a separatist literary history and locate Chicano/a literature within the broader discursive history that has often produced competing literary nationalisms and the cultural values that privileged publicly some narratives (even if politically dissenting) as symbolically meaningful to the nation–state, while relegating other narratives to the margins of denationalized history.

Using one method of complicating both theories of continuity and resistance, this study joins the efforts of Paul Lauter and others in advocating a comparative approach to American literature.[7] Such an approach will help bring Early American literature into a sorely needed conversation with current theories on ethnic literature. Just as importantly, it will encourage students to study Puritan writings, and their attending scholarship, as one means of understanding contemporary ethnic writers and the postmodern moment in general. Betsy Erkkila writes:

I would like, that is, to call for a reconceptualization of American literary and cultural studies as a field of comparative studies—a radically comparative field of cultural encounter, dialogue, and exchange in which American literature(s) and culture(s) would be studied not only, as in the traditional model of comparative literature, in relation to European continental literature but also in relation to the multiple and different cultures that have constituted the history and literary history of the Americas—North as well as South, Mexican as well as Caribbean. (564)[8]

Thus, the goal is not to reify Puritan myth and history over all literary history, but to understand the effects of a New England legacy on ethnic writers, and the effects of ethnic writers on the New England legacy. This goal fosters a more culturally and racially integrated national literature, no longer ordered by a single literary history.

More broadly, this study responds to two anxieties that have emerged from the New American Studies. The first resulted from one of the surprising consequences of the multicultural debates of the 1980s: an unprecedented desire and enthusiasm by commercial presses, mainstream readers, in addition to academics, to publish and read works by minorities. An unanticipated outcome of this phenomenon has been an anxiety in academic circles over what *should be* the relationship between mainstream literary figures and the newly emerging writers from the colonial period to present.[9] One response—which I wholeheartedly support—has been to institute a comparative approach both to literary history and criticism. Paul Lauter has argued that the nineteenth century is replete with examples of how to devise a comparative literary history for Anglo and African American writers of the same nationalist moment. This comparative history would also simultaneously take into account divergent aesthetic creations that mark their social differences (be those race, citizenship, class, or cultural iconography). Thus, when reading Harriet Beecher Stowe's *Uncle Tom's Cabin*, one should be able to contextualize the novel, not only within Garrisonian abolitionism or the "Feminine Fifties," but also as in dialogue with slave narratives like those by Frederick Douglass and Harriet Jacobs.

While this comparative approach is gaining ground within American studies, a "resistance theory" paradigm whose legitimacy was earned in the 1980s nonetheless holds steadfast in ethnic studies. Herein lies the second anxiety, since at a fundamental level a resistance theory paradigm is incompatible with a comparative approach. Resistance theory was strengthened, in fact, by the sweeping canonization of certain contemporary writers whose works challenged the racist, heterosexist, and other hegemonic foundations of U.S. society. It was in the 1980s that Alice Walker, Toni Morrison, Gloria Anzaldúa, Audre Lorde, and so many others became new academic touchstones for critical practice and social critique. Their broad appeal to critics and students encouraged the republication of earlier writers such as Zora Neale Hurston, Zitkala-Ša, and Américo Paredes. However, in implicit opposition to emerging comparative and more integrated critical approaches, ethnic scholars have generally proceeded by a more separatist critical philosophy, arguing for the need to develop literary histories that are more focused on, and sensitive to, minority issues.

However understandable, the effort to historicize literary works completely ignored and repressed by mainstream critics of the twentieth century has sometimes come at the expense of producing histories for ethnic communities that falsely separate them from the mainstream populace, reproducing in fact the very same asymmetrical power relations that are routinely denounced in calls to reform the American literary canon. That is, the tendency of resistance theory to presuppose a monolithic white national hegemony has had a totalizing effect on the field such that resistance critics have had a hard time with writers or texts that do not categorically "resist" the hegemonic influence of Anglo America. Such writers are recovered rather astonishingly as rebels or "subalterns" in spite of politics that suggest otherwise, or are typically identified as assimilationists, or worse, behind hushed whispers, as "sellouts." These individuals are perceived as having internalized their minority status so completely that they serve as vehicles for disciplining members of their own community.

Because of its acknowledged importance to the field's founding premises, resistance theory has created anxiety among some Chicano/a critics—myself included—about the future of Chicano/a literary studies.[10] Ironically, this anxiety is being fueled by the popularity of minority texts that worry mainstream critics to "do the right thing." For Chicano/a critics, the success of writers like Sandra Cisneros and Gary Soto with mainstream audiences has opened up the field to non–Chicano/a critics, who identify Sandra Cisneros and Gary Soto not only as Chicanos/as but as

American writers. While this might seem like cause to ring the victory bell, the crossover of Chicano/a writers to publishers such as Random House, Knopf, and Simon and Schuster has troubling implications for critics whose political philosophy was born in the fields of Cesar Chávez's boycotts of California grapes and sharpened against the police brutality of the 1970 National Chicano Moratorium. These critics have not strayed very far from their original political roots. For them, Chicano/a cultural identity has long depended on working-class experience to derive community narratives. For them, the label and reality of being "outsiders" to institutions of education and power fueled the need to create viable, alternative cultures of being.

For other Chicano/a critics, especially those coming of age politically since 1980, the mainstream acceptance of old and new U.S. writers of Mexican descent signals a time of reckoning the past with the present. The current cultural moment that finds value in being Hispanic–from Edward James Olmos to Salma Hayek, from Henry Cisneros to George P. Bush the Mexican American–requires an understanding of political gains and losses in terms that include, but are not exclusively reliant upon, 1960s and 1970s radical and civil rights politics. Indeed, the reckoning has been under way for quite some time, but never so much in need of articulation since the 2000 Census Report confirmed that Latinos/as will become the single largest U.S. minority group by the year 2010. Within this category, people of Mexican descent will constitute the majority. Further, in some regions of the Southwest and West, people of Mexican descent will represent, certainly by the end of the decade, the majority of eligible voters in local and national elections. How to make sense of all these changes is vastly important.

While this book purposely begins and ends with the nation-state that is the United States from 1848 to 1998, I nevertheless mean to reconstitute the field imaginary of American literature, and therein recast the literary history of Mexican America beyond a portrayal of Mexican Americans as primarily the subordinated objects and subjects of Manifest Destiny and toward a more complicated account of their agency and presence in the national symbolic. The chapters in this book are therefore divided into two major parts. Part I, "Foundational Histories: The Future of Chicano/a Literary Studies," develops two histories, Chicano/a and Early American studies respectively, as the basis for establishing a literary history of Mexican American literature since 1848. Further, these histories frame how a comparative study of Mexican American and U.S. canonical writers might envision a more integrated American literary history. Part II, "Nuestra Literatura Americana: Toward an Integrated Literary History," lays out three general categories of identification that serve to locate Mexican American literature within history, culture, and politics. These categories of identification are taken up one by one in chapters 3–5, and consist of (1) writings that exhibit competing colonialisms at work; (2) texts that engage with the supposition that the Puritans were reinvented as the ideal model of immigration to the United States in the early twentieth century; and (3) literature that is reflective of a literary binationalism.

Although each category is developed with a specific historical context in mind, in no way are these categories absolute with regard to periodization. The fact that these categories might overlap transhistorically is actually indicative of their primary value as foci of study. For example, evidence that Mexican American literature embodies a cultural memory of a prior colonial status as either Spanish or Mexican, or both, can be found readily in much Mexican American writing, but the most expressive period for this embodiment was from 1848 to 1900. Similarly, while immigration has been a constant in Mexican American experience and culture since 1848, its overall reflection in literature as an organizing principle of aesthetic, political, and economic issues is overwhelmingly present from roughly 1900 to 1960. The period beginning with the Civil Rights Movement, right through the founding of Chicano/a studies, represents the contemporary period when an effective counternationalism also politicized the long-term history of Mexican Americans in the United States. The consequences of a dual nationalist literary heritage are quite clearly in the minds of writers of this period, more so symbolically and rhetorically than in any previous period. Taken as a whole, this conceptual framework, I argue, suggests that current Mexican American literature, and criticism too, has been on the verge of a new imaginative horizon for well over a decade.

The gap between the two parts of the title of chapter 1, "Making the Case for the New Chicano/a Studies: Recovering Our Alienated Selves," is emblematic of our current cultural moment. "Recovering Our Alienated Selves" refers to the institutional agenda that has been Chicano/a studies' mission since the Chicano Movement. To put it succinctly, Chicano/a studies has been in the business of recovering the ruptured, alienated culture and history of people of Mexican descent since the Treaty of Guadalupe Hidalgo in 1848. In short, Chicano/a studies has chronicled and analyzed the legacy of racism and discrimination that this minority group has endured as U.S. citizens. This agenda is not at issue in this chapter. Indeed, this chapter weighs in on the recovery of the alienated selves of Chicanos and Chicanas with urgency. What I argue in this chapter is that the dominant character of Chicano/a studies, in relationship to its mission, has dramatically evolved over the last twenty–five years, hence "Making the Case for New Chicano/a Studies." The current praxis of this field focuses on aspects of alienation–cultural, historical, political, and so on–that would have been unimaginable in the past. In general, Chicano/a studies is still activist but antiromantic, historical but antiprogressive, communitarian but transnational.

This chapter firmly acknowledges and supports the ethnic studies imperative to write previously silenced histories of culture and literature. It also recognizes the limitations of Chicano/a studies, especially when it relies on a myth of origins that narrowly frames Mexican descendants in the United States as the ideal inheritors of Aztlán but also as the colonized subjects of Anglo "manifest destiny" and racism. Chicano/a studies' dependence on erecting a myth of origins that is a righteous counterweight to Anglo society will invariably ignore or discount writers and histories that portray Spanish and Mexican people as colonizers, imperialists, and elitists. It will do so in order to protect its own self–image in a political arena that still seeks to scapegoat people of color and the poor for the social ills of the United States. This chapter encourages Chicano/a studies to be more tolerant of an "un–usable past" and simultaneously make a finer distinction between scholarship with a political cause in mind and scholarship with a social conscience. Although the distinction may be small, the latter is less likely to produce an untenable orthodoxy of ideas that forecloses scholarship.

On the other hand, efforts to revise the U.S. literary canon are far from complete. Reformulating the canon to reflect the historic presence of minority writers continues to be priority. Chapter 2, "Literary Origins in an Age of Multiculturalism," proposes a broad integration of both canonical and noncanonical figures in American literature. This chapter notes that the dominant trend of twentieth–century American literary criticism identifies American literary history with a Puritan past. In Puritan writings, early scholars found the origins of American literature.

Nevertheless, a Puritan myth of origins has also been used to misrepresent the nature of competing colonial histories in North America and to ignore relationships of non–Anglo Puritans to this same myth of origins. How, I thus ask, did that Puritan myth of origins affect Chicano/a literature and criticism in the twentieth century? Fifty years after its consolidation during World War II, its nuancing during the Cold War, and its critique in the cultural protests of the 1960s, how are we to make sense of Chicano/a literature's alternative origin myth of Aztlán? What role does a search for literary origins play in the constructions of canons, counter-canons, and literary nationalisms? These questions are important because discourses involving literary origins have periodically shaped critical discussions of literary history, aesthetic criteria, canon formation, and national politics in this century. Reliance on a Puritan past will continue to frustrate efforts to revise the canon. This chapter argues how an alternative colonial history, literature, and culture might inform an interpretation of canonical Puritan writings and an assessment of American literary history in general.

Chapter 3, "All Strangers in a Strange Land: When Anglo and Mexican Histories Collide," takes up directly the general impact of competing colonial histories on the literature and experiences of people of Mexican descent in the nineteenth century. The chapter deals primarily with the life and writings of María Amparo Ruiz de Burton, and in particular her first novel, *Who Would Have Thought It?* (1872). Though she was not representative of the "100,000" or so Mexicans who became part of the United States in 1848, Ruiz de Burton's life and writings do reveal the general complexities of her times. By 1872, the Mexican–American War may have been long over, but a war continued between the cultural memories and values of two distinct colonial enterprises: one Spanish Mexican and the other Anglo Puritan. Refusing to articulate clear ideological positions against the U.S. government, Ruiz de Burton's novels evidence instead a spectrum of political judgments that run the gamut from celebrating a Spanish Mexican colonial past, to a condemnation of U.S. ethnocentrism and imperialism, to the supposition that Mexico always exists culturally, if not always conditionally in the national sense, for elite Mexicans like Ruiz de Burton herself. In the end, Ruiz de Burton's "imagined community" remains, for better or worse, north of the Rio Grande.

Chapter 4, "One Nation under New England: Immigration, Citizenship, and Representation," proposes that we study the issue of literary origins in American literature as problematic, and not as an ongoing self–evident discourse. If we treat literary origins as one of the most important issues that writers and critics have faced in the twentieth century, we can begin to unfold a relationship between this issue and the creation of various literary nationalisms. To do this, we need to historicize the construction of a Puritan myth of origins as a "usable past" for literary studies. I go against the grain and ask why the ascendancy of Puritan studies in academic circles occurred at precisely the same historical moment as the cultural and political growth of the Mexican American community. Or to put it more unconventionally, can Chicano/a studies today explain why the ascendancy of Puritan studies paralleled the cultural and political growth of the Mexican American community in roughly the same period? I believe it can, and in an area of study in which the field commands unquestionable expertise: immigration. This chapter thus sets up the historical context by which the New England Puritans became this country's ideal "immigrant community," and how in turn this construction had the effect of distancing Mexican Americans from their own ethnic culture and history. An extended review of literature written and published between 1900 and 1960 demonstrates how Mexican American writers drew upon a variety of strategies for dealing with the effects of Anglo Puritan discourses that unjustly demonized Mexican immigrants for both wanting and failing to uphold the American Dream.

Chapter 5, "From Camelot to Barrio on a Hill: Contemporary Chicano/a Literature and the Puritan Crucible," demonstrates how a comparison of Chicano/a literature with early American works that became part of the canon in the twentieth century reveals the extent to which mainstream models of literary "dissent" were internalized and redeployed by Chicano/a writers to reflect a non–Anglo ethnic history. This was especially true during the initial phases of the Chicano Movement when the myth of Aztlán served not only as the foundation for a new literary and cultural nationalism, but as the rhetorical basis from which to challenge Anglo social, educational, and political institutions. While Chicano/a writers and critics of this period drew from the perceived differences of their communities to middle–class America, they nevertheless proceeded on paradigms that had evolved over the previous sixty years. Indeed, as a field, Chicano/a literature often mirrors not only alternative traditions, as in African American literature, but also the subversiveness of many canonical writers, from Walt Whitman to Ernest Hemingway, that came to be identified within the purview of American studies. A comparative analysis is thus used throughout the chapter to theorize the binational character of Chicano/a literature.

The bulk of the chapter establishes a methodology and critical language that enables the comparison of contemporary Chicano/a authors with Puritan writers from seventeenth-century colonial New England. Although differently expressed, each reading sets out to intervene on the singularity of an Anglo Puritan hegemony in history. In short, this chapter makes sense of a canon that now stretches, for example, from Anne Bradstreet to Sandra Cisneros and does so without sacrificing history and "difference." Our ability to read Chicano/a and Puritan writers together continues the work of deconstructing the basic literary tenets of the post-1945 canon. In seeking to establish more concretely the binational character of Chicano/a writing, this chapter dovetails with the rest of the book in calling for an integrated literary history that is simultaneously multiethnic, multiracial, and multicolonial.

When We Arrive owes its genesis and political motivation in large part to the growing national debate on curricular changes with a multicultural emphasis. Multiculturalism, as a social and academic discourse, provides a platform—albeit confusing because it is so co-optable by conservative forces—by which to reexamine the relationships between subfields of American literature and the larger issue of canon formation. I believe that it is possible to attend to a history of marginality and liminality within hegemonic discourses without sacrificing the histories of counterhegemonic struggles. These histories, I argue, have shaped Chicano/a literature as both minority literature and American literature. Contemporary Chicano/a writers, like their nineteenth-century predecessors, must constantly negotiate their embodiment of a dual national experience. This experience is characterized by a pre-Columbian and Spanish Mexican past, conditioned by a shared history as oppressed subjects in the United States, and finally thoroughly grounded in the discourses that celebrate the United States and "Americans" as immigrant champions of democracy and defenders of pluralism. The challenge of these writers, and our challenge as readers, is to appreciate the complexities of traversing nationalist borders while simultaneously enlarging our notions of what counts as U.S. literary history and culture.

PART I

Foundational Histories

The Future of Chicano/a Literary Studies

CHAPTER ONE

Making the Case for
New Chicano/a Studies

Recovering Our Alienated Selves

I begin with a murder, a fictional one portrayed in Lucha Corpi's 1992 detective novel, *Eulogy for a Brown Angel.* Why a murder? Because Corpi, in narrating her protagonist's search for the killer of four–year–old Michael David Cisneros, also constructs an unusual story about the Chicano/a Movement at its height. It is a story that encourages readers to return to the heady activist days of the 1960s in order to usher in a different con-sciousness for the 1990s. The symbolic backdrop for this murder mystery is the National Chicano Moratorium of August 29, 1970, held in Laguna Park, East Los Angeles. As Chicano historian Edward J. Escobar has shown, on the day that twenty or thirty thousand people mounted the single largest peaceful demonstration by a community of Mexican de-scent, the Los Angeles Police Department put into action a plan they hoped would turn public opinion against the Chicano/a Movement.[1] In the resulting mayhem of police brutality, tear gas, and illegal arrests, Laguna Park was emptied of its peaceful protesters. Men, women, and children were indiscriminately chased down and terrorized into submis-sion. What had begun as a protest against the Vietnam War and the sus-piciously high casualty rates among Mexican American soldiers ended in the deaths of three people—*Los Angeles Times* journalist and activist Rubén Salazar being the most prominent. Dozens of others were incarcerated and paraded in front of the media as society's worst enemies.

The violence committed by the Los Angeles Police Department on August 29 enshrines this moment as an archetypal event in Chicano/a history because it marks society's intolerance for Mexican Americans who protest national policies. Lucha Corpi's novel explores the ambiguities of social dissent in a liberal democracy by putting into motion a murder mystery where all the major characters are Mexican Americans, some more deracinated than others, some more powerful than others, and some darker than others. Corpi's revisionist story of the Chicano/a Movement is important for the differences it shows existing within the Mexican American community back then, differences that widen because of class and race issues affecting the nation during the 1980s, and finally differences that become the crux of the social alienation faced by legal and illegal Mexican people in the 1990s.

In the end, the child's murder in Corpi's novel is a reflection of the racism and violence committed en masse in Laguna Park in 1970, and of the economic war waged during the Reagan/Bush administrations in the 1980s and early 1990s. Significantly, the murderer is not some sniper in the bushes, but rather the culture at large, including Mexican Americans, who support or nurture the gaps and rifts between rich and poor, white and dark, citizen and alien. Corpi's murder mystery is thus a reminder that while the Chicano/a Movement provides hopeful archives for historians and writers, its stories wait to be fully told, fully disclosed. What lurks in the ethnic closet are the skeletons of a communal psyche badly in need of healing and direction, even if we must sometimes turn out our own *raza* in the process. The examination that follows offers itself as medicinal and spiritual food for thought, at attempt at mediating the movement of the past with the challenges of today. Indeed, in order to embark on any new literary history of Mexican American literature, it is vital to understand how the current institutional moment frames this study.

Chicano/a studies is, and has been, moving in directions that are decidedly at odds with its origins in the Chicano/a Movement. While much of Chicano/a studies' ethical, political, and philosophical base remains the same—attention to the historic consequences of Mexican Americans' minority status within the United States—recent scholarship in history and literature has nevertheless opened the field to questions that challenge its institutional foundations. Today, the field is dominated by the cultural politics made famous by Gloria Anzaldúa's trope of "borderlands." Although many of the ideas discussed in this essay share basic premises with borderlands studies, it will also become clear that I apply and extend the borderlands concept without reservations about where the research may lead and what political conclusions it may suggest. If Chicano/a studies since the late 1960s has unmasked the questions that kept a historic ethnic community marginal, New Chicano/a Studies advocates revealing the history of this community on its own complicated internal terms, not simply terms that suggest an oppositional relationship to Anglo America.

New Chicano/a Studies imagines a dialogue between scholars about how we might historicize and theorize what is difficult to accept about Chicano/a culture and history: namely, that Chicanos/as are the descendants of colonizers, as well as the colonized; that historically mestizos experienced a more preferable legal status than Native Americans, both in Mexico and the United States; that the nineteenth century is replete with Mexicanos who initially welcomed the Anglo invasion; that Nuevo Mexicanos rode alongside Theodore Roosevelt up San Juan Hill; that "whiteness" matters in Mexican and Chicano/a societies; that patriarchy, sexism, and homophobia are all daily facts of life in Chicano/a communities, past and present; that NAFTA enjoys considerable political support among Mexicanos/as and Chicanos/as all along the U.S./Mexico border; and, finally, that for many Mexican Americans coming of age since the mid–1980s, being identified as Chicano or Chicana has lost its magic.

By making the case for New Chicano/a Studies, I do not mean to suggest "new" as of today, now, with me as the primary spokesperson. But rather "new" as of the last ten years and based on the critical work of people such as Norma Alarcón, Angie Chabram–Dernersesian, Rosa Linda Fregoso, Chela Sandoval, Rosaura Sánchez, José Limón, Ramón Gutiérrez, David Gutiérrez, Antonia Castañeda, Ramón Saldívar, José David Saldívar, Renato Rosaldo, Carl Gutiérrez–Jones, Martha Menchaca, Patricia Zavella, David Montejano, Emma Pérez, Genaro Padilla, and Nicolás Kanellos. Indeed, my argument for renaming ourselves institutionally takes its intellectual and philosophical lead from the many Chicana feminists who have renovated and continue to renovate the field. The collection of essays entitled *Building with Our Hands: New Directions in Chicana Studies* (1993) is only one of many instances where the leadership of Chicana scholars has opened a virtual bonanza for the field as a whole.[2] This chapter fully recognizes the meaning and significance of their efforts to my own.

While I am opposed to fetishizing generational differences, ideological splits, or disciplinary divides as a way to make my case, I do claim that a historic change has occurred within the material culture of people of Mexican descent in the United States. But, I would hope to avoid the kind of misunderstanding that followed Donald Pease's invocation of New American Studies, or Patricia Limerick's naming of a New Western History.[3] My goal is not to unleash an unhealthy and self-destructive intensification of the divisions within our field. And yet, every field, mainstream or otherwise, has divisions. Why should Chicano/a studies be any different? The point of this essay is to offer instead a meaningful narration of the divisions that have occurred within Chicano/a studies since the 1970s, divisions that have now come to a critical head, and significantly so since the 150th anniversary of the Treaty of Guadalupe Hidalgo. I make the case for New Chicano/a Studies not as a way to mend fences and say to the world "all is fine" with Chicano/a studies, nor to "hang out our dirty laundry," but rather to persuade us all to take full advantage of our differences in order to narrate more effectively the world that greets us every morning.

"Making the Case for New Chicano/a Studies" is thus a recognition of how far the field has traveled by its ventures into gender studies, queer theory, and analyses of the new global economy. It is also a call for a new lexicon better equipped to deal with a postmodern Mexican American culture, one that exports pop stars, like Selena, to Mexico, commands the attention of Madison Avenue advertising executives, and celebrates the national status of politicians like Henry Cisneros. Despite this mainstreaming of Mexican American culture, ours is a community that suffers from a widening gap between the rich and the poor, between the long settled and the recently arrived, and between an increasingly visible intellectual elite and a growing underclass of poorly educated Chicano/a youth. A change in nomenclature is also required in order to explain why significant numbers of Mexican Americans are increasingly voting in favor of conservative measures like California's Propositions 187 and 209. All these aspects signal Mexican Americans' political departure from the ideals guiding the Chicano/a Movement.

Although I argue that the field imaginary of Chicano/a studies is no longer what was imagined during the 1970s, I do not mean to give an extraordinary sense of unity to either the Chicano/a Movement or the founding of Chicano/a studies. I agree with Juan Bruce-Novoa and the late Lora Romero that it is erroneous to think of the Chicano/a Movement as homogenous, harmonious, free of internal dissent and debate.[4] There is nothing to be gained by reifying some reductive unified representation of the Chicano/a Movement only to then deconstruct it. Nevertheless, what seems historically clear is that the activists within the various parts of the movement succeeded, through gestures toward unified community, in constructing a potent symbolic and rhetorical narrative that argued for the civil rights of Mexican Americans during the 1960s and 1970s. No amount of conservative backlash during the 1980s and 1990s can undermine the history of the Viva Kennedy Clubs, the Delano grape strikes, La Raza Unida Party, or even the protesting of the harmful effects of advertisements like the "Frito Bandito" on children of Mexican descent. Without a doubt, the Chicano/a Movement made historic gains. Chicano/a studies exists today precisely because activists produced a narrative of unified ethnic community, a narrative forged amid a great diversity of opinion, immigration history, class status, regional loyalties, linguistic traits, educational backgrounds, ethnic ties, and local struggles.

Nevertheless, Homi Bhabha's insight into how "the claim to be representative provokes a crisis within the process of signification and discursive address" aptly describes the dilemma that 1960s Chicano/a leaders encountered in their attempts to forge a counterhegemonic, nationalist movement.[5] From iconography, like images of the Virgen de Guadalupe to contest the hypocrisy of the Statue of Liberty, to manifestos, like "El Plan Espiritual de Aztlán" to shame believers of the U.S. Constitution, to scholarship, like Rodolfo Acuña's classic *Occupied America*, which made visible the lie that Mexican Americans had no history, Chicano/a activists, scholars, mothers, fathers, teenagers, Vietnam veterans, and *los mas abajo*—the pachucos, *cholos*, and inmates of the judicial system—all had to concede, mask, disguise, and erase the differences that existed historically among Mexican American populations from Houston to Los Angeles, from Chicago to Brownsville, and, even more importantly, differences *con el otro lado*, Mexico. Thus, *la raza*—people who were not previously a racially politicized community—came into being to facilitate and lay claim to that larger historical event known as the Civil Rights Movement.

The Chicano/a Political Imaginary

To revisit the Chicano/a Movement, let us immerse ourselves in the rhetorical record of la raza. I go to Luis Valdez, not only because he was there at the beginning, as a Cesar Chávez supporter and founder of El Teatro Campesino, but because his artistic biography stretches from writing socialist plays such as *Bernabé* to directing Hollywood films such as *La Bamba* and *The Cisco Kid*. His biography thus provides a metanarrative that charts the evolution of Chicano/a studies. For now, let's consider Luis Valdez as he writes on behalf of the Chicano/a community in 1972:

> It is the task of all literature to present illuminating images of mankind. This, as most writers are surely aware, is not easy to do. It takes the clearest, most unassuming effort on the part of the poet to speak for Man. This effort is very often confused and frustrated when the writer is a victim of racism and colonization.
> . . .
> Man has been in the Americas for more than 38,000 years. White men have been around for less than five hundred. It is presumptuous, even dangerous, for anyone to pretend that the Chicano, the "Mexican–American," is only one more in the long line of hyphenated–immigrants to the New World. *We are the New World. . . .*
> We are, to begin with, Mestizos—a powerful blend of Indigenous America with European–Arabian Spain, usually recognizable for the natural bronze tone it lends to human skin. Having no specific race of our own, we used poetry and labeled ourselves centuries ago as La Raza, the Race, albeit a race of half–breeds, misfits, and mongrels. Centuries of interbreeding further obfuscated our lineage, and La Raza gave itself other labels—*la plebe, el vulgo, la palomía.* Such is the natural poetry of our people. One thing, however, was never obscured: that the Raza was basically Indio, for that was borne out by our acts rather than mere words, beginning with the act of birth.[6]

There's much to admire in Valdez's bold, denunciatory, inflammatory language, its courageous understanding of racism and the dominance of Western culture in the Americas. This is after all the early 1970s. The

Vietnam War rages, taking on new victims in Cambodia. At home, as I have noted, the National Chicano Moratorium of August 29, 1970, ends tragically. Elsewhere, supporters of civil rights for people of color, women, gays, and lesbians continue their protests against an oppressive society. Meanwhile in Washington, the Watergate Hotel soon reveals the depths to which some powerful men plunge in the name of more power.

And yet, thirty years later, we must also admit to ourselves that latent in Valdez's shared language with thousands of Chicano/a activists and scholars was the deployment of a homogenized Mexican American nation, underwritten by notions of a unified Chicano/a cultural identity. In analyzing the Chicano/a Movement, Rosa Linda Fregoso and Angie Chabram write:

> Chicano identity was a static, fixed, and one-dimensional formulation. It failed to acknowledge our historical differences in addition to the multiplicity of our cultural identities as a people. This representation of cultural identity postulated the notion of a transcendental Chicano subject at the same time it proposed that cultural identity existed outside of time and that it was unaffected by changing historical processes. The notion of cultural relations that this concept of cultural identity subscribed to appealed to a cultural formulation composed of binaries: Anglos vs. Chicanos. But more importantly, what this mimetic notion of representation obfuscated was the fact that the naming of cultural identity was not the same thing as cultural identity.[7]

Bhabha's notion of a crisis of representation and Fregoso's and Chabram's suggestion of an obfuscation are dramatically illustrated by Valdez's gendered language about the universalist "Man." Recall, too, Valdez's claim that Chicanos/as can unproblematically embrace the statement "We are the New World." In combination, these statements, while aiming toward political dissent, nevertheless reinvent Rousseau's "noble savage." Compared to the Anglo, the indigenous Chicano/a stands on unquestionable moral ground. Furthermore, in order to attack Anglo racism and forward the "natural" dignity of la raza, Valdez invariably resorts to statements about liberty and freedom and ontology, concepts whose cultural origin lies in the very same Enlightenment ideology he seeks to overthrow. Further complicating his formation of "the people" is the paradoxical relationship that the "poet" assumes between articulations of "the nation" and the society "he" means to represent. The poet must stand inside and outside of the people in order that the nation might survive in language, away from the heterogeneity of the people. Ironically, the poet becomes the nation by virtue of his access to representation, while the people become a static entity, subsumed within the cultural ideals and politics of the new nation.

Even as a racist Anglo European narrative of oppression is being highlighted and contested, a complicated performance of race is under way that carries its own problematic implications. Valdez's emphasis on dark skin and la raza as "basically Indio" works at a superficial level to reidentify Anglo whiteness as the enemy of la raza, and assimilated Mexican Americans as "Uncle Toms." But on another level, Valdez's celebration of darkness suppresses the anxiety that "Brown Power" won't work. Here "whiteness" has a dual history of signification: one derived from U.S. contexts that Valdez addresses, but the other residing in the histories of Spanish and Mexican colonialisms that Valdez has no intention of addressing. To do so would complicate the more graspable and politically effective opposition between Anglo and Chicano/a.

Although Valdez clearly states that mestizos are "a powerful blend of Indigenous America with European–Arabian Spain" and thus "a race of half–breeds, misfits, and mongrels," his celebration of the people nevertheless fuses a spectrum of different identities and histories under the homogenizing imagery of la raza as "naturally bronzed." "Bronzed skin" is how this people can be recognized. Ironically, the point of reference here is not la raza but Anglo America. Anglo America in 1972 can only see dark–skinned Mexicanos. Anglo America cannot see what Richard Rodriguez, Cherríe Moraga, and countless other writers see and have seen: that "whiteness" also plays a social and cultural role within Mexican and Mexican American discourses of race. In the heyday of the Chicano/a Movement, one couldn't be "güero" (a person of Mexican descent who looks or passes for white) and be "authentically" Chicano/a. Much like speaking fluent Spanish, bronze skin was one of the essential preconditions for membership in la raza.[8]

In speaking to and for la raza, Valdez enacts what Bhabha considers most primal in the formation of modern nations: the balanced ambivalence of a social identity that relies, for coherence, on material culture–Bhabha's scraps, patches, and rags of daily life–and yet is guided by a rhetorical ideal, even if negatively conceived, that contradictorily and mischievously hails the people as one. Bhabha writes:

> The scraps, patches, and rags of daily life must be repeatedly turned into the signs of a national culture, while the very act of the narrative performance interpellates a growing circle of national subjects. In the production of the nation as narration there is a split between the continuist, accumulative temporality of the pedagogical, and the repetitious, recursive strategy of the performative. It is through this process of splitting that the conceptual ambivalence of modern society becomes the site of *writing the nation*. (297)

Rereading Valdez some thirty years later, we can better appreciate that his writing of la raza as nation introduced to activists and artists an opportunity for turning material history into a national culture. But at what cost? This question is posed not to suggest that there was a viable alternative available to Chicana/o activists during the Chicano/a Movement, but rather to clarify Bhabha's "process of splitting" as it is applied to minority discourses in the United States. Once one departs from an analysis of the hegemonic forces of a nation, it is inevitable, as Bhabha suggests, that ambivalence and its consequences take different forms when one's attention turns to narratives of counternationalism. With historical hindsight, it is easier to see that the cost of this splitting was high, indeed too high to be sustainable given the larger context of the Civil Rights Movement. In the case of Chicanas, we can see poignantly how the cost of splitting required a sustained critique of Valdez's and others' phallocentric representation of la raza, and a refusal to back down from their criticism for the sake of ethnic unity or because of the intense and painful backlash they endured from their Chicano brothers.[9]

If early Chicano/a activists confronted a dilemma in forming an alternative, counterhegemonic movement, why in its early days did Chicano/a studies remain so committed to its origins in the Chicano/a Movement? Part of the answer must be the compelling myth of origins that was constructed with Aztlán at its center. The myth of Aztlán, legendary homeland of the Azteca people, gave poetry to the cause. It identified a territory, a series of landscapes located in the Southwest, that coincidentally matched up perfectly with the territories lost to the United

States in the Mexican–American War. Furthermore, it created a set of dialectical relationships that on the surface united all Mexican Americans in the name of past glories, past injustices, but more importantly the future reclamation of a lost patrimony. The final paragraph of "El Plan Espiritual de Aztlán" makes all these claims clear: "Brotherhood unites us and love for our brothers makes a people whose time has come and who struggle against the foreigner 'Gabacho,' who exploits our riches and destroys our culture. With our heart in hands and our hands in the soil, We Declare the Independence of our Mestizo Nation. We are a Bronze People with a Bronze Culture. Before the world, before all of North America, before all our brothers in the Bronze Continent, We are a Nation, We are a Union of free pueblos, We are *Aztlán*."[10] However compromised this language might seem to us now, we must admit the power of its romanticism. The deeply moving and challenging response is: Why not us? Why can't we determine our own lives? Why can't we stand and be recognized? The myth of Aztlán responds compassionately with "you can." What we hear in this manifesto is the unexpurgated desires of a newly imagined community that posits its political and national future in nostalgic and Edenic terms, terms that locate Chicanismo before the arrival of Columbus, terms that nevertheless operate with, rather than against, the set of narratives that wrote the New World as paradise long before Cortés set foot in Montezuma's court.

Homi Bhabha writes that "the people" inscribed in narratives of the nation are constructed in "double time." By this, Bhabha argues, the people are both "the historical 'objects' of a nationalist pedagogy" and "the 'subjects' of a process of signification that must erase any prior or originary presence of the people" (297). In light of Aztlán, what might Bhabha say to a scenario where the "originary presence" is not erased but rather reconstructed in the name of the people? He would probably say that the Chicano/a Movement is one of dozens of post–1945 anti-colonial movements that must invoke a nationalizing mythology of origins in order to steer away from the burden of colonizing narratives of occupation. It is a necessary fiction of nation–building that nonetheless takes its cue from Western culture in that it, too, looks for a wellspring of identity by which, as Bhabha notes, "the national life is redeemed and signified as a repeating and reproductive process." Similarly, Fregoso and Chabram argue that "whereas the basis of Chicano identity as formulated by Chicano cultural nationalism postulated that collective identity was simultaneity and continuity between the object and its representation, the critical points of difference were often overlooked. These critical points of difference and experience of rupture and discontinuity also shape[d] our identities in decisive ways, for instance, the heterogeneous experiences of migration, conquest, and regional variation."[11] The unanticipated consequence of the narrative of counternationalism supported by the Chicano/a Movement was thus the suppression of some people's history and culture from within, a suppression deployed as an attack on the colonizers. If this is "double time" with a colonial twist, then we must consider what this doubleness erases. If what the Chicano/a Movement produced was a celebratory counternationalist narrative, it also suppressed those less than celebratory narratives that also were part of a Mexican American past. These darker, more troubled narratives, although a part of the historical record since 1848, are only now seeing the scholarly light of day

Chicano/a Marxism and the Foundations of Chicano/a Studies

It would be misleading to suggest these troublesome narratives were unknown to members of the Chicano/a Movement. They were known, but they occupied so contradictory a role in the formation of Chicano/a culture that they acquired an apocryphal identity as activist gains became academically institutionalized. What Chicano/a studies needed was a usable past that included revolutionary figures like Emiliano Zapata—not elitist aristocrats like Miguel Antonio Otero, Jr., the first territorial governor of New Mexico. Yet, the apocryphal would surface from time to time. For instance, if one were to conduct a detailed study of the institutionalization of Chicano/a studies in its early phase, one would immediately note a profound tension between cultural nationalists on the one hand and neo-Marxists on the other. These tensions are well documented, for example, in the early volumes of *Aztlán: Chicano Journal of the Social Sciences and the Arts,* and especially among the editorial staff who were themselves proponents of a politically unified Chicano/a community but consciously wary of the pitfalls of cultural nationalism as a paradigm guiding scholarly study. It was the Marxist scholars, committed to historical praxis, who kept the apocryphal from disappearing completely.[12]

While not the only journal to articulate the aims of Chicano/a studies in this period, *Aztlán* was undoubtedly the most visible and influential of the set. Headed by Marxist historian Juan Gómez-Quiñones, the journal took its name and social identity directly from the 1969 "El Plan Espiritual de Aztlán." As proof of its allegiance to this manifesto, the journal reproduced the text in both English and Spanish in its very first issue, spring 1970. It prominently cited "Corky" Gonzalez's Denver conference as the origin of this cultural text. By reproducing "El Plan Espiritual de Aztlán" as an authenticating text of Chicano/a culture, the journal rhetorically joined its academic scholarship with activism in the streets, communicating, at a symbolic level, that the goal of the Denver conference could continue in the pages of the journal. Yet, almost instantly, the allegiance to cultural nationalism inscribed in "El Plan Espiritual de Aztlán" was met by an ambivalence that would thereafter characterize the role of scholars in this journal and their continuing interface with Chicano/a studies.

One way to understand this ambivalence is to see the participants of the journal as engaged in a highly conscious effort to create and sustain at least two different cultures of activism within the evolving domain of Chicano/a studies. Despite inevitable conflicts, the end result was a compromise among neo-Marxists to accept a strategic form of nationalism necessary for political organization and activism. The other culture, largely academic, needed to struggle from within humanist structures of cultural authority. That culture selectively employed the humanist model of autonomous selfhood to force academia to admit to its implication in exclusionary practices based on race, ethnicity, language, class, and culture. To a large degree, both cultures of activism recorded early historic successes, because they were able to claim an identified constituency and therefore effectively deploy a unified group identity. In retrospect, the journal undertook the supreme task of hailing and consolidating these two activist cultures whenever possible.[13]

One can see directly this process of hailing and consolidating in a study of group identity formation by sociologist Deluvina Hernández.[14] In the second article of the first issue of *Aztlán*, Hernández tackles head-on the cultural nationalist dimensions of this identity issue vis-à-vis the organizing role of "El Plan Espiritual de Aztlán" in activist politics: "The Plan of Aztlán is a design for Mexican American unification and organization; its symbol is La Raza; among its objectives are unity and economic control of Chicano communities; it calls for action from everyone in all spheres of Chicano or Mexican American existence. The prime objective is the liberation of the Chicano or Mexican American people from social bondage: 'EL PLAN DE AZTLAN–IS THE PLAN OF LIBERATION'" (20). By identifying la raza, the people, as a primary symbolic point of identification, Hernández's objective is to understand how the myth of Aztlán stimulates group identification from diverse Mexican American populations and yet encourages differentiation among individuals based on their own unique regional and social grasp of Aztlán. This internalized diversity, in an otherwise unified political community, is a curious balance to strike, since by spring 1970, the Chicano/a Movement had yet to reach its peak. What we see here are Hernández's efforts to consolidate a larger nonacademic political identity while also promoting university leadership of that constituency, a blueprint for future organizing and for the movement vanguard.

Because Marxism was notoriously obtuse to the racial dimensions of class oppression, Hernández makes a point to observe this ethnic group's skillful departure from classic Marxist principles:

> The Mexican American, although included in the proletariat, is not an oppressed class, per se, it is instead an oppressed ethnic group. Thus identified, the Mexican American *ethnic* group will not readily seek to abolish itself in order to abolish the oppressive conditions, as Marx would have the oppressed classes do. The reverse is in fact the case: Mexican Americans seek to maintain their identity while abolishing the oppressive conditions, utilizing the concept of nationalism as the ideological framework for community organizing. (25)

Hernández implies that working–class Mexican Americans in this period would not or could not oppose oppressive class conditions effectively unless under an ethnic–nationalist framework–though this had not been true of labor strikes earlier in the century where Mexicans and Mexican Americans joined with other ethnic groups to combat abusive U.S. labor practices.[15] It might be true, in 1970, however, if one took seriously the spectrum of classes within contemporary Mexican American communities. The middle and upper classes of any ethnic group historically have been adverse to collective action in the United States, except where ethnicity is the primary basis for political action; the Mexican American community proved no different. Therefore, Hernández's analysis is in some respects an admission that the Chicano/a Movement, while overtly conscious of its working–class dimensions and objectives, could not have succeeded without an appeal to and the involvement of the middle classes. For the middle class to be involved, ethnicity and upward mobility had to be foregrounded and stressed. In this way, all classes could claim a united ethnic ethos even if everyone did not suffer the same material and social deprivations.

While the journal advocated strategic nationalism as prudent and essential, there was also a subtle but significant countervailing voice in the figure of Juan Gómez–Quiñones. As the chief editorial architect of the journal, Gómez–Quiñones demonstrated over and over again his counternationalist allegiances, but he also theorized a long–term approach to the issue of Chicano/a identity and politics. In the journal's first special issue, which was devoted to history, Gómez–Quiñones doubled as special issue editor and contributor. His essay, "Toward a Perspective on Chicano History," appeared first and set the mark by which the accompanying essays were to be judged.[16] Significantly, Gómez–Quiñones strikes an academic, disciplinary stance with regard to the future of writing Chicano/a history. Instead of using a militant, cultural nationalist voice, he opens with a humanist vision:

> Clearly Chicano history is an exciting field for the historian. Research in this field will provide insight into nineteenth– and twentieth–century América, particularly the West, from a vantage point often overlooked. Similarly, it will contribute to the comparative understanding of ethnic–minority history, within an international as well as national framework. . . . The most important aspect however, for those who are Chicano, is that in writing the history, they will contribute modestly to the heritage and self-knowledge of the community, and perhaps contribute a structural analysis for positive action on behalf of the community. (1)

"Structural analysis for positive action" is Gómez–Quiñones's only overt rhetorical indication that writing a previously unwritten history might be deployable in a political arena. Otherwise, his vision for Chicano/a history evidences little of the myth of Aztlán, or the rhetorical vehemence of a cultural nationalist. For Gómez-Quiñones, the production of Chicano/a knowledge will follow well-known disciplinary habits of writing history, including inventing new narratives and methods, but will not include overt political organization. Furthermore, and this is a key element in his vision, Chicano/a history will be produced in a comparative framework with other ethnic minorities globally. In such a framework, cultural nationalism becomes a feature of study rather than an outright goal of cultural production. In other words, producing histories of a specific community is not the same as mythmaking on behalf of a community.

Gómez-Quiñones influenced the evolution of Chicano/a history in the early 1970s by balancing the need to organize through a unified narrative of resistance with a historical analysis that went beyond presentist strategies of activism. Writing to the converted, as much as trying to win over new converts, Gómez-Quiñones concludes his essay with the following exhortation:

> Chicano history is, and must continue to be, innovative. It is innovative because it calls for a reconceptualization of history and the role of history in society. This means the use of new methods of inquiry and a reconstruction and reinterpretation of available sources. Thus, it would chronicle a union of history as discipline and history as action on behalf of a community in its struggle for survival. It must be viewed critically because Chicano history is not an adjunct to U.S. Anglo history. It is not the listing of "important" names and contributions of "Mexican Americans" to the development of "this great country." Chicano history is not exclusively the relationship of the Anglo as oppressor and the Chicano as oppressed, but must realistically reflect the historical context of the Chicano community vis-à-vis other oppressed groups in U.S. society. (39)

Chicano/a history, according to Gómez-Quiñones, should provide a critique of the imperialist history of the United States. It should not lend itself to an effacement of class struggle, racial discrimination, and cultural harassment of minority communities. It should not lend itself to a pluralist model of ethnicity that toothlessly celebrates the political and cultural institutions of the United States. And yet, Gómez–Quiñones tactfully reminds Chicano/a historians to be careful not to create in their own paradigms the same exceptional theses of a "unique and special" people that have driven most U.S. historiography since the mid–nineteenth century. He doubts the saliency of analyzing Chicano/a oppression outside of a comparative global framework, because an exceptional thesis of oppression risks not only obscuring the historical record of Chicanos/as but also impeding a firmer understanding of the evolving capitalist dimensions of racial oppression everywhere. In other words, the singular advancement of one minority group is not liberation.

Gómez–Quiñones, and others, were therefore well aware of the essentializing confusions that could come about if Chicano/a cultural nationalism were narrowly contingent, for example, upon a territorial reclamation of the Southwest. Gómez–Quiñones's emphasis on "other oppressed groups" raises the specter that any serious advocacy of territorial reclamation would instantly erase the historical record of southwestern Native Americans who were systematically harassed, killed, converted to Catholicism, forced into slavery, dispossessed of their tribal lands, and forcibly inducted into European systems of socialization under Spanish and Mexican colonialisms. Aztlán would have to remain a myth to succeed as an organizing text for the Chicano/a nation. The Chicano/a Movement could never have succeeded in a contest with the American Indian Movement over native sovereignty as a political or moral right.[17]

As the activist cultures that sustained counternationalist identities began to wane in influence in the later 1970s and early 1980s, the topic of "Chicano/a culture" became an increasingly contentious site for discussions about the successes and failures of the Chicano/a Movement. Scores of assessments of the movement's goals appeared in sundry journals. Gómez–Quiñones himself took a leadership role on the question of culture, especially how expansive it should be and what relation it should have to activism. In the aptly entitled essay "On Culture," Gómez–Quiñones alludes to theoretical debates ongoing within Chicano/a studies circles by the mid–1970s: "This essay deals with culture among people of Mexican descent of the United States. The problem of culture consists of understanding its makeup and its process historically and in contemporary times and understanding the relation of culture to conflict both conceptually and politically."[18] Reinvented for the Chicano/a Movement, the myth of Aztlán had little or no room for alterna-tive cultures of activism that did not prioritize heterosexual, masculine notions of race and nationality as the most salient and expeditious fea-tures of political engagement. When alternative narratives of activism would appear, debate was sure to follow. But rather than contain debate, Gómez–Quiñones regarded the tensions of the early postmovement pe-riod as an opportunity for reconsolidation of activist cultures. He writes: "In sum, this essay explores the 'problemática de ser Mexicanos y traba-jadores' [the problem of being working–class Mexicans]. The task is to work to bring about cultural unity on a given basis to a given end" (29). In the rest of the essay, Gómez–Quiñones attempts, in broad strokes, a re-theorization of Chicano/a culture that is "historically derived, fluid, com-posed of both positive and negative aspects and is malleable to conscious action" (29). In short, he aims for a new theoretical understanding of cul ture that could serve as a basis for replicating the community–building feat of "El Plan Espiritual de Aztlán," but with a lot less nationalism and a lot more flexibility about courting new cultures of activism.

However illuminating Gómez–Quiñones's "On Culture" was to a va-riety of scholars, and it was very influential, the task of producing a new synthetic narrative of activism had to take a backseat to historical assess-ment. In 1978, a year after "On Culture," Gómez–Quiñones published a provocative monograph.[19] This time his focus was on the Chicano/a student movement. While he writes a detailed account of the student movement's origins, growth, and activist roles, he also delivers a sober-ing critique of the Chicano/a Movement in conjunction with these stu-dent groups:

> For some time a variant of Mexican–"Chicano" nationalism was the most pervasive tendency within the student movement. It was seen as the *key* to organizing but not necessarily the end goal.... Nationalism was a mystique that offered the potentiality for binding a heterogeneous and fragmented community, pro-viding the basis for operational unity, and the concomitant re-sults. (28)

> The student movement manifested a series of contradictions; principal among these were those which were strictly objectively sociopolitical in character, and those that were subjective.... The

student movement was directed not only against the status quo of the dominant system but also at the status quo allied with domination within the Mexican community. (29)

Among students there was a lack of understanding of the student situation, its limitations and its role in a struggle for democratic rights in behalf of an oppressed nationality. The student groups were underlaid with socially constructive and self–destructive tendencies. (29)

While completely supportive of the students' efforts, Gómez–Quiñones's frank assessment of the movement seemed to suggest that the "writing was on the wall." In the end, he writes: "At their best, students are the key contributors to struggle, at their worst they are a self–indulgent dis-organizing element. . . . Students must assume the historical respon-sibilities incumbent upon them as a sector of the Mexican people with the seriousness this entails" (46–47). Given all the accomplishments of the student wing of the Chicano/a Movement, and they were many and profound, this admonition by Gómez–Quiñones was also warranted.

For Chicanas, a new narrative of collective activism could not be theorized, much less forwarded, without a well–developed assessment on the status and history of the "Chicana." As noted earlier, the Chicana feminist critique of the movement, for example, was swift and to the point, though of course it did not proceed from a vacuum. Roberta Fer-nández argues that "El Plan Espiritual de Aztlán" and the racial con-sciousness it encouraged was enabling for many early feminist Chicana writers: "Although Chicano nationalism was indeed grounded in a mas-culinist rhetoric, many women activists viewed the nationalist discourse as an emancipatory discourse for Chicanos as a people, and Chicanas played an active role in the efforts of the Chicano community to organize itself. Out of this participation came a growing consciousness of the Chicana's sexual as well as racial and ethnic oppression."[20] For Ignacio M. García, gender consciousness developed from the Chicano/a Move-ment's general intervention into western history on behalf of people of Mexican descent, which later encouraged Chicanas to intervene on mas-culine historical narrative itself: "The reinterpretation of history pro-vided Chicanas an opportunity to discover their Aztec goddesses, their union organizers, their radical journalists, their *soldaderas*, and their historical importance."[21] Yet, as Fernández goes on to show, the need for feminist Chicanas to investigate the gendered dimensions of culture within the Chicano/a community was driven also by the lack of attention or sensitivity of their male counterparts to the oppressiveness of patriarchy (30). The silencing of this issue was particularly hurtful because of the contributions of these same Chicana activists to the Chicano/a Movement. It would be up to Chicanas themselves to explore, critique, and reinvent the culture of activism that had given them their first identities as empowered political subjects. But where to go for this exploration was the key question. Fernández writes: "They [Chicana feminists] recognized that in order to transform human relations within Chicano/a culture, feminism was necessary as a theory, a method, and a practice" (30). As for their male predecessors, the place of investigation would often be in the writing of literature. García adds: "In a history of struggle against oppression, Chicanas fought against the greatest odds, and most remained faithful to their ideals. The cultural renaissance which made the third phase [of the Chicano/a Movement] possible depended heavily on women writers and poets" (13).

Given that it was "literature," of the kind Luis Valdez and Alurista wrote, that had engendered cultural nationalism in all of its exclusive tendencies, it seems inevitable that literature would become the site of countercultural formation for Chicana feminists as well. Even Gómez-Quiñones, in his essay "On Culture," concedes to art the power of raising political consciousness and building community. Despite his training as a historian, and the role that Western-trained historians play in the maintenance of nationalist narratives, Gómez-Quiñones argues: "A strong community means a national culture, which provides for satisfaction, progress, a critical awareness, group solidarity, values of self-sacrifice for the common good, and a world view. Art is central to this process" (44). Art is central to the process of community formation because, unlike the unique situatedness of most political manifestos, art transcends the limits of time and context, to join disparate parts of a community. More importantly, art inspires the development of a body politic necessary to contest hegemonic structures of power and discipline: "The forms and ethos of one art must be broken—the art of domination; another art must be rescued and fashioned—the art of resistance" (44). The art of resistance becomes the key link for Gómez-Quiñones between the Chicano/a Movement and the future. However untidy art might be for political strategists, it nevertheless holds an advantage over Chicano/a history: it does not have to wait for an audience; it can create one as it goes along.

Despite contemporaneous critiques by leftist Chicano/a scholars who worried over rhetorical devices like that of the myth of Aztlán, it was the cultural nationalists who won the political stage during the Chicano/a Movement. Though contested by scholars like Juan Gómez-Quiñones and Deluvina Hernández in the pages of *Aztlán*, cultural nationalism, combined with burgeoning identity politic coalitions, succeeded in winning university and college concessions for Chicano/a studies programs throughout the Southwest and California. Over a short period of time, these successes gave the impression that cultural nationalism was just another name for political activism. Although round after round of negative critiques of cultural nationalism were produced from the mid-1970s on, and mostly from Chicano/a historians and feminists, cultural nationalism survived in the various arts that Gómez-Quiñones hoped would flare up—especially in Chicano and Chicana literature.

Long after the demise of the myth of Aztlán as an effective organizing tool for political activism, the myth surfaced and resurfaced as the operating metaphor of many Chicano/a literary projects. When even that waned, Aztlán was transformed into a generalized, if vague, resistant cultural politic, somewhat like that imagined by Gómez-Quiñones, except that that method of community-building had the unsalutary effect of replicating many of the initial exclusionary habits of cultural nationalism. Even Chicana feminist texts would fall into similar traps of essentializing paradigms. What was missing from this literature-as-activism was the kind of Marxist historical perspective and comparative framework called for by Gómez-Quiñones and others. Ironically, the success of Chicano/a literature in the 1980s, both among Chicano/a and mainstream readers, distanced literary producers and consumers from the need to assess anew the Chicano/a community. As a result, cultural nationalism that once led to political activism now became literary nationalism, with activism reduced to the role of identity politics in universities, programs, majors, syllabi, and academic presses. If there was a collective sense of national Chicano/a politics, it came from literature and not grassroots political actions. By the mid-1980s, the activists that remained visible, in a national sense, were mainly writers and a handful of critics associated with these writers. Neo–Marxist scholars and activists lost the rhetorical and symbolic ground of community formation to literary critics, who succeeded in arguing that activism and cultural nationalism could be found in a unique form of resistance literature.

The political utility of contemporary Chicano/a literature, with its working–class protagonists and race–conscious plots, was self–evident and easily distinguishable from the more ambivalent legacies of historic figures such as Lorenzo de Zavala, Juan Seguin, Pió Pico, and M. G. Vallejo. Early community–building required narratives that mirrored the contemporaneous efforts of activists such as Cesar Chávez, Dolores Huerta, and "Corky" Gonzalez. In the final analysis, leftist Chicano/a historians, even if producing prize–winning labor histories like Rodolfo Acuña's, could not compete with the metaphoric content of literature by Chicanos such as José Montoya, Alurista, Tomás Rivera, Rudolfo Anaya, Rolando Hinojosa–Smith, followed by Chicanas such as Gloria Velasquez and Lorna Dee Cervantes. Thus, the literary critics of the movement surpassed their counterparts in history, or for that matter most social scientists, by becoming the gatekeepers of Chicano/a culture and identity. Even today, though highly respected and awarded countless prestigious forms of scholarly recognition, Chicano/a historians, unlike their Anglo American counterparts, have yet to assume a position like that of literary critics in shaping the material culture of a Mexican America. For better and worse, Chicano/a literary criticism has dominated the direction of Chicano/a studies since the mid–1970s.

I believe the time has come for Chicano/a studies, especially Chicano/a literary studies, to enact a model of ethnic scholarship that seeks historically sensitive methodologies for understanding culture as fluid with regard to race, class, gender, sexuality, and political affiliations. In essence, I call for a return to the internationalist, comparative arguments of the early Chicano/a Marxists that understood cultural nationalism as a finite, strategic organizational moment in community–building, and not the pretext for establishing a romanticized, idealized notion of la raza. The myth of Aztlán, in this context, would have been better understood, argues Wilson Neate, "as a question of localized practices of self–empowerment and self–determination which would, in turn, evolve into a platform for broader, unified political action," rather than as the more rhetorical basis of a militant reclamation of the Southwest.[22] I agree.

The Difference Mestizaje Makes

If Chicano/a studies owes its genesis to the hard work of historians and social scientists, like those whose writings are found in the early pages of the journal *Aztlán*, then its growth was prophesied and actualized in the writings of movement authors and literary scholars. The ten–year period from 1977 to 1987 that culminated in the publication of Gloria Anzaldúa's *Borderlands/La Frontera* (1987) witnessed tremendous changes in the foundations of Chicano/a studies. Nowhere was this change more evident than in Chicano/a identity politics. From its reliance on Aztlán in the early 1980s, Chicano/a studies evolved to incorporate new notions of *mestizaje* by the end of the decade. In the wake of Anzaldúa's *Borderlands*, the invocation of mestizaje has produced a whole new language of signification, which includes borders, differences, multiple racial and ethnic histories, varying sexual and political orientations, and alternative geographies of labor and gender formation. By being both a historical description of violent collision between Old and New World boundaries, as well as a postmodern signifier of power through multiplicity, mestizaje has emerged as the compelling critical framework for the next century. Yet, *Borderlands* did not evolve from a singular voice. For this reason, it is worthwhile to review how Chicano/a studies has come to identify itself with borderlands studies.

Despite their initial readerly reception, one politically conservative, the other progressive, the two major Chicano/a autobiographies of the early 1980s, Richard Rodriguez's *Hunger of Memory: The Education of Richard Rodriguez* (1982) and Cherríe Moraga's *Loving in the War Years: Lo que nunca pasó por sus labios* (1983), are ironically more responsible than anything else for the eventual displacement of the myth of Aztlán in Chicano/a studies.[25] How can this be when "resistance theory" was itself gaining ground and vitality in Chicano/a studies all during the 1980s, peaking in Ramón Saldívar's *Chicano Narrative: The Dialectics of Difference* (1990)? The short answer is that both autobiographies speak to and construct a cultural imaginary willing to confront the exclusionary practices of the Chicano/a Movement even as they broadly identify with la raza. All the same, the la raza each identifies with differs from that of the other and differs, even more, from that of activists likely to look to Aztlán for solutions in a postmodern world. In a very concrete way, both Rodriguez's and Moraga's tales begin a larger introspective examination within the Mexican American community. Although many other Chicano/a authors were writing toward similar ends in this period, none, save Anzaldúa, had the cultural impact of these two writers. Ultimately, the real cultural work of these texts lies in their respective reimagining of a Mexican American community where Aztlán is not a centering idea, or a political ideal.[24]

Think about this: Is there a way that Chicano/a studies can claim a positive legacy in Richard Rodriguez?[25] This question explicitly asks that we not rehearse why Rodriguez has been a foe to progressive Chicano/a politics, but rather ask how his politics have constructively challenged Chicano/a scholars and activists to retool their positions in an increasingly conservative environment. Richard Rodriguez remains a pariah in most Chicano/a studies circles primarily because he renounced any Mexican American ethnic identity as central to his formation as a U.S. individual. For most of his critics, his infuriating nonethnic ethnic identity is at the heart of his politics. Indeed, it helps to explain his opposition to two key tenets of Chicano/a activism in the late 1970s and early 1980s, namely, affirmative action and bilingual education. Because he sees arguments for legal intervention in ethnic oppression as faulty, Rodriguez maintains steadfastly that the key to social justice lies in individuals' efforts to become competent citizens. For Rodriguez, to set apart one group for special treatment based on a history of racial and ethnic discrimination treads too dangerously close to validating another racialized history that figures Mexican Americans as stereotypically incapable and unworthy of citizenship. In public life, by contrast, Rodriguez has consistently shown readers, television and radio audiences, and critics his overwhelming credentials as citizen. In short, Rodriguez, as an individual of Mexican descent, has made a writerly and journalistic career of dispelling cultural and racist stereotypes without ever claiming a history of oppression.

Because, as writer and journalist, he acts as social commentator, Rodriguez has been an appropriate target of criticism. But his celebrity status protects him; unlike activists and scholars, Rodriguez can more easily walk away from criticism. Chicana critic Rosaura Sánchez sums up the collective view of Richard Rodriguez held by many Chicano/a scholars: "Why devote so much attention and so much paper to a writer who has clearly been groomed and strategically deployed by the political right?"[26] While I agree with Rosaura Sánchez that Rodriguez's texts should be subject to critique—on this ground he receives the same treatment any other writer would from me as a teacher—I nevertheless disagree that he is a self-serving puppet of the conservative Right. While it is true that Rodriguez is often deployed by servants of the Right, he himself is not the Right. He is neither a cultural nationalist of Aztlán, nor, I argue, a cultural nationalist of Anglo America. Though I agree with Sánchez that Rodriguez often draws out some pejorative comparisons between an Anglo America and a Spanish Mexico in *Days of Obligation* (Sánchez, 161), he never acts more un–American than when he goes against popular history and informs his readers that the Puritans sailed to the New World, not because they were persecuted freedom fighters, but because they rejected the Old World.

Pointing out that Rodriguez is not the Right does not give a stamp of approval to his politics, but rather supports his right to self-representation, however frivolous and ahistorical. I agree with Kevin R. McNamara's assessment: "*Days of Obligation* performs a more complex interrogation of identity as Rodriguez attempts to conceive what the mixing of these cultures [Anglo Puritan and Spanish Mexican] portends."[27] But this same process, I would argue, is already under way in *Hunger of Memory*. Indeed, the hybridization of "life and culture" (106) that marks *Days of Obligation* as a California story for McNamara is first present in *Hunger of Memory*. This is a critical distinction to make if we are to acknowledge how Richard Rodriguez has inadvertently encouraged Chicanos/as to come up with more sophisticated answers to questions of citizenship, immigration, justice, and history. His penchant for viewing the United States as always hybridized, and increasingly so in a postmodern economy, underscores a heretofore unrecognized positive legacy of Richard Rodriguez to Chicano/a studies. However problematic his views have been to Chicano/a progressives, his current role as a New World Saint Augustine of social commentary—both as editor at the Pacific News Service and as commentator on *The News Hour with Jim Lehrer*—dramatizes his complex cultural power to shape public opinion, to be visible as a gay journalist of color. He is thus equally comfortable talking about the rise of evangelical Protestantism in Latin America and meditating on the Sotheby's auction of Jackie Onassis's belongings.[28] Having broken ethnic ranks, in recent years his cultural power has only increased.

Surely, there is a lesson to be learned from Rodriguez's brand of hybridization. Despite the celebration of his autobiography by conservatives, we can see retrospectively that Rodriguez had a radicalizing effect on readers who did not identify with the Chicano/a Movement but still wanted to claim their civil rights. It was not his notoriety among conservatives, whether or not ultimately deserved, that helped to erode the myth of Aztlán as much as his eloquent, anguished portrayal of a second–generation immigrant, male child. In reading his recollection of grade school, we see how this child of immigrant parents desperately wants to fit in American society. Put aside disagreements with Rodriguez's views on bilingual education and affirmative action, and especially with his narcissistic division of the public and private realms of experience, and one has to admit that Rodriguez got the story of the male immigrant child right. This memory anchors Rodriguez's biography and explains why he identifies so little with Chicano/a activist mythology.

For his generation of la raza and for those few whose circumstances afforded middle–class aspirations, the desire to belong to America, to be called upon as Americans, to feel kinship with Catholic President John F. Kennedy, and to read the "classics" as if they were truly one's own, represented the social realities that Mexican Americans dreamed of possessing before the tumult of the late 1960s.[29] For better and worse, where Rodriguez finally lands by the end of his autobiography–alone, disconnected, centered on no single culture, cynical, and deracinated–is on the "American" side of Mexican American. Rodriguez achieves through art his own self-construction as an American. He loses his ethnic soul, but gains a public audience.[30] In short, what is cryptically attractive about Rodriquez is that he becomes the "American Dream." Never mind his *moreno* looks. His racial darkness, as he notes early on, is well on its way to commodification. Exoticized good looks can be traded upon profitably in a postmodern economy. For Chicano/a studies, the success of *Hunger of Memory* is a constant reminder that the American myth of immigration is alive and well. It is also a cautionary tale about the limits faced by alternative nationalist discourses when the desires of a community include mainstream acceptance, and when calls for ethnic solidarity run up against equally compelling individual and communal desires for self-expression.[31] As I will argue shortly, Rodriguez's break with ethnic solidarity is not unusual and not always condemned. His refusal to identify himself as a minority, as a victim of a conqueror's history, was also a refusal to be relegated by history to the ranks of the unknown and powerless. In this regard, who can fault him?

Keeping in mind Rodriguez's ability to occupy multiple cultural sites (even if mestizaje is underappreciated among them), it is fascinating that Cherríe Moraga's popularity in women's studies circles works from opposite attractions: it is largely predicated on her acceptance of her routine estrangement from society. This is not to say that her marginality as a woman, Chicana, and lesbian was ultimately a happy coincidence because it led to her rise as a sought-after author. No one can draw this conclusion given the painful and soulful revelations of *Loving in the War Years*. Rather, if Richard Rodriguez represented the Chicano gone public American, Cherríe Moraga represented the public American gone private Chicana.[32] Hers is an "ethnic" story that nonetheless made it possible for a mainly white women's studies audience to see her as telling their stories–those of daughters of white fathers who must retrieve their mothers' stories to forge a different female identity in U.S. society. In finding a home in women's studies, Moraga has had her most profound effect on American criticism and Chicana feminism. In many ways, Moraga's text can be credited with opening up white audiences to other mestiza and Chicana writers. I would even say that Sandra Cisneros and others owe their mainstream popularity to this California community activist who went to New York City to learn Spanish and write her story.

Moraga's role in undermining the myth of Aztlán derives from her desires to confront within, as well as without, racism, sexism, and homophobia. As with Rodriguez, Moraga's story is a studied examination of how the public arenas of society call out for the ethnic other to fit in and be absorbed. Unlike with Rodriguez, Moraga's *güera* looks, courtesy of her Anglo father, made entry into public America a given. Seeking a return to her mother's raza, however, proved more difficult. It required that she, as woman and lesbian, critique her Mexican American family and then come to terms with that critique. In effect, she had to create a social text that would allow her to claim her racialized identities as a mestiza, Chicana, and Latina. In this regard, Moraga is an interesting link between Richard Rodriguez, whose critique of his family at the end of *Hunger of Memory* denies him the family connection he purportedly mourns, and Gloria Anzaldúa, whose critique of the "borderlands" moves her to a new configuration of family and community altogether.

In *Loving in the War Years,* Moraga places a premium on the benefit of dialogue to weather difficult differences, whether in the family, the barrio, or society at large. For Moraga, it is not enough to claim hybridity as the ground of agency; this must be balanced with a sense of responsibility and respect for each culture occupied, wherein even ethnic celebrations are open–ended and nonexclusionary.

Moraga's conclusions pose a conundrum for Chicano/a studies in the 1980s: "I am the daughter of a Chicana and anglo. I think most days I am an embarrassment to both groups. I sometimes hate the white in me so viciously that I long to forget the commitment my skin has imposed upon my life. To speak two tongues. I must. But I will not double–talk and I refuse to let anybody's movement determine for me what is safe and fair to say" (vi). Moraga's sense of obligation as a writer, that she make all of herself understood, is an explicit rejection of separatist politics. Though ardently Chicana, she writes for all readers. Further, she rejects that brand of identity politics that would privilege one set of essentializing cultural traits over another. Why? Her life story is the unfolding of experiences that originated in the policing mechanisms inherent to both Anglo and Mexican American cultures. Continually negotiating her release from all systems of social policing, how could she then self–impose her own prisonhouse of "acceptable" experience? She cannot. This is why she rejects the orthodoxy of any movement, however well intended. This is why she must accept her Anglo father and her Chicana mother, because any less is a denial of the complexity of her life, her past, her future. If the choice is between the grayness of complexity and the fantasy of uniqueness, Moraga chooses complexity.

Moraga's writing and thinking as a feminist Chicana lesbian challenged Chicano/a studies in the 1980s to unlink separatist ideology from progressive activism in U.S. politics. In response to Moraga's uninvolvement in the Chicano/a Movement, critic Lora Romero observes: "By the end of *Loving in the War Years,* it is clear that Moraga will never again stand on the sidelines when her *brothers and sisters* take the streets" (122). In making this ethnic identification, in choosing ethnic solidarity in political struggles, Moraga seems by the end of her tale to concede that some form of strategic separatism is inevitable. But lest we read brothers and sisters too reductively (and Moraga is rarely simplistically reductive), she offers the following: "Any movement built on the fear and loathing of anyone is a failed movement. The Chicano movement is no different"

(140). Moraga's political position in *Loving in the War Years* is not only to sharpen the divides between man and woman, Chicana and Anglo, straight and gay, but also to commit herself to straddle these divides productively, humanely. Moraga's lasting contribution to Chicano/a studies may well be that in accepting the "whiteness" of her father, she reminds all mestizas and mestizos of their "white" fathers, past and present.

By the late 1980s, the centrality and relevance of Aztlán to Chicano/a studies had slowly faded. In its place, the current ruling metaphor of borderlands emerged. In its embrace of divisions, splits, ruptures, gaps, silences, wounds, and absences, Gloria Anzaldúa's *Borderlands/La Frontera: The New Mestiza* (1987) captured the critical imagination. In telling contrast, the rhetorical power of Aztlán had lain in its ability to confirm wholeness, coherence, and continuity on behalf of a marginalized people. But remember, Anzaldúa is not opposed to Aztlán. Her first essay is entitled, "The Homeland, Aztlán/El Otro Mexico." Yet Aztlán as utopia cannot adequately describe the social conditions of Anzaldúa's life. She narrates early on: "I am a border woman. I grew up between two cultures, the Mexican (with a heavy Indian influence) and the Anglo (as a member of a colonized people in our own territory). I have been straddling that *tejas*–Mexican border, and others, all my life. It's not a comfortable territory to live in, this place of contradictions. Hatred, anger and exploitation are the prominent features of this landscape" (preface). The text Anzaldúa created out of her willingness to explore "this place of contradictions" without apologies, without regrets, was the one that Chicano/a literary critics were longing to find in the 1980s. Further, *Borderlands* answered the question, "Can there be a meeting place between 'an authentic Chicano/a critical discourse' and Anglo/European theory?" By the late 1980s, Chicana critics such as Tey Diana Rebolledo were openly alarmed by the increasing adoption of Eurocentric theory by Chicano/a scholars: "This priority of placing our literature in a theoretical framework to 'legitimize' it, if the theory overshadows it, in effect undermines our literature or even places it, once again, in a state of oblivion. Privileging the theoretical discourse de–privileges ourselves."[33] In other words, Rebolledo voiced the concern among many ethnic scholars that poststructuralist theory in the 1980s threatened to reobscure the ethnic historical subject.[34]

In this light, *Borderlands*'s curious mixture of history, theory, analysis, poetry, essay, and manifesto was the perfect tonic for allaying fears that the ethnic subject would be lost in the world without a story. Indeed, *Borderlands* forecloses such a possibility by imagining a critical terrain conducive to the multiple agendas of writers, critics, and popular cultures, wherein contradiction and difference ally themselves in the defense of narration. Angie Chabram echoes Anzaldúa's own praxis when she writes in 1991 about the need for new metanarratives for criticism:

> As we rapidly move into what proves to be a rich and productive phase in the development of Chicano critical discourse, we will be faced with the substantial challenge of defining the perimeters and objectives of this discourse in ways that would no doubt seem inconceivable to that early generation of Chicano critics, who boldly inaugurated it with their admirable struggles within the institution of literary criticism. Our success in responding to this challenge will depend largely upon our ability to circumvent those 'strategies of containment that would sever Chicano critical discourse from its multiple determinants and expressions and upon our ability to reconceptualize it within various domains of its influence, directing it toward values, practices, and social realities that engendered it.[35]

Although one can debate whether or not in the intervening years Chicano/a criticism has become more accessible to a nonacademic audience, Chicano/a literature has become more accessible, thus validating the social and cultural role of Chicano/a critics in the study of Chicano/a discourses. Hence Anzaldúa's *Borderlands* both fulfilled a critical need and renewed the faith that studies of material and popular cultures could have a political, as well as aesthetic, utility.

Still, one can, and should, claim the same for Ramón Saldívar's *Chicano Narrative: The Dialectics of Difference* (1990), published only three years after *Borderlands;* it impressively weaves Fredric Jameson's notion of the "political unconscious" with the material condition and literary production of Chicano/a writers. By complicating the deconstructionist tendency to view all texts as fictional, especially historical narrative, Saldívar's "dialectics of difference" manages to combine poststructuralist theory with the material and political history of the racialized other. Saldívar clarifies why Mexican Americans do not have the luxury of jettisoning history. For the racial other, to reduce history to the status of fiction is to overprivilege claims of difference by those who can socially and politically stand outside of official history when strategically useful. By contrast, the racial other, who may or may not desire the empowerment of official history, is always already implicated as the disfranchised other. He or she can only appear in official history as subjugated. To achieve a critique that actively opposes the static position of Mexican as other, *Chicano Narrative* invokes "difference" and material culture as twin engines of analysis; anything less reifies the broader status quo of the Mexican American in society, hence Saldívar's "dialectics of difference." In this regard, Saldívar's critical assessments are very similar to Anzaldúa's border meditations.

Yet, the dissimilarities between the two texts are also clear. Hector A. Torres writes: "As a reduction to history, [Saldívar's] dialectics of difference are suspicious of the transcendentalizing tendencies of metaphysical thinking."[36] This is especially true in light of the historical framework Saldívar adopts. As Torres observes, Saldívar rehearses the historical evolution of Mexican American quite deliberately. He begins with the Mexican–American War and the consequences of the Treaty of Guadalupe Hidalgo and then proceeds to the contemporary labor/economic evolution of the Mexican American as working class. Saldívar reiterates a narrative of Chicano experience that was, by 1990, *the* foundational history of Chicano studies. When Torres implies that Saldívar finds fault with Richard Rodriguez's ahistoricism, or is wary but respectful of Chicana writers, like Cherríe Moraga, who prioritize spirituality, he calls attention to the specific "structures of feelings" contained within standard Chicano/a historiography. In retrospect, Saldívar's "dialectics of difference" might have been suspicious of the metaphysical, but it is perhaps more accurate to say that his use of Chicano history had more in common with (or validated the metaphysical thinking of) someone like Luis Valdez than it did with writers like Rodriguez or Moraga.

Rather than relying on Chicano history as its primary, organizing principle and ideological center, Anzaldúa's text offers a series of metaphors, each revolving around the "border," that draw out the importance of the "borderlands" to some of society's most vexing questions. There is of course "history" in Anzaldúa's text, but not a historian's notion of history. Wilson Neate writes: "For Anzaldúa, the pre–Columbian period does not comprise a recuperable chronotrope but rather, she draws on that tradition to find new metaphors for a revision of the terms of

Chicano/a identity and community" (24). If the personal is political, Anzaldúa stretches the personal to be historical, and vice versa. This is the story of a people resurrected from the margins of official history. As outsiders, they become realized as "*Los atravesados* [who live on the bor-derland]: the squint-eyed, the perverse, the queer, the troublesome, the mongrel, the mulato, the half-breed, the half dead; in short, those who cross over, pass over, or go through the confines of the 'normal' " (3). Here "normal" also includes what goes for the status quo in Chicano/a stud-ies. As much as Saldívar's scholarly work opened Chicano/a studies to new horizons, his adherence to a canonical history and the "structure of feeling" that accompanied it limited *Chicano Narrative* even as it achieved authority to speak on behalf of Chicano/a literary criticism. The cul-tural work of Anzaldúa's text has gone further precisely because her metaphysical world has yet to find itself fossilized in any kind of offi-cial history.

Fifteen years after the publication of Anzaldúa's *Borderlands,* from public policy to histories of sexualities, the metaphor of borderlands has energized not only Chicano/a studies, but fields as distinct as postcolo-nialism and medieval studies. While Gloria Anzaldúa's autobiographical quest for the "New Mestiza" might get lost in its adaptations by non-Chicano/a scholars, what is not lost, I'm sure, is how her text helped to redefine Chicano/a studies. Critical studies since 1987 show either the direct influence of Anzaldúa or her shaping of a critical "reader re-sponse" to borderlands as an analytical paradigm. Books such as *Criticism in the Borderlands; The Dialectics of Our America; Dancing with the Devil: Society and Cultural Poetics in Mexican-American South Texas; Telling Identities; Rethink-ing the Borderlands; Movements in Chicano Poetry;* and *Home Girls* suggest that the dominant discourse of Chicano/a studies today has its rhetorical origins in *Borderlands/La Frontera,* and in its wake, Chicano/a studies has come into a new maturity.

Why is that? And how can it be? Especially when Anzaldúa's ten-dency to essentialize her "New Mestiza" sends up so many red flags? When in fact she constructs la raza of the border in exclusive terms? And lastly, but most importantly, when her text is also clearly implicated in nationalist discourses?

But first I should grant Anzaldúa's nationalist statements are never stable. They disappear as quickly as they appear. In Anzaldúa's mind, the "borderland" is certainly home, but not necessarily homeland. To read *la frontera* as homeland is to reduce the field imaginary and direct attention to narrow political ends. Anzaldúa herself often intertwines the moral and the "national" with the universal and cosmic. For example: "On that day [December 2], I search for essential dignity as a people, a people with a sense of purpose–to belong and contribute to something greater than our *pueblo*. On that day I seek to recover and reshape my spiritual identity. *¡Animate! Raza, a celebrar el día de la Chicana"* (88). Anzaldúa's talk of the *pueblo* and spirituality is appropriately reminiscent of "El Plan Espiritual de Aztlán," with one exception. Anzaldúa's vision does not begin or end with some realized new national community. She certainly hails la raza on behalf of the Chicana, but her ultimate vision is of a personal spiritual rebirth, a process available to all if it's available to only one person. Anzaldúa defines her society by its ability "to belong and contribute to something greater than" itself. What this is or means Anzaldúa leaves purposely vague and mystical, but I think it effectively brackets any kind of romantic illusion that the New Mestiza is the forerunner for a new nation. Instead, the New Mestiza, a state of mind, is the manifestation of a universalist agenda, a mission that goes well beyond traditional borders of time, space, nation, and experience, even while, simultaneously, Anzaldúa means to hold up people of Mexican descent to special attention.[37]

The short answer to the question, How has Gloria Anzaldúa changed Chicano/a studies? lies in the symbolic synthesis that the idea of borderlands has generated for the field. In moving away from the myth of Aztlán as a nationalist project, Chicano/a studies has nevertheless claimed a geopolitical imaginary that is related to but separate from the everyday policed border between the United States and Mexico. While the idea of borderlands is always caught in the web of narratives about the nation (both the United States and Mexico), "border" subjects never take up residence unambivalently in either country. Even ambivalence is so culturally charged that it precludes overarching, stable concepts of "nation." This symbolic realm is thus at once a field of knowledge, experience, peoples, histories, conflicts, and futures, as well as a conduit for ideas, discourses, images, economies, languages, and immigrants. It is also a place of negotiations between nations, commerce, narratives, families, and individuals. And because the concept of the borderland opens up to two different nations, the idea of a bicultural society becomes instantly quantifiable and readable in ways unavailable before 1987.

Borderlands as a concept has resolidified the institutional mission of Chicano/a studies. The fractious, indeterminate nature of the borderlands has given the interdisciplinary nature of Chicano/a studies new life, new authority. Given the effects of the conservative and centrist control of the U.S. presidency and Congress for the last fifteen years, from issues such as immigration policy to affirmative action, from the demonization of higher education to support of the Persian Gulf War, from NAFTA and the WTO to the current war against terrorism, Chicano/a studies has been ably qualified to interrogate and examine these issues as they affect the local and the global. The result has been a high degree of relative exposure over the last twenty years.[38] "Borderlands" has enabled Chicano/a studies to adopt a discursive identity that is neither keyed to a singular nationalist vision, nor invested in reifying patriarchal traditions in the name of cultural preservation. Yet it remains in a position to imagine la raza, to recover repressed histories, especially as the experiences of people of Mexican descent in the United States change over time. Philosophically then, Chicano/a studies, since Anzaldúa's *Borderlands*, has been open to the "queering" of its identity, whether that means in the study of sexuality, gender, history, literature, or even ethnic solidarity. For Neate, "mestiza consciousness endows Chicano/a identity and community with 'a tolerance for contradictions, a tolerance for ambiguity'" (24). Ironically, Chicano/a studies' embrace of multiplicity, nonlinearity, discontinuous narrative, transnationalism, and colonial history have put it more at the center of academic discourses than ever before. This is a tantalizing phenomenon given the historical displacement of mestizos and mestizas from hegemonic narratives of the nation–state.

Because of the dominance of the trope of borderlands, we may conclude in another twenty years that this was a period of fantastic growth in Chicano/a studies, especially in the recovery of specific histories, peoples, and literatures. I have in mind the tremendous archival and cultural work that the Recovering the U.S. Hispanic Literary Heritage project has already produced. Without the electric draw of Anzaldúa's *Borderlands*, it would be hard to imagine the Recovery Project's own initiation of new paradigms of study–especially those required to understand recovered texts that preceded the reinvention of Aztlán. Indeed, the Recovery Project has already republished texts that challenge us to consider people of Mexican descent as one–time colonizers, texts that champion the nonpopulist side of Venustiano Carranza in the Mexican Revolution.[39] One has to wonder if such formerly taboo subjects would have been possible without Anzaldúa's autobiography. Perhaps Anzaldúa's "New Mestiza" is ultimately an apt figure for all that is or has been taboo in Mexican American culture and history. If so, mestizaje scholarship within New Chicano/a Studies should be understood as consciously refusing the enigmatic chain of events that often makes certain narratives more prized than others, certain histories more central than they were, that erase discontinuities in favor of usable pasts, even if a shared goal is the production of a counterhegemonic, postnationalist set of discourses.

The Future of Chicano/a Studies

In his historical review and cultural analysis of Aztlán, Rafael Pérez-Torres offers a reading of the Chicano/a Movement and Chicano/a studies that is sympathetic to what I have laid out. He writes:

> One image central to Chicano/Chicana intellectual and social thought has been the figure of Aztlán. Too often, the name of this mythic homeland is either dismissed as part of an exclusionary nationalist agenda or uncritically affirmed as an element essential to Chicanismo. In refiguring Aztlán, we move toward a conceptual framework with which to explore the connections between land, identity, and experience. Significantly, these connections become centrally relevant as the political, social, and economic relationships between people and place grow ever more complicated and fluid.[40]

However, instead of arguing for an overall paradigm shift in Chicano/a studies, Pérez-Torres's article focuses on the recuperation of Aztlán as an empty signifier that has played a historic role "in shifting the horizon of signification as regards Chicano/a resistance, unity, and liberation" (16). In other words, for Pérez-Torres, Aztlán marks the historical changes that have occurred in Mexican American culture and Chicano/a studies since the early 1970s. As an idea that encapsulated countercultural activism, Aztlán was meaningful to activists and intellectuals during its reinvention; as the basis of a conceptual framework for scholarship, Aztlán continues its cultural work under new identities such as borderlands studies. In the course of his article, Pérez-Torres persuasively and passionately argues for a retention of a renovated Aztlán that is fluid, non-nationalist, and nonexclusionary. Otherwise, "any fixed significance ascribed to Aztlán erases the vast differences that inform the terms 'Chicana' and 'Chicano'" (33).[41]

While Pérez-Torres's analysis is encouraging about the possibilities the term "Aztlán" might have in the future, more significant is his observation that the term–like the term "Chicano" or "Chicana," I would add– resides increasingly within academic circles: "But, to be fair, for many in the Chicano 'community,' Aztlán signifies little; it is the political, social, and cultural Chicano/a elite of a particular stripe for whom Aztlán resonates as an icon imbued with some historical meaning. Five hundred years of European presence in the Americas is contested by an assertion of the indigenous, by an affirmation of native civilizations, by the recollection of Aztlán" (17). The difficulty of joining the minority object of study with some kind of "real" politics in the streets or Washington, D.C. is not exclusive to Chicano/a studies; this notorious problem is shared throughout ethnic and women's studies programs in the country today. Ironically, as Pérez-Torres notes, by declaring independence, or, as he says, a "union of free pueblos," and declaring it on the site of New World difference, the declaration of rebellion over time cannot help but remind us of the same rhetorical strategies used by Puritans or revolutionaries of 1776. In this case, it seems to me, Chicano/a studies, as an archive and cultural center for Mexican American intellectual production within Western academia, becomes at best a conservatory rather than a fundamental catalyst for all that is truly vital or different in the Mexican American community. So the challenge for the Chicano/a scholar who resides within humanist structures of knowledge and authority is to quixotically resist the lure of stability, canonicity, and elitist measures of value, and to reject the mainstream role of cultural gatekeeper, in favor of that of the eyewitness, chronicler, storyteller, community elder.

So long as the desire for activist scholarship remains alive, Chicano/a studies can never wholly become a vehicle for cultural elitism. Nor can it accrue to itself some cultural existence outside of nationalist or counternationalist contexts. Like other postnationalist critical studies of the United States, Chicano/a studies will always have to assume a highly conscious but fluid sociohistorical relationship to its objects of study. Just as Cherríe Moraga has taught that the personal is political precisely because identity is always in dialogue and debate with an evolving political environment, Chicano/a studies, as a field that has historically identified itself with people of Mexican descent in the United States, must endeavor to keep up with a Mexican America that itself is forever changing politically, and unevenly at that.

For Pérez-Torres, Aztlán is a fiction that was given context and political content for historical reasons. It remains in our lexicon because intellectuals cannot survive outside of history, or the history of ideas. Whether or not Aztlán exists now in something called the "community," however, is an important question. If it does not, the cultural history of the Chicano/a Movement has nevertheless forever enshrined its significance, because Aztlán has been transformed, as Pérez-Torres observes, into a process of liberation (37). It is upon this process that I posit New Chicano/a Studies as a new critical paradigm necessary to understand our current social text. By "this process," I include our evolving consensus that if Aztlán contains a history of contradictory meanings, then only a new critical paradigm can effectively embrace those meanings. This paradigm is especially needed to anticipate the day when concepts like "Aztlán," or for that matter "Chicano/a," will become obsolete and replaceable by terms more suited to a future political moment—thus ensuring that even the notion of "fluidity" remains fluid. Nevertheless, as Daniel Cooper Alarcón argues: "it is important to realize that even a fluid, shifting model of cultural identity is potentially exclusionary—and it is this exclusionary power that must be acknowledged and examined if we are to move toward a sophisticated understanding of how and why identities change" (35).

In these troubled political times, understanding the interplay between ethnic identity and representation has never seemed more vital to grasp. This interplay is especially crucial to the long-term survival of Chicano/a studies and the further development of fluid ethnic studies paradigms. However, if the field's principal preoccupation is either the decline of the Chicano/a Movement, or the inability of Chicano/a studies to be the staging ground for mass community activism, Chicano/a scholars will be institutionally discouraged from asking the obvious: Who are Chicanos/as today? And how is this group recognized? Instead of this "either/or" approach, we might view the cultural politics of representation as an illustration of an evolving social context—a look at the "I's" and "we's" of Chicano/a identity–by which to evaluate the goals and strategies of activist scholarship at the local and global level.

Consider the following positions on representation from Norma Alarcón and Angie Chabram–Dernersesian:[42]

> Thus, the feminist Chicana, activist, writer, scholar, and intellectual on the one hand has to locate the point of theoretical, and political consensus with other feminists (and "feminist" men), and on the other continue with projects that position her in paradoxical binds: for example, breaking out of ideological boundaries that subject her in culturally specific ways, and not crossing over to cultural and political arenas that subject her as "individual/autonomous/neutralized" laborer. Moreover, to reconstruct differently the raced and gendered "I's" and "We's" also calls for rearticulation of the "You's" and "They's." Traversing the processes may well enable us to locate points of differences and identities in the present to forge the needed solidarities against repression and oppression. Or, as Lorde (1984) and Spivak (1988) would have it, locate the "identity–in–difference" of cultural and political struggle. (Alarcón, 71)

> It is ironic that, although we live in a period that prizes the multiplicity of identities and charters border crossings with borderless critics, there should be such a marked silence around the kinds of divergent ethnic pluralities that cross gender and classed subjects within the semantic orbit of Chicana/o. So powerful is the hegemonic reach of dominant culture that fixed categories of race and ethnicity continue to shape the production of social identities within the alternative sector. Few are those who have cut through the nationalist or pluralist registers that promote an all–or–nothing approach to writing the intersections between underrepresented transnational ethnic groups and their heterogeneous social movement toward one another. (Chabram–Dernersesian, 269)

If we can imagine Norma Alarcón's call to seek solidarities across multiple feminist lines, despite global structures of power that limit radicalism, as only one side of a coin, the other side is Angie Chabram–Dernersesian's argument that Chicano/a studies is now in a position to link transnational studies of ethnicity with studies of "divergent ethnic pluralities" within the Chicano/a community. For me, the ability to imagine this coin is the ability to reimagine the status and currency of Chicano/a studies today, to move away from the either/or trajectory noted above toward a sense of possibility. Together, Alarcón's and Chabram–Dernersesian's visions challenge us to reformulate activist, interventionist scholarship as well as rekindle large-scale community-activist formation, through nonessentializing, non–nationalist new narratives of community-building. While one may be possible without the other, there hasn't been an effective, all–encompassing narrative of activism since the Chicano/a Movement, and even my own assessment, as I have suggested, depends entirely on what one means by effective and for whom. The politics of representation are thus key to any reconfiguration that would have Chicano/a studies be a site where scholarship and activism are joined, compromises and all.

In this chapter, I have been interested in what lies between the two sides of the Alarcón/Chabram–Dernersesian coin. I have argued that Chicano/a studies is, and has been, moving in directions that do not disavow the Chicano/a Movement even if they show increasing affinity for the positions marked above by Alarcón and Chabram–Dernersesian. All these changes suggest that an opportunity exists to mint a new currency to be passed among us equally, as well as between us and our allies. While the political imaginary embodied in Aztlán enabled past leaders to lobby for the civil rights of Mexican Americans by inventing a "usable past" that mirrored our vexed history, the trope of borderlands and the political identity of mestizaje has opened the future to new leadership.

And that's good. Because the Southwest is no longer home to all people of Mexican descent. New field imaginaries are being assembled outside and beyond Aztlán. Nontraditional places like Seattle, Minneapolis, Des Moines, Madison, Atlanta, and Philadelphia increasingly are home to Mexican American communities. According to a recent study, Mexicans are "one of the newest and fastest–growing immigrant groups in New York City."[43] What will happen to our collective imaginations when we start educating Chicano/a students from points further north, New Haven, Providence, Boston, and, dare I say, Canada, is currently beyond comprehension. Perhaps the dream of Aztlán and the Chicano/a Movement succeeded beyond the wildest expectations of the activists. Yet, we must grant also that the lure of jobs and the willingness of corporate capitalists to take advantage of cheap labor is equally behind these new demographics. Some things have changed for the better, some for the worse. Chicano/a studies is the same and yet different from its origins in the Chicano/a Movement. I hope it's clear that the original mission of Chicano/a studies to recover our alienated selves is far from done. While a difficult task lies ahead, New Chicano/a Studies has never been in a better position to advocate for the powerless, the uneducated, and *los olvidados*, the forgotten, of this country.

With this thought, I return to Lucha Corpi's detective novel, *Eulogy for a Brown Angel*, for a final look. Through her protagonist, Gloria Damasco, Corpi allegorizes what she perceives as the necessary tools for understanding a postmodern society where the Cold War no longer orients our ideologies, where nationalism no longer guarantees a regional economy, and where centrist politics has made progressive activism nearly impossible. What you need, according to Corpi, are family, friends, and a good measure of clairvoyance. Gloria Damasco's psychic ability as a detective is the only kind of alchemy left in a world overly dependent on technologies to solve the dilemma of human connection. Corpi's literary use of clairvoyance is an interesting choice, not only for her novel, but as a trope that describes our current generation of Chicano/a writers and activists in search of a new horizon for Chicano/a politics. At the beginning of the new century with so many things uncertain, clairvoyance–that non-Western, nonscientific frame of alternative knowledge that negotiates the invisible–may be the skill most needed to understand the past, present, and future of Mexican Americans in the United States. Making the case for New Chicano/a Studies is one way to make visible the understanding that an ethnic community stands on its own merits, but is also united with the countless other communities that seek a more just society in our time and throughout the world.

CHAPTER TWO

Literary Origins in an
Age of Multiculturalism

By the end of *The House on Mango Street* (1984), Sandra Cisneros's alter ego, Esperanza, comes to a crossroads. If she stays on Mango Street, she risks atrophying her soul. If she gives flight to her soul's desire, she might never find her way back. Her home–its street, the cracks in the pavement, dysfunctionality made bittersweet by compassion–functions like one grand symphony of fictional autobiography. Esperanza is forever locked in finding the best of herself in the worst of circumstances. This is why she meets her dilemma of staying or going by proposing a paradoxical resolution: she will leave so that she can eventually return. Though Esperanza explicitly rejects the social/spatial hierarchies of a City on a Hill, she nevertheless imagines returning to a socially just community not unlike the one found in John Winthrop's "A Model of Christian Charity" (1630). But her community has been "ethnicized," and in it there will always be room for "bums in the attic." She can leave the physical trappings of Mango Street without rejecting the psychic impression they have made, or her sense of belonging, even if the rest of the world cannot, will not, understand. Her future lies in going out into the world, so that the world and its forbidden knowledge might eventually establish a foothold on Mango Street.

Cisneros's carefully crafted tensions reflect her writerly understanding of being an American writer of Mexican descent, of writing in a society that measures literary greatness in terms of familiarity, not difference, of being a woman writer beset doubly by mainstream and Mexican American cultures alike. For her, "the portrait of a young artist" in the wake of the Chicano/a Movement necessarily looks and feels like a journey into the unknown. What signposts exist are tremendously written over and previously claimed. All she can do is what others–Native Americans, lonely white women on the frontier, former slaves and their descendants, political exiles and social outlaws–have always done in response to their rhetorical and literary dispossessions: claim the unclaimable, the unwanted, the lowly sites of creation, the disreputable; claim irony without transcendence, art without history, history without glory. Many would say that Sandra Cisneros has written herself into a quintessentially American tradition of alienation, a tradition made famous by Cotton Mather, Jonathan Edwards, Benjamin Franklin, Washington Irving, James Fenimore Cooper, Nathaniel Hawthorne, Edgar Allan Poe, and the list goes on.

But if that were the case, why is it that *The House on Mango Street* found its literary worth framed so exclusively within a 1980s multicultural curriculum? How is it that, on the one hand, multiculturalism provided Esperanza a home in anthologies and syllabi, but, on the other, relegated her to a "room without a view" in the mansion of American literary history? Even if we concede that the discourse of multiculturalism has been an honest response to the Civil Rights Movement in educational circles, a broad–based movement to desegregate a national curriculum that did not reflect the existence, the contributions, or innovations of women, people of color, and gays and lesbians, I would observe still that something happened in the translation of this social/legal body politic into a cultural praxis. Proponents of multiculturalism had no adequate models of change to guide their vision, nor time to conceive of alternatives that answered everyone's objections. From the beginning, too, these proponents had to spend considerable energy fending off the hostile attacks of cultural nationalists from the political right as well as the left. As a result, the effort to revise literary canons, to make histories more inclusive, to champion the personal and private as political, dissolved into a strategy of civic pluralism.[1] In literary criticism and pedagogy, the literary canon came face to face with the "melting pot," and the effect was devastating. One could boast that there were more chairs at the table of American literature, but the sense of segregation was enhanced rather than eliminated. Newly arrived guests could achieve familiarity only by leaving their differences at the doorway. By contrast, ethnic scholars fiercely, and understandably, fought the impetus toward a universal literary nationalism, only to find themselves making a Faustian pact with exceptionalism as their defining identity. By the end of the 1980s, multiculturalism had succeeded in arguing for space at the table, but the table itself remained unchanged.

If we stop to consider why the debate about multiculturalism has engaged so many followers on either side of the divide—whether it is rescuers of American literature from colonizing habits or protectors of Western civilization itself in North America—what is pronounced is a confusion over the role that origins myths play in the service of the nation and the production of citizenship. In hindsight, it was reasonable enough for activists of the various civil rights movements to desire a cultural transformation of the character of American identity. But the move to change the national unconscious meant that they had to meet anonymity with visibility, silence with voice, history with alternative history, high art with folk art, and so on, creating a new set of dialectical social relationships that never finally transcended local politics (like the UFW organizing successes) in favor of a bona fide national political program. This privileging of the underprivileged placed supreme value on historic differences, thereby postponing true literary integration—and the renarration of American literature that would come with it. The governing literary metanarrative of Plymouth Rock, and Puritan immigration to the New World, thus remained unchanged, and in the hands of an angry Allan Bloom, and others like him, the Puritan mythology of a Christian brave new world found new life as the Cold War came to an end.[2] Like a Thanksgiving dinner at the local homeless shelter, room was made for the noncanonical, but the cultural ritual itself, and its annual reinvention of a singular national identity, remained central to civic participation.

Proponents of multiculturalism in the 1980s also profoundly underestimated the centrality of canonical cultural texts (like the ritual enactment of Thanksgiving) to social and cultural contexts outside of the university classroom and academic environs.[3] Part of the resistance to questioning canonical cultural practices was fueled by conservative reaction that demonized higher education throughout the 1980s and its "politically correct" professorate. This conservative reaction has advocated everything from the return of school prayer and the local control of public schools to the funding of chartered schools through public tax monies known as vouchers.[4] In the hands of the New Right, multiculturalism became pluralist "diversity," something to celebrate. Furthermore, a hungry publishing industry saw profits to be made from the culture wars. In the end, the debate over revision culminated in a numbers game that afforded minority writers visibility in anthologies and undergraduate courses. But if we look elsewhere in grade school and high school curriculums, resistance to change in "official national culture" has been and continues to be intense.

Nowadays, the practice of comparing nineteenth- and twentieth-century American writers with Puritan figures is typical of American pedagogy and within literary criticism. It seems "natural" to begin a study of American literature with the Puritans. Even some groups of writers for whom colonial literature seems an unlikely literary antecedent, say African American writers, can be seen as having some relationship with Puritanism. For example, current historical periodization and regional identification frame Phillis Wheatley and Anne Bradstreet well within established theories of literary and historical continuity that foreground their shared, if unequal, New England colonial status. Intertextuality, another variant of continuity, convincingly links slave narratives, such as that of Harriet Jacobs, with Mary Rowlandson's 1682 captivity narrative. The presence and evolution of Protestantism on the eastern seaboard speaks to an intriguing and complicated history between African and Anglo Americans. In addition, the sacrifices of African Americans since the Battle of Bunker Hill underscore their contributions to the establishment of this country's political ideals. Hence, on religious, economic, military, and political terms, African Americans are linked to early American history and thus find their way relatively surely into the national imagination.

Other continuities are produced whenever intellectuals, artists, and politicians reinterpret the past for the present. Consider the important legacy of Massachusetts–born, Fisk and Harvard educated W. E. B. DuBois to African American letters, or the case of contemporary poet Michael Harper. In his poem "History as Apple Tree" (1977), Harper takes on the figure of Roger Williams, drawing out a seventeenth–century multiracial narrative and claiming, on the roots of Williams's legacy, a new green shoot for African Americans. Or consider how Langston Hughes's poem "Let America Be America Again," itself an obvious revision of the Puritan "errand into the wilderness," was invoked by Bill Clinton at the 1992 Democratic Convention.[5] In his acceptance speech as the party's presidential candidate, Clinton called upon the legacy of Hughes not only for a poetic characterization of the 1980s as ultimately un–American, but for a populist vision of America that dovetailed (ostensibly) with his political platform. Thus, it is possible (if rare) to read in African American letters a complex dialogue with a Puritan past.

If, as I said before, it seems "natural" to begin a study of American literature with the Puritans, any study of Chicano/a writers instantly reveals the constructed nature of theories of continuity, how "unnatural" in fact they can be when applied universally. Such theories show themselves to be ideologically prescriptive, eclipsing and then diffusing the presence of competing colonial histories. As David Weber points out, early historians of the Southwest went out of their way to portray Mexican Americans as part of a failed Spanish colonial past and thus proof of the racial and cultural superiority of Anglo–Saxon peoples.[6] In the twentieth century, as scholars of Puritanism promoted a uniform ideal of nationality as white, male, Anglo–Saxon, and Protestant, Mexican Americans did not find their way at all onto the national map. Hence, peoples with historic claims to more than one national origins tale became, by definition, marginalized, scapegoated as "alien," and written out of dominant national history. In short, theories of continuity that insistently join writers over the past three centuries into an "American" tradition have been historically burdensome for Chicano/a writers and their binational voices.

On the surface, these barriers would suggest that, unlike African American writing, Chicano/a literature exists somewhat independently of continuities that hark back to seventeenth–century New England. Indeed, Chicano/a literary criticism since the late 1960s has evolved primarily in pursuit of Spanish and pre–Columbian origins and precisely in opposition to the dominant Puritan paradigm. Yet, while I read a Puritan myth of origins as oppressive to Chicano/a writers, I would nevertheless argue for a more sophisticated understanding of literary nationalism, including the relevance of Puritan paradigms, so that the complexities of a binational literature, like Chicano/a literature, can be better understood. Rather than treating Puritan origins as the site from which Chicano/a writers can create only a separate, singular, counternationalist literary tradition, we should also focus on a Puritan myth of origins as a motivating discourse that enabled minorities to write their bicultural, binational narratives. Certainly Mexican American writers of the twentieth century have written in no more of a vacuum than their Anglo contemporaries, and in fact, have been quite aware of, if not both challenged and driven by, the idea of literary origins—be they Mexican, American, or something in between.

The Puritan Legacy of Self-Invention

"Puritanism"—as culture, myth, and history—has been reinvented and redeployed by a host of individuals over the centuries and in realms that range from the literary to the political.[7] This has been especially true when writers have articulated a crisis of national identity and purpose: from Mather's *Magnalia Christi Americana* (1702) to the political rhetoric justifying Desert Storm, the U.S. war with Iraq in 1991. As Sacvan Bercovitch has shown in *The Puritan Origins of the American Self,* Cotton Mather's histories began a tradition that rendered his grandfather's generation as the mythic, and hence figural, basis for later generations' grasps of the future. In his own period, says Bercovitch, Mather responded to his community's sense of crisis through an accumulating nationalist language:

> Mather's continual reference to himself as an American, like his concept of Winthrop as "Americanus," signifies not a secularization of "New Englander" but, on the contrary, an amplification of the figural import of the colony. . . . His method in this regard (as in others) is symptomatic of the movement from colonial to national identity. Early New England rhetoric provided a ready framework for inverting later secular values—human perfectibility, technological progress, democracy, Christian socialism, so simply (and comprehensively) the American Way—into the mold of sacred teleology.[8]

Accordingly, Mather aligns "America and American" as a trope and literary figure, with the sacred history of the Puritans of New England as pretext. It is sacred because the first generation of Puritan settlers are assumed to have entered the heavenly congregation of Puritan saints, and sacred again because their migration to New England was the fulfillment of a biblical promise to the faithful. With the arrival of these Puritan faithful, New England, and America by extension, was transformed as both the site and means of Christ's eventual return. As Bercovitch presents it, Mather enabled later writers to invoke the Puritan myth through history or figure. As sacred history collapsed into the figural representation of America, to write about "America" or as an "American," especially during moments of communal or national crisis, was to automatically assert yourself as one of the "solitary keepers of the [Puritan/American] dream" (136). Bercovitch places Jonathan Edwards and Ralph Waldo Emerson in this tradition.

In "The Ends of American Puritan Rhetoric" (1990), Bercovitch applied this mode of authoring history to later moments in national history. But his focus shifted. Instead of citing Mather's legacy purely in religious and literary writers, he sees what he calls the "genre of auto–American–biography: the celebration of the representative self as America, and the American self as the embodiment of a prophetic universal design" also expressed in overtly political texts:

> I mean Christianography in a broader metaphoric sense than Mather intended. The publications through which the republic established itself were political rather than theological, they appealed to reason, they celebrated civic virtues, and they addressed "a largely, new class of readers, Franklin's middling class," which they "came increasingly to treat . . . as the very definition of the American." But the same conditions applied in kind to Puritan New England. The transition from colony to province was not a process of secularization. It was an expanding sacred–secular process of textual self–identification from the *Arbella* covenant through Timothy Dwight's epic of the Revolution, *The Conquest of Canaan.* (174–75)

What is important about this shift is that Bercovitch demonstrates how this genre of "auto–American–biography" can also be maneuvered for cultural and ideological purposes. Though his interests remain largely literary–especially as he acknowledges the different traditions of W. E. B. DuBois and Langston Hughes as ones that still embrace a literary figure of Puritan America (187)–Bercovitch acknowledges the broader resonance of Puritanism in U.S. history: "The legacy of this ritual mode [of history as "auto–American–biography"] may be traced through virtually every major event in the culture, from the Great Awakening through the Revolution and the Westward Movement to the Civil War, and from that

'Armageddon of the Republic' to the Cold War and the Star Wars of our latter days" (186–87). Thus, Puritanism as myth, culture, and history has been pushing beyond its own historical boundaries since the seventeenth century. What Bercovitch's thesis affirms is the ideological range of the trope of "America"–whether used by Langston Hughes in his poem "Let America Be America Again," or Ronald Reagan in an inaugural speech that uses Winthrop's biblical figure of "city on the hill" (187). In both examples, despite political differences, "America" is deployed both as proof of the country's sacred history and as the figural landscape upon which to remake oneself outside of history and its constraints.

A historical appreciation of Puritanism helps to contextualize the emergence of Puritan studies as an academic field in American universities. It allows us to see the institutionalization of Puritan studies as part of a national response to the economic, political, and cultural condition of the United States during the 1930s. With the backdrop of the Great Depression and the rise of fascism in Europe, Puritan studies participated in a national search for an identity that would rescue the country from its economic and political crises. Historians like Perry Miller–aware that New England Puritans confronted bleak political and cultural crises with a fierce belief in providence–provided histories that performed the cultural work of revitalizing America's sense of identity and destiny.[9] The Allied victories in Europe and Japan during the middle 1940s confirmed the implicit narrative of these histories: the Puritans were a hardy and intellectual lot that earnestly believed America would be the site of God's fulfillment of his promise to Abraham, and that consequently America and its inhabitants would ultimately lead the world toward prosperity and moral righteousness.

In addition, by adapting the modernist aesthetics of T. S. Eliot–especially his critical stance on canon formation as argued in "Tradition and the Individual Talent" and "The Metaphysical Poets"–Puritan literary scholars, such as Thomas H. Johnson, were able to claim in a person, like Edward Taylor, the discovery of America's own John Donne.[10] The effect of this claim was to catapult the literary output of this earlier colonial period out of "the poorer cousin's realm." Puritan studies could not only claim a significant Anglo Protestant tradition, but with works like Perry Miller's *The New England Mind: The Seventeenth Century* (1939), it could also claim a continental philosophical tradition that linked New England theology to Saint Augustine. Elsewhere, F. O. Matthiessen's

American Renaissance (1941) privileged a list of male authors that tilted considerably the evaluative scales toward New England Puritan writers.[11] Matthiessen's reading of nineteenth-century literature *necessitated* a Puritan origin in order to justify an American poetic tradition through Emerson, and a novel tradition through Hawthorne and Melville.[12] The combination of these claims—which further promoted the legitimacy of studying American authors—came as American literature fought to be institutionalized in universities. With American literature now on equal footing with the "great literature" tradition of Old World England, Americanists could point to a literary canon that was symbolically and intertextually linked, and for years to come these symbolic and textual gestures were markers for the literary merits of a work by an American writer. A work could enter the academic canon only as long as it announced its allegiance to a Puritan myth of origins.

A Pledge of Literary Allegiance

My use of "allegiance" is not casual given what World War II meant for the evolution of American studies in the postwar years, and the subsequent renarration of American literature within a Cold War ideology. The origins of American studies can be traced to the turn of the century itself, but it is the 1946 publication of the massive *Literary History of the United States* (*LHUS*) that consolidated a dozen or so trends into one narrative.[13] Further, the production and publication of *Literary History of the United States* took on a character that paralleled the course of World War II.[14] In this context, it is a unique and concrete example of Bercovitch's "ritual mode" of a Puritan identification/reinvention in a moment of urgent national consciousness. The publication of this literary history is thus particularly noteworthy to my own discussion of literary origins because of the webs of allegiance—patriotic, aesthetic, and moral—it pressed on all who read its conclusions.

At the heart of this allegiance is the theory of literature Robert Spiller espoused as general editor. He advocated, and his contributors either supported or tolerated, an evolutionary and organic theory of American literature that, Spiller argued, resulted in cycles of great literature.[15] In the main, his theory argued for cultural continuity as the basis for a literary history. Not surprisingly, American literature's genesis begins on the Atlantic seaboard. The British colonies, New England in particular, are important cultural sites for the importation and adaptation of European thought and English literary traditions. Separated from Europe by their collective experiences in the New World, they return, in times of need, to their own colonial origins for spiritual and creative regeneration. According to this theory, the writers that follow this path are increasingly "American." Spiller's theory illustrates one means by which the Puritan myth of origins was institutionalized in key scholarly texts.

The project was begun in 1939 as an MLA-sanctioned project. Spiller eventually encountered such a diversity of opinions and personalities that it dissolved into the private enterprise of a few scholars.[16] Despite the initial wranglings, the project overcame a host of internal critical differences, war-related logistical problems, late submissions, poor writing, and other obstacles, to produce, in 1948, a three-volume literary history, comprising over eighty chapter entries, written by more than fifty scholars. This monumental effort was presented as the collaborative effort of a diverse set of scholars and writers. Nevertheless, the project incurred harsh reviews from the likes of Perry Miller, Arthur Schlesinger, Jr., Oscar Cargill, and Jay B. Hubbell. Early on, only Norman Holmes Pearson granted the new literary history a favorable review. Yet, if its publication history into a fourth edition (1974) is any indication, Spiller's literary history succeeded where few dreamed it would. As both Annette Kolodny and Kermit Vanderbilt recall, the *Literary History of the United States* was a major part of graduate education in American literature, extending even into the early 1980s.[17] Given its pedagogical role in the training of Americanists, it would seem important to ask what Spiller's theory of American literature taught in the ensuing thirty-plus years.

Spiller theorized American literary history as divided into two cycles, 1830–1870 and 1870–1910; each period marked an outpouring of great literature. In addition, his own contemporary period, the 1940s, was producing literature that validated the strength of the theory. To account for the early colonial period's relationship to the whole, Spiller argued that the British colonies assimilated the Old World, thereby providing the basis for the emergence of a new culture and nation. Kermit Vanderbilt reports: "The stages of this development were 'importation, modification, fertilization, and dynamic return.' The four themes that recurred 'with a fair degree of consistency' were (1) the revolt against authority in religion and philosophy, (2) the revolt against authority in government, (3) the illusion of infinite resources, and (4) the skepticism of scientific inquiry" (432). Vanderbilt argues that these four themes proved to be the foundation for Spiller's two–cycle theory. They represent, writes Vanderbilt, what Spiller learned from Norman Foerster: that Puritanism, the frontier, romanticism, and realism are the pillars of American literature. For Vanderbilt, the four themes "combined with Foerster's phrase 'European culture and American environment' to govern much of the argument of the entire *LHUS*" (432).

According to Spiller's theory, American literature figures as an expression of Western European traditions, whose American identity is a consequence of the cultural and political revolt from England and Europe of the "original" thirteen colonies. What's significant is the degree to which Spiller's language of revolt values texts in which dissent plays a nationalist role on North American soil. These texts are themselves organized under headings that stress a postcolonial nation–building enterprise. *LHUS* begins with "The Colonies," but it quickly proceeds to "The Republic" and "The Democracy"; it later features "Expansion" and "The Continental Nation" to explain the growth of the nation and its regional diversity, and it ends with "The United States" and "A World Literature" to reflect a political and literary coming of age (ix–xii). The cumulative suggestion of these headings is that the United States can boast of an anticolonial dissenting tradition of literature, one that (even if ironically) has underwritten the country's eventual establishment as a world power. Implicit is a consciousness about the power of narrative to establish meaning, and the need to make sense of the past in light of the current nationalist moment. Ultimately, the editors of *LHUS* drew upon a rebellious colonial past, especially its rhetoric of dissent, to secularize and update the idea of religious providence as a scholastic humanist enterprise that validated their work and asserted American literature's future global importance.[18]

Apart from praising Spiller's diplomacy with the other editors and contributors and his maintaining of a stylistic integrity, Vanderbilt congratulates Spiller's romantic theory for making the whole project "remarkably lucid and readable for a cooperative work so extensive and scholarly" (527). Approvingly, Vanderbilt reiterates that one of the lasting contributions of Spiller's work was the conception of a national literature as the unfolding, "organic expression of American life closely experienced by our major writers in their time" (527). According to Vanderbilt, the two–cycle theory resolved for Spiller two formative questions:

First was the aesthetic question of what great literature is and who the great American writers are (Spiller figured that they numbered somewhere from six to twelve). Second was the definition of what is American–the issue of nationalism amid our heterogeneous races, languages, customs, traditions, and occupations. Spiller discovered the answer to both questions in a romantic formula applied to American backgrounds and writers. In his theory, "only a romantic movement can create great literature," though within such a welling–up of expression must come also "a degree of control through self–criticism." (431)

In his retrospective assessment–some forty years later–Vanderbilt agrees with Spiller that the whole of American literary history can indeed "be described organically, this time in the metaphor of cyclical birth, growth, flowering, and decline" (527). Spiller's theory for unifying American literature was not the only one available at the time, and was not without its critics. Nevertheless, Vanderbilt credits Spiller's editorship with having sparked among Americanists "the drive toward assimilation, compromise, and synthesis while affirming the integrity of literary art and the organic unity of art and life" (526).

Vanderbilt's comments on Spiller's two-cycle theory and LHUS are an inadvertent gloss on theoretical and institutional changes that have occurred in the academy since the late 1960s. What Vanderbilt celebrates as the achievements of LHUS underscore the limitations of a totalizing theory of literary history unconcerned with alternative traditions or writings by women and/or people of color, much less with historical issues involving race, gender, and class as categories of analysis. Spiller's resolution of his formative questions reveals the extent to which a T. S. Eliot-like canon of masterpieces predetermined the content and trajectory of his literary history. Ideally, this literary history functions to support the cultural legitimacy of a few select texts and to subordinate the significance of all other texts to this selection. Spiller's notion that there exist six to twelve "great" authors not only seems incredibly subjective, but it demonstrates how theories of continuity underlying grand critical enterprises can contribute to the construction of ahistorical literary histories, which speak not to a past history but to present and presentist scholarly values. One can see how, over time, so–called minor works, like those written by white women in the 1850s, lose prestige and credibility among younger scholars, and are therefore written out of the literary record, presumably because they have not lasted the test of time. Furthermore, the presumption of an elite group of texts makes moot Spiller's second question about "What is American?" Editorially, Spiller resolves "the issue of nationalism amid our heterogeneous races, languages, customs, traditions, and occupations" by selecting Emerson, Thoreau, Hawthorne, Melville, and Whitman as the representative master writers of the first cycle, true champions of democratic values.[19]

The Achilles' heel of this theory is self–evident. It is self–replicating and self–validating, and ultimately ahistorical. Thus, the experiences and thoughts of a few select writers–how "they" unite art and life in their work–are the vehicles and basis for a totalizing literary history, which makes universal what is actually a predominantly male Anglo Puritan tradition. Even differences among these writers are modified or effaced in favor of the organic metaphor. This metaphor, which Vanderbilt praises, serves to naturalize continuity as progressive and inevitable, while discontinuities, like popular literature or alternative literary traditions, appear as aberrations or a function of "decline." Indeed, when the expected literary renaissance, as predicted by Spiller, failed to appear after 1945, the 1953 edition added a chapter that corrects not the cycle theory but the timing of the cycle![20] Given the hermeneutic circularity of Spiller's cycle theory, this kind of fine–tuning can go on forever without disturbing its core texts, tenets, or the narrative of origins it implements.

Vanderbilt laments that a project like *LHUS* became a "lost art" among scholars in the decades that followed. A fact further exacerbated, in his opinion, by the variety of critical directions "the profession was moving in . . . after 1948" (521). That *LHUS* represents a "lost art" should be viewed in the context of the synergy expected from collaborative national projects, not unlike the unifying Allied effort against the Axis powers during World War II. The better explanation for why projects of *LHUS*'s ambition were rarely attempted thereafter lies in an earlier statement by Vanderbilt:

> Perhaps the final magnitude of this enterprise even had a slightly
> menacing effect on would–be literary historians. The output of
> such an impressive army of scholars and critics, together with
> expenditures by Rockefeller, Macmillan, ACLS [American Coun
> cil of Learned Societies], APS [American Philological Association],

and various universities of the contributors, brought about the sense of an ending. A huge scholarly undertaking such as this could not soon be duplicated or surpassed. (521)

Embedded in Vanderbilt's assessment is a glimpse into the economic allegiances underlying *LHUS*'s production. The "investment" of these various institutions in *LHUS* was, I would argue, motivated in part by a sense of patriotism. That this scholarly patriotism should find itself in a monied venture was not unusual in a political climate that equated a defense of democracy with the virtues of capitalism. That Vanderbilt ascribes "a sense of an ending" to *LHUS*'s publication is also not surprising. As in Vanderbilt's language of armies, the publication history of *LHUS* doubles as a narrative for the war effort. Like U.S. participation in the war, *LHUS* endured monumental obstacles and initial setbacks, but in the end it emerged victorious, bringing to an end a half–century effort to represent American literature as a world literature. Further, the initial postwar years of returning GIs, the GI Bill, and the end of wartime rationing enabled not only the resumption of a consumer–oriented economy but the patriotic consumption of all things "American," from cars and clothes washers to a variety of American art forms. In this context, the postwar reconstruction of U.S. capitalism at home and abroad underwrote the longevity of *LHUS* and no doubt added to a mythology of its growing importance to American criticism.

Certainly, this economic analysis can be extended to other publications, scholars, theories, and even the proliferation of American studies programs during the 1940s. They all contributed to the institutionalization of American literature in universities and, by fiat, its dependence on a Puritan myth of national origins. An economic analysis also calls attention to issues of resources and capital distribution often overlooked in critiques of postwar scholarship and the canon. It explains how research grants and funds wound up supporting the status quo rather than more "marginal" or "radical" approaches to American literature. For example, Edmund Morgan, in celebrating the 100th year of the founding of the Colonial Society of Massachusetts, remembers the contributions of several past members to early American scholarship. One scholar he cites is Ted Shipton. Morgan says of him: "the achievement that puts us all in his debt was the publication on microcards at the American Antiquarian

Society of every book and pamphlet printed in America before 1800."[21] In a short amount of time, Shipton updated "on microcards the entire text of every book and pamphlet listed in [Charles Evans's *American Bibliography*]." Morgan credits Shipton for having made available to graduate students and professors primary material otherwise locked away for safekeeping.

The significant story being told here is of the earmarking of financial resources for expensive projects that in the end reinvented and validated the British colonial experience. Morgan's "America" added up to a narrow set of texts. Like *LHUS*, Shipton's microcards represent an economic commitment to a fairly stable narrative of literary and historical origins that emphasized the importance of the Anglo Puritan legacy in U.S. culture. The research infrastructures these kinds of projects put in place at midcentury would determine graduate education and scholarship for decades to come. Despite all the theoretical changes that have occurred in the field since the late 1960s, the surprisingly late arrival of the *Heath Anthology of American Literature* in 1990 demonstrates not only the staying power of the postwar ideology of texts like *LHUS* but how that ideology could be effectively contested only when market forces allowed it.[22]

In retrospect, the period 1939–48 that made Spiller's two-cycle theory and *LHUS* possible had tremendous consequences for the definition of American literature, what would be studied and how, and finally who would be its scholars. The consequences for these "other" scholars were also tremendous. Here, it is crucial to consider how the institutional infrastructure of any literary history is as important as the theory that enables it, and potentially just as exclusionary. Bercovitch's argument of the omnipresence of "auto–American–biography" in American culture and history—a rhetorical template for identifying and actualizing an Anglo Puritan experience—is clearly at work in the example of *LHUS*. Yet, this cultural production, while aiming to be pluralistic and democratic in its invocation of what is American literature, is also, ironically, fascistic on what constitutes allegiance to a literary nationalism. While *LHUS* constitutes a wonderful manifestation of a "ritual mode" of Puritan identification during a period of crisis, it is an open question how this solidifying of a Puritan legacy influenced ethnic writers it never imagined as its readers.

What's Puritan about Chicano/a Literature?

In the years following World War II mainstream writers inherited a revitalized cultural and institutional Puritan myth of origins. Mexican American writers were no less a part of that revitalization, despite their forced social invisibility and marginality. Mexican American writers just had to deal with both their presumed disconnection from this Puritan national identity and connection with identities that were more local, regional, and binational in character. If a national identity was fundamentally impoverished in civic terms, Mexican American writers nevertheless explored their binational experience within the more retrievable local and regional dimensions of their identity. I argue that the neo–Puritan culture of this period exerted its influence and extolled reactions at different levels from the Mexican American community. One could not consider the significance of being American of Mexican descent without pondering the meaning of an Anglo Puritan America. Yet, how did one contend with a myth of origins so recently reinvented to authorize official literary history? Ideally, one would search for an alternative myth of origins, a literary history more in keeping with the local dimensions of civic, racial, and regional identities. What then became of a national identity? Where could a Mexican American find an alternative myth of origins that could be the basis of any literary identity and still be considered an American writer? Where was the "ritual mode" of Anglo Puritan identification to be found?

Answers to these questions required that society itself become, at a minimum, accepting if not tolerant of hyphenated U.S. identities. It would take a World War II generation of Mexican Americans to create in the next generation the desire to fulfill the dreams of their predecessors. In short, it would take the Civil Rights Movement, the counterculture, student protests around the world, the Vietnam War, and the United Farm Workers boycotts all rolled into one to create a political vision. This vision had to be sustained long enough to reinvent a myth of origins suitable for the evolving Chicano/a Movement, and its literary companion, the Chicano Renaissance. As seen already in chapter 1, to articulate the unspoken desires of a minority community in the United States required a flexible cultural nationalism that would inspire ethnic pride while simultaneously providing a historical critique of European colonialism, U.S. imperialism, and economic disfranchisement. Though this cultural nationalism was obviously political, its deployment fell upon the shoulders of a generation of writers who saw their work as literary, not just propaganda. Even academics complemented their disciplinary analyses with outpourings of protest poems, short stories, and novels.[23] Soon enough, political demonstrations became inseparable from cultural productions of art, and vice versa.

Indeed, the explosion of Chicano/a protest writing in the late 1960s was intended to promote and accompany the struggle in the streets.[24] As a very early essay (1971) by Philip D. Ortego notes, the Civil Rights Movement sparked and nurtured a desire to read the writers of one's own ethnic heritage: "In recent years there has been an increasing social and political consciousness, leading to demands for reformation of the socioeconomic structure that has kept Mexican Americans subordinated these many years. With this increasing social and political consciousness has come the awareness of their artistic and literary heritage. Through out the Southwest the sleeping Mexican–American giant has begun to flex his dormant muscles."[25] As this literary flexing continued into the 1970s, Ortego envisioned Chicano/a literature as widening its readership from its ethnic base to a larger mainstream audience. In fact, he foresaw what would become, by the 1990s, a whole industry, from editors to academic scholarship, redefining "American literature as a fabric woven not exclusively on the Atlantic frontier by the descendants of New England Puritans and southern Cavaliers" (295).[26] In his view, the Chicano Renaissance of the 1960s can be appreciated for its political and literary dismantling of a Puritan colonial past.

Ortego imagined the day this politically awakened ethnic group would participate more directly in the nationalist revisions of American literature and culture. Ortego's generation of Chicano/a scholars thus fashioned a literary history faithful to a broad Chicano social politic. Along the way, though, they made aesthetic choices that represented a conflict in their resistance to the mainstream canon. Precisely because they aimed to be nationalists, they had to confront what was Puritan in the mainstream canon in order to carve out an alternative political identity. Yet, this identity, I argue, also had to function within the models of political and literary resistance offered within U.S. history, or else poets and writers, as a group, risked further historical erasure as an "American" civic community.

As Ortego points out in "The Chicano Renaissance," for Chicanos/as the challenge of dislodging the preeminence of a Puritan experience is the challenge of rewriting history. Entailed in that revision is a pronounced confidence that an ethnic literary history will complement the general movement for civil rights. By its sheer reintroduction into historical consciousness, a Chicano literary history will make clear the terms of oppression that have afflicted American citizens of Mexican descent. Ortego writes:

> Heretofore, Mexican Americans have been a marginal people in a sort of no man's land, caught between the polarizing forces of their cultural–linguistic Indo–Hispanic heritage and their political–linguistic American context. They have become frustrated and alienated by the struggle between the system that seeks to refashion them in its own image and the knowledge of who and what they really are. As a result, this cultural conflict has debilitated many Mexican Americans. (296)

Aided and abetted by a capitalist need for cheap labor, this "political–linguistic American context" supplanted a Mexican literary heritage. And thus, according to Ortego, perpetrated the erasure of a literary tradition for Chicanos and non–Chicanos alike. But for the Chicano, the loss amounted to a loss of cultural pride:

> Mexican Americans actually have a rich literary heritage. That they have been kept from it bespeaks a shameful and tragic oppression of a people whose origins antedate the establishment of Jamestown by well over a century (and even more, considering their Indian ancestry). Moreover, the shame and tragedy are compounded when Mexican–American youngsters learn about their Puritan forebears but not about their Hispanic forebears about whom they have as much right–if not more–to be proud. (296)

Hence, the recovery of these "Hispanic forebears," Ortego thinks, will authenticate and elevate the presence of an "Indo–Hispanic" people within the political confines of the United States. From this recovery, an alternative nationalist experience will arise that will compete with a Puritan literary tradition.

One might think this recovery would begin with actual literary figures, or at the least with Spanish and Mexican colonial history. Instead it began with an adoption and promotion of the Mayans and Aztecs. In Ortego's understanding, "the significance of the [1960s] Chicano Renaissance lies in the identification of Chicanos with their Indian past" (302). By embracing the historical and legendary achievements of the Aztec and Mayan Empires in south central and southern Mexico, Chicano literary artists, acting as both activists and writers, reintroduced a pre-Columbian nationalist experience that could compete with their Anglo Puritan subjugation. Ortego writes: "They have thus cast off the sometimes meretricious identification with the Spanish templar tradition foisted on them by Anglo American society because of its preference for things European. To reinforce their identification with their Indian past, Chicano writers have appropriated for their literary symbols Aztec and Mayan figures, including the great Aztec calendar stone" (302). The overall effect of this adoption was simultaneously literary, cultural, and political. And since the achievements of the Mayans and Aztecs predated any European influence, it celebrated a distinct prenationalist relationship to the New World. For those who viewed themselves as "Montezuma's children" (302), a prior claim on the land was fundamental in challenging the socioeconomic and legal domination of an "Anglo American society." This pre–Columbian claim to the land eventually led to a very deliberate use of the myth of Aztlán as a way to identify the southwestern United States as the rightful homeland of Chicanos/as.

In the late 1960s, activist–poets, such as Alurista and Rodolfo "Corky" Gonzalez, advanced the myth of Aztlán as a means of actualizing the goals of the Chicano/a Movement. As discussed in the previous chapter, their use of Aztlán was more clearly separatist. Alurista saw it as a "symbol of liberation, pride, unity, and self–determination for Chicanos."[27] The myth of Aztlán promoted a unified cultural identity as a means to contest Anglo oppression of people of Mexican descent.[28] According to critic Gustavo V. Segade, this search "for the primordial communal values of ancestral earth and a mythic past" encouraged "talk of acquiring lands and establishing separate Chicano communities. . . . Not everyone could have land; 80 percent of the Chicano population live[d] in an urban setting. But everyone could share a mythic past, and the knowledge that their forebears were buried in lands now lost to strangers."[29] In a short time, the geographic location of Aztlán in myth could also represent the actual location of Chicano/a communities in the Southwest, from California to Texas. This ethnically claimed homeland, as discussed in chapter 1, became the basis for challenging the dominant culture and for inspiring an all-out artistic attempt to locate Aztlán in contemporary life.

For a time, Aztlán became, among this generation of poets, writers, and scholars, the means of shaping their community experiences and in turn shaping Chicano/a reading communities. It became the organizing symbol for Chicano literature, especially in the 1970s, and in formulating a new myth of origins, it provided a political platform by which to challenge the status quo in the canon.[30] Yet Aztlán also confirmed Chicanos/as' paradoxical relationship to U.S. history and culture as binational citizens. While Chicano/a writers and scholars advocated a non-Puritan myth of origins for Chicanos/as, they enacted categories of national identification that invariably dialogued with a discourse of literary origins that posited a Puritan past as part of their dual nationality. Aztlán is not a City on a Hill. On the other hand, the kind of utopia constructed with Aztlán at the center has all the symbolic and cultural expectations of a City on a Hill. It invokes the rights of the native as part of an organic theory of history and homeland; it promotes the notion that people of Mexican descent are special and exceptional; and invariably Aztlán holds up the wonders of the Aztec civilization as a counterweight to Western culture. Yet, this recognition must contend with an Aztec cosmology that viewed Aztlán as a kind of "earthly paradise" turned wasteland once the ancestors of the Aztec left to pursue its prophesied "promised land."[31] Aztlán, though a paradise, was not the future site of the Aztecs' evolving sacred providence. Aztlán of the Chicano/a Movement and literature is clearly a cultural construction of its time. As a result, what's ultimately Puritan about Chicano literary history is that it engages in the secular Puritan process that Bercovitch identifies as writing oneself and/or one's community into U.S. history. Without a doubt, the myth of Aztlán enabled this literary entry into official history writ large.

Calls for Change in American Literary History: Two Views

In "Narrative, Ideology, and the Reconstruction of American Literary History," Ramón Saldívar articulates a rationale by which we can better understand Chicano/a literature's relationship to mainstream processes of American literary culture. Building on the oppositional analyses of scholars like Philip Ortego and the economic model of internalized colonialism as proposed by scholars like Rodolfo Acuña, Saldívar begins with the obvious: "Chicano literature and its literary criticism [has] been systematically excluded from the traditional framework of American literature".[32] Consequently, he argues for "reading Chicano literary texts as a group of works that intentionally exploit their peripheral status to and exclusion from the body of works that we might call majority literature" (11). The purpose of this interpretive strategy lies in the "developing" nature of Chicano/a literature. Because such a reading method requires an awareness of the function of ideology in the social/cultural world that creates realms of exclusion, it will help "shape the direction of an art that is, to paraphrase Gates, in the process of 'imagining' and 'figuring' a world" (12). Saldívar's "dialectical critical awareness" (11) argues for a social order that does not exclude Chicano/a writers or critics and thus sees Chicano/a literature not only as a means to critique the dominant culture but the site to envision how society might refashion itself altogether.

Crucial to my argument that a critically constructed Puritan ethos influenced twentieth-century Chicano/a writers is Saldívar's identification of the ideology that is the basis for Chicano/a literature. To make his case, he draws upon Sacvan Bercovitch's studies of ideological formation in early American writers and history.[33] Important for Saldívar is Bercovitch's thesis that U.S. society can call upon an "American ideological consensus" that has "already built into itself a way of dealing with, and neutralizing, 'alternative and oppositional forms' of social formation" (14). This consensus legitimized "a canon based on the works of the Puritan forefathers," as well as it internalized a Puritan ethos that validated an imperialist narrative about "America's" future and its role in the world (14).

Equally important for Saldívar is Bercovitch's analysis that ideology is a product of historical conditions. A society's ability to produce representations of itself as universal and natural is related to the ability of certain groups to disguise their historical agency through a reliance on notions like self-evident truth or the pursuit of happiness.[34] To establish the historical conditions for Chicano/a literature's exclusion from the mainstream canon, Saldívar uses Bercovitch's definition of ideology:

An ideology will thus repress alternative or oppositional forms when they arise. The ideology of the Puritan colonies, for example, did not simply exclude Native Americans from the colonists' consensus about the new world being fashioned from the wilderness. The native inhabitants were seen as the very embodiments of the evils most threatening to the creation of the new Jerusalem. This ideology of exclusion remained central to the American creed throughout the nineteenth century. And we see its effects in other historical and literary moments. (14)

In short, Saldívar points out how an ideology—itself clustered around the historically evolving term "Puritan"—succeeded indirectly over time to exclude groups that are figured antithetical to this "new Jerusalem," and in addition, how this ideology is the primary basis for the mainstream canon and thus the force behind the exclusion of Chicano/a writers. In his estimation, Chicano/a narrative "carries out a counterhegemonic resistance to the dominant ideology at the level of symbolic languages, attempting to figure what we might call . . . an 'alter–ideology'" (17). In terms of American literature as a whole, Saldívar argues, "these other marginal texts serve to highlight the ideological background of the traditional canon, to bring to the surface that repressed formation that Jameson has called the 'political unconscious'" (17).

Saldívar's use of Bercovitch does not come without some critique as well. He takes Bercovitch, as well as Werner Sollors, to task for offering a "new integrative model [that] can in practice turn out to be a counterhegemonic move to renew, defend, and modify, not to undo, the earlier forms of dominance" (19).[35] In Saldívar's view, a truly integrated U.S. literary history would not, for example, omit "the literary tradition of the Southwest" because of a desire to create a unitary model of literary origins that solely features "American culture or an American ideological consensus [as] arising from a Puritan, New England, middle–class perspective" (20). Saldívar's cautionary critique of Bercovitch and Sollors is a reminder of the institutional elitism of certain narratives. Indeed, this kind of persistent academic elitism has made separatist strategies all the more critically and institutionally necessary.

In contrast to a limited unitary model, Saldívar proposes "an oppositional reconstruction of American literary history [that] would recapture those stories [of colonization and exclusion] and use them to construct a dialogical system." (20). He posits twentieth–century writing by Mexican American men and women as a "direct resistance" to F. O. Matthiessen's argument that Renaissance writers fulfilled " 'the potentialities freed by the Revolution, [and provided] a culture commensurate with America's political opportunity' " (20).[36] Saldívar explains that this political opportunity was realized only via "the colonized oppression of the native people of the Southwest and the exclusion of their writings from the canon of American literature" (20). To reverse this historical tendency in a new literary history, he argues for a dialogical system that would "help us understand both the canonical master works that were sanctioned by the American ideological consensus and the antagonistic works that were not. By placing the masterworks in a framework that includes the voices to which the master texts were covertly opposed, voices that were silenced by the hegemonic culture, we might indeed begin to formulate a truly integrated American literary history" (20). Thus, Saldívar ends with a sense of possibility for an integrative literary history. It can happen even as Chicano/a literature develops within its own canon. It can happen as long as a history of oppression is foregrounded and a history of resistance is highlighted. And it can happen alongside the masterworks of the traditional canon. But it cannot happen, and this is one of the important issues in my argument, with a unitary vision of American literature's origins.

Saldívar's "dialogical system" outlines the rationale for a more specific study of Bercovitch's "American ideological consensus" as it influenced Chicano/a writing during the twentieth century. The rhetoric of dissent and nationalism inherent in the traditional canon alone should alert us to the literary models of resistance that were and are available to minority writers. All this rhetoric, history, and biography–both literally and symbolically presented in the traditional canon–about the power of individuals to write themselves and their communities into a national narrative during crises could not have been lost on the Mexican American writer, especially if he or she were taught in an educational system predominantly governed by the mainstream canon. What is the collective myth of the New England Puritans in the twentieth century if not a model for how to defend against the hostilities of the world while simultaneously believing in America as the site for a City on a Hill?

For Saldívar, Chicano/a literature "illuminate[s] the gaps and silences that are the limits of the ideological consensus of American literary history" (18). My study does not see "the consensus" in quite such mono-lithic terms. Rather, by exploring beyond these limits, by looking at the fault lines of the border, if you will, "the consensus" is revealed as vul-nerable to and appropriated by those groups it sought to exclude. One area of vulnerability has always been the appropriation of this collective myth of origins by those deemed as Other. I ask that we consider not only how latter-day salvific visions of "America" overlap and compete with the Puritans' "errand into the wilderness," like those thousands of Mexican immigrants in this century who have treated the Rio Grande as their own River Jordan, but how Chicano writers might symbolically transform a City on a Hill—as John Rechy, for example, did in *City of Night*.

Like Saldívar, but from the vantage point of Early American stud-ies, R. C. De Prospo considers seriously the ideological implications of a canon and myth of origins that promotes exclusionary practices. In "Marginalizing Early American Literature," he argues that Early Ameri-can criticism continues to suffer because of its service to twentieth-century literary nationalism. De Prospo critiques both a scholarly cult of American exceptionalism that aligns twentieth-century literary na-tionalism with a colonial past, and progressive revisions of literary his-tory that highlight the critical importance of the seventeenth century but only by superimposing social or political categories of analysis ahistori-cally onto the literature examined.[37] The combined effect of these two trends has been a marginalization of Early American literature that un-dermines serious study of the period for its own sake. To counteract this marginalization, De Prospo proposes specific study of the Early Ameri-can period. Its benefits are twofold. First, it would serve to deconstruct this century's literary nationalism and its penchant for theories of con-tinuities that link New England Puritanism with modern American liter-ature. Second, it would contribute to the ongoing body of scholarship that theorizes modern humanism. In the end, writes De Prospo, "Early American literature must be redeployed, no longer as the progenitor but as the necessary companion of modern American literature, as the Other according to whose *différance* we modern humanists may come better to know ourselves" (255–56).

The upshot of De Prospo's critique is that a desire for origins in literary history implicates continuity as the best means to achieve it. Such a literary history "will inevitably be deemed continuous, because origin and continuity are inextricably bound to one another within the organic figuration that silently informs such neo–romantic historicizing" (243). According to De Prospo, this results in a "condescension toward early American literature" (245) that is further aggravated by the marginalizing tendencies found in the latest anthologies. By marginalization, he means that "the compulsion to establish origins [even if renovated for a multicultural audience], and to trace continuities, dominates the introductions to early American literature, and ensures its diminution" (247). That is, such introductions paint the importance of the early period only in regard to later trends or issues deemed more significant, like the romantic period of the nineteenth century, exploration and settlement of the continent, the founding of democratic institutions, and so on. In addition, De Prospo charges such anthologies with presentist agendas, such as the *Heath Anthology's* portrayal of multiculturalism as a transhistorical phenomenon traceable to the seventeenth century (248). The culmination of such treatment is that the early period is given no critical importance on its own merits, while the study of American literature is simultaneously committed to a "crude occidentalism that has been long decried by scholars with an other–than–exclusively–Western orientation" (250–51).

In short, argues De Prospo, the continuing "compulsion to establish origins," with all the limitations of its organic neo–romanticism, demands that the traditional assumptions behind American literary history and criticism be challenged. Quoting Elaine Showalter, De Prospo includes among these assumptions "'periodic divisions (such as 'the American Renaissance') that were exclusively based on male literary landmarks[,] to the underlying ideas about genre, the literary career, and the role of the critic'" (251). This challenge will enable and promote "comparatist approaches" to American literature, which De Prospo considers an advantage since they function against the inertia of the status quo. Such approaches "will have an impact not only on how literature is studied but how the institution is structured," and by extension they might reveal how such institutions affect society (252–53).

"What needs ultimately to be done," proposes De Prospo, "is to theorize American literary history not as a diachronic passage from past to present–continuous, discontinuous, or whatever–but as the synchronic differentiation of past from present" (255). Not only would this retheorization mark the liberation of Early American scholarship from the ills of American exceptionalism and ethnocentric nationalism, it would align the study of Early American literature with current projects to historicize modern humanism. De Prospo contends that the "marginalizing of early American literature by modern American literary historiography can thus be taken as a synecdoche of the universal humanist enterprises, and opposition to it accordingly can become a part that signifies the whole of the deconstruction of the sciences of man" (255). De Prospo links the scope of this undertaking with international investigations into "the possibility of the existence of a so-called counter-discourse, which possibility is implied most notably in Michel Foucault's fascination with atavism, and which has become a primary focus of post-Foucauldian commentators on Foucault" (256). But in the end, De Prospo finds the more pertinent goal of this project closer to home. Taking his cue from William C. Spengemann, De Prospo reminds his readers that "we are the authors of early American literature, not Smith and Bradstreet, and if we can create a marginal Early American literature in the narrow interest of preserving American literary nationalism, we can recreate a more mobile Early American literature in the broader one of deconstructing American literary nationalism" (258).

De Prospo's argument substantiates many of the claims made by this chapter: that the institutionalization of Puritan studies paralleled and aided the study of American literature at the university level; that the treatment of the Puritans by enthusiasts, like Perry Miller, gave scholarly credence to popular conceptions of the Puritans as the "founding fathers" of the United States; that scholars, in their zeal to establish a history of a "national" literature, sought out in writers democratic ideals such as religious freedom and dissent from oppressive authority; that tracing a national legacy through Anglo Puritan colonial tradition canonized certain authors at the expense of erasing and marginalizing the contributions of women and/or people of color, including those writing out of non-Puritan colonial traditions; and finally, that a comparative approach to American literature holds out the promise of complicating established literary history without sacrificing the history of criticism, both mainstream and alternative.

Despite these overlaps, De Prospo underestimates the significance of continuity in criticism and creative writing of this century. He is right to point out that scholars have created the university category of "early American literature," not Smith or Bradstreet. But have scholars also created the twentieth-century writer or poet who individually participates in a Puritan myth of origins? Discourse theory would have us believe that this is not only possible but inescapable. Yet American writers must themselves be partly responsible for creating an interest in origins and legacies. In the nineteenth century, Hawthorne's guilt-ridden fascination with a colonial past was preceded by Catherine Maria Sedgwick's character Hope Leslie (1827), who believed that New England Puritan history held some importance for her own times. Or, more recently, what are scholars to make of Thomas Pynchon's pre-Columbian narrative in *Vineland* (1990)? What discourse theory illuminates is that theories of continuity produce realities of their own—more complicated and contradictory than accounted for in De Prospo's thesis of marginality. Therefore, the problem is not whether theories of continuity should exist or not, or that upon close reading, presentist politics, ideology, or nationalism eventually rear their ugly heads. Rather, is it possible to write literary history without invoking a "compulsion to establish origins"? As most historians will concede, any narrative that intends to mark change over time necessitates some point of origin. How to do it better has been the debate for the last thirty years.

Everything else aside, De Prospo provides an exciting glimpse of a possible future. His idea "to theorize American literary history . . . as the synchronic differentiation of past from present" bodes well for a revision of the Puritan myth of origins, because it allows for the differentiation between a history of criticism and a history of the cultural work of that criticism. This kind of differentiation would be most useful in developing comparative approaches to literature, where the theoretical tension is always in maintaining alternative literary histories despite the ahistorical tendencies of comparisons. Rather than doing away with this compulsion for origins entirely, I believe it is presently better to embrace it as part of the complicated apparatus in making or revising literary history. Scholars and students would be better served if the cultural work of this compulsion were developed into institutional histories, because it is ultimately the institutions of higher learning in the United States that control the process of intellectual change, and over time influence broader changes in popular thinking. This view of the cultural role of literary histories underscores the need for a comparative method by which to explore the effects of a Puritan myth of origins on Chicano/a literature and criticism.

Opportunities for Comparative Approaches

A comparative approach of the kind suggested above has been in the making since the early 1990s. In "Letting Go Our Grand Obsessions: Notes towards a New Literary History of the American Frontier," an essay in the March 1992 issue of *American Literature* that inaugurated Cathy Davidson's debut as editor, Annette Kolodny launches an argument for a "literary history of the American frontiers" that will free "American literary history from the persistent theories of continuity that have made it virtually impossible to treat frontier materials as other than marginalia or cultural mythology" (2). Kolodny wishes to decenter a British model of colonial experience that symbolically and ideologically continues to shape features of U.S. literary history: "my approach necessarily complicates the notion of earliness but, at the same time, promises liberation from the stultifying habit of regarding that literature merely as a precursor to an authentic literature yet to follow or as transition pieces between British forebears and American identities" (3). In this context, Kolodny embraces colonial histories of other European powers as a way to work against the inherent nationalism in American literary history. She is also interested in representing a necessarily more complex history of early North America that is more attentive to the current discourse on multiculturalism: "by acknowledging the many different configurations of indigenous peoples, immigrants, and immigrants who came in contact over time on a variety of landscapes, we allow the literatures of the frontiers to stand—accurately at last—as multilingual, polyvocal, and newly intertextual and multicultural" (11–12). Kolodny's proposal is both an acknowledgment of the current curricular debates fostered by advocates of multiculturalism and a response to the field's growing appreciation of New Historicist praxis.

Kolodny's call for change is in explicit agreement with De Prospo that the current American literary history distorts the historical record of the colonial experience in North America. But, all the better, she directly links her argument with a language that has been forged in dialogue with discourses of race and ethnicity, of which the multicultural curricular debates is just one. Kolodny's expansion of colonial experience would denaturalize the New England experiment. Her literary history would present New England as only one of many colonial experiences, some of which dramatically reveal different linguistic, religious, and historic pasts. Thus Kolodny argues that in developing Spanish, French, Dutch, and other colonial histories, scholars might be able to study the interactions of indigenous peoples with these non–British cultures. The result would be an assemblage of histories, texts, and experiences that would forever change our perception of early North America.

In terms of race and ethnicity, Kolodny's comprehensive literary history would facilitate understanding the emergence of an African American literary tradition or a Chicano/a literary tradition. That is, by shifting the critical gaze toward the "multilingual, polyvocal, and newly intertextual and multicultural," Kolodny is purposefully helping to reconceive the marginality of "other" literary histories. Just at the linguistic level, attention to the multiple languages present in seventeenth-century North America implicitly legitimizes the presence of different languages in the twentieth-century United States, and undermines the social perception that the continental United States has always been a predominantly English-speaking country. In this revised history, English is only one language, which competed for cultural primacy with not only indigenous languages but other European languages. Under this paradigmatic frame, the bilingualism in most Chicano/a works, for example, might become a more central feature of a literary canon that posits the multilingual as part of its definition of a literary history. In turn, the multilingual might then become a category of acceptance, even prestige, within a canon rather than a site of alienation and dispossession. In all, Kolodny's literary history stands to make substantial structural changes in the study of Early American literature that will better reflect the social identities of current U.S. students.

Kolodny's call for change goes even further. She challenges American literature departments to accept a new role in the formation of literary histories of the "frontier," a role that would necessitate an interdisciplinary approach and would encourage the dismantling of American literature as a single discipline. Thus, Kolodny's structural change in literary history actually forces an institutional one. This latter change dramatizes what is at stake when the canon and/or literary history is fundamentally questioned, namely, the institutional means by which students are socialized into a cultural and political past. As Paul Lauter writes, "the canon is, after all, a construct, like a history text, expressing what a society reads back into the past as important to its future."[38] In part, Kolodny marks her call for change as "revolutionary" precisely because she has in mind the diverse student bodies entering colleges and universities in the 1990s where they would invariably be confronted with the cultural and political issues of that time: race relations, gender relations, sexuality, the opportunity for access to institutions of political, economic, and cultural power, and access to representation itself (whether in student newspapers or Third World Centers).

Kolodny's implicit support for a comparative model of literary analysis links her with Paul Lauter, who identifies his comparative project by way of presentist concerns:

> The United States is a heterogeneous society whose cultures, while they overlap in significant respects, also differ in critical ways. A normative model presents variations from the mainstream as abnormal, deviant, lesser, perhaps ultimately unimportant. That kind of standard is no more helpful in the study of culture than is a model, in the study of gender differences, in which the male is considered the norm, or than paradigms, in the study of minority or ethnic social organization and behavior, based on Anglo–American society. (9)

Though Lauter structures his argument around literary examples from the nineteenth and early twentieth century, he concedes his critical position is formed by presentist social concerns and by the legacy of reading reception theory in the 1980s. "The diversity of audience response to literature in late twentieth–century America" (29), Lauter states, has convinced him not to treat the classroom as "neutral ground for literary study, within which differing works can, whatever the context of their original articulation, be studied with equal success and without a great deal of attention to differences among students apart from the levels of literacy" (29). Lauter here comments that the canon, like literary history, performs profound cultural work upon the students who receive it as a matter of course. Because of the canon's exclusionary tenets, students, as they study the canon, are also socialized to read "alternative" writers or texts as the canon does: as marginal.

The importance of a comparative model of literature is thus fourfold: it justifies the need for a more integrated literary history of literatures that historically developed in North America; it denaturalizes "Anglo–European, male writing as but one voice, albeit loud and various, in the chorus of 'American' culture" (11); it argues that a "full literary history of this country requires both parallel and integrated accounts of differing literary traditions and thus of differing (and changing) social realities" (12); and finally, it theorizes the pedagogic effect a canon and literary history has in the classroom and, concurrently, how the social constitution of classrooms should alert instructors to the classroom's political relationships to the larger world.

At the moment, there are three important obstacles for new comparative methodologies. First, comparative study requires a great deal of training and knowledge that the field of American literature for the most part is not set up to facilitate. To follow a comparative model, an instructor must navigate various barriers of difference while maintaining those same differences for the sake of historicity. In other words, an instructor can make a transhistorical, transcultural comparative analysis as long as it is not reductive in formal and historical matters or politically naive about the power relationships transacted between the dominant and marginal members of society. Second, a comparative vision of the scope of Kolodny's requires intensive work in the following areas: textual recovery of works from the sixteenth and seventeenth centuries that are pertinent to a literary history of the "frontier"; translations of these texts into English; the actual editing and publishing of these texts; the writing of histories appropriate to other non–British colonial experiences and their various cultural contacts with indigenous groups; and finally the interdisciplinary training of scholars in fields of literary analysis, history, and anthropology, or in other relevant disciplines. In short, Kolodny's project requires a degree of specialization, as well as intellectual breadth, largely unavailable in American universities today. Finally, for a viable comparative approach to thrive, scholars need synthesizing models of analysis that simultaneously call attention to differences in form, literary tradition, and cultural and political production.

Fortunately, one such model of analysis is unfolding in a project known as "Recovering the U.S. Hispanic Literary Heritage." With the hope that their efforts might lead to an earnest revision of U.S. literary history, Chicano and Latino scholars met in 1990. As director of the

Recovery Project, Nicolás Kanellos has guided a ten–year–plus effort to reclaim authors and texts of Hispanic origins from the colonial period to 1960. The sheer volume of recovered material will likely develop the project into a major center of Hispanic and Chicano/a studies in the near future. Just as important, this project poses an unprecedented opportunity for Americanists to reconceive literary history. Specifically, the recovery of texts and writers since the sixteenth century will challenge literary historians to construct narratives that can account for traditions that mediated British colonization of the Americas. In this respect, the Recovery Project has the potential not only to revolutionize Chicano/a and Latino/a studies beyond its formative Civil Rights roots, but to denaturalize the "exceptional" status of Anglo American literary tradition in criticism and historiography.

Nevertheless, the Recovery Project occupies many problematic positions. In terms of identity politics, how does Chicano/a studies incorporate a corpus of literature that preceded the Chicano/a Movement and the whole discourse of Chicanismo? On racial and feminist grounds, the project goes counter to the efforts of the last twenty years to incorporate women and minorities into the canon. The Recovery Project, because its aim is to recover a Hispanic literary past from the sixteenth century to 1960, will ironically favor male Eurocentric writers. As in other arenas, the archival record favors male production. Further, the recovery in effect documents historical eras in which fierce patriarchal control was maintained over women's labor, bodies, and social and political relations. Related, some recovered texts narrate, approvingly, the colonization of North America and the displacement and, at times, annihilation of Native Americans. The overall recovery of what is turning out to be a very Eurocentric Hispanic past has created ambivalent responses among participating scholars, especially because recovered materials highlight the need to reframe current theoretical paradigms. How might racist, sexist, and elitist texts find their way into literary histories and canons primarily aligned with the progressive politics found in literatures and criticism inspired by the Civil Rights Movement?

Within Chicano/a studies, the potential of the Recovery Project has been met with a mixture of excitement and dread. As Project Director Nicolás Kanellos broadly notes:

This is the largest project of its kind undertaken in the history of scholarly efforts to study Hispanic culture in the United States. Its importance lies in filling the large gap which exists in American literature: the Hispanic contribution. . . . It will shape for decades to come academic scholarship in the disciplines of literature and history and it will have a major influence on the curriculum and teaching of English, Spanish and bilingual education in K–12 schools as well as in institutions of higher education.[39]

Kanellos's sense of the future dovetails extraordinarily well with Kolodny's aspirations for American literary scholarship and pedagogy. Yet there's another side to this recovery that Chicana critic Erlinda Gonzales-Berry makes clear: "This long over-due project, Recovering the U.S. Hispanic Literary Heritage, by its very nature places us in the rather uncomfortable position of creating a literary canon, that is to say, in the position not only of codifying an ethnic literary identity, but also of assigning a standard of value to a corpus of texts."[40] When Gonzales-Berry notes her discomfort, what, again, is at issue here is the realization that contemporary scholars, in canon-building efforts, invariably occupy the powerful role of cultural authority not traditionally assigned to or claimed by scholars of marginalized literatures.

Like Gonzales-Berry, Chicano critic Charles Tatum is mindful of the inherent contradictions in fashioning a canon:

If the last decade of canon wars in the academy and in professional associations has taught us any one lesson, it is that scholars such as ourselves . . . can wield tremendous power over future doctoral dissertations, the nature of curricula and programs from elementary through graduate school, and even what publications are accessible to the general reading public. As individuals who are all too familiar with how U.S.–Hispanic literatures have historically been excluded from the canon of American literary studies, we should approach our project already sensitized to the dangers implicit in significantly expanding and redefining this present canon we have identified as U.S.–Hispanic literature.[41]

In essence, both Gonzales-Berry and Tatum agree that the Recovery Project is a wonderful opportunity, but they remind their audiences that the burden of responsibility rests with them. Critics' uneasiness is not only reasonable but instructive; it signals the perceived dangers posed by any kind of canon formation, whether mainstream or minority. Given this, both critics agree that the Recovery Project has consequences too important to bypass; the scope of recovery–"all conventional literary genres as well as such forms as letters, diaries, oral lore and popular culture by Cuban, Mexican, Puerto Rican, Spanish, and other Hispanic residents of what has become the United States" (Kanellos 13)–entails nothing less than a wholesale reorientation of the collective imagination of what is America and what is American. Given the potential of the Recovery Project, its architects feel the need for a scrupulous, historically grounded analysis. Gonzales–Berry writes that "we must begin by recognizing that we are engaging in an act of political interpretation, and that interpretive acts, as Elizabeth Meese reminds us, 'inevitably install us in a matrix of difference and differential relations, and an (ex)tended field of tensions which are reduced to or contained only with limited success as pure *identity* '"(129). On this slippery ground of identifying a "pure" literary culture with a specific community, Tatum adds a further cautionary note. He agrees with Rosa Linda Fregoso and Angie Chabram that in light of the Chicano/a Movement, "mimetic notion[s] of representation led to equating the naming of cultural identity with cultural identity itself, a notion that ignored critical points of difference and the experience of rupture and discontinuity that also shaped Chicano/a identities in decisive ways" (200). Tatum also agrees with Chicana critic Rosaura Sánchez that to keep a historical handle on the inevitable avalanche of new information about a Hispanic past–its people, immigration histories, documents, politics, colonial practices, and stories–intertextuality, multiplicity, and contradiction will be hallmarks of the Recovery Project itself (200). In other words, the architects of the Recovery see in this heteroglossia an opportunity to narrate literary histories without a sacrifice of "difference."

This last point underscores how the Recovery Project has responded to its own recovery of a Eurocentric Hispanic past. Halfway into the project's timetable, the co–editors of the Recovery's second volume of essays, Gonzales–Berry and Tatum, write: "Initially, the so–called 'shapers' of the Recovery Project ... were eager to privilege those texts that met our present day expectations: texts that resist cultural assimilation or demonstrate working class alliances, that is, the predominant cultural nationalist ideology of the Chicano/a Movement."[42] Because the recovered material easily tasked contemporary notions of identity politics and resistance, more recent scholarship has moved to expand "the ethnic, gender, and class perimeters of the Hispanic literary heritage" (19). In effect, recent scholarship has been able to insist upon the integrity of the Recovery Project and its importance to ethnic and American studies without having to apologize for the racist, sexist, and elitist ideologies contained within recovered texts. Indeed, these "negative" aspects have been the touchstones by which contemporary theorists of culture and history have come to understand the constructions of race, gender, and class formation in a Hispanic America. Even so, the Recovery Project has its critics, especially in Chicano/a studies, who are wary of what they see as an assault on the field's progressive politics and who also worry about the political consequences of the loss of a separatist identity.

Mindful of a similar trend in Asian American studies, Sau–ling Cynthia Wong in *Reading Asian American Literature: From Necessity to Extravagance* presents an approach to reading Asian American literature that can serve as a model for how to maintain the cultural integrity of an ethnic literature outside of a separatist strategy while moving toward a more integrated and complete literary history.[43] Like Asian American scholars, many Chicano/a scholars have been legitimately cautious about moving away from separatist philosophies. Hegemonic appropriation of ethnic literatures has tended to flatten out historical differences in favor of "continuities" that remarginalize the ethnic writer. Wong frames her argument between the concern "about the misreading, appropriation, and co–optation of this literature by white readers and critics" and the question, "Does the study of a marginalized literature require membership in the given group, participation in appropriately typical historical experience, 'insider' cultural knowledge, and a group–specific methodology?" (4). She bridges these two seemingly exclusive concerns by foregrounding "Asian American literature's interdiscursivity in history and in contemporary life" (8). Both concerns resolve themselves, once we decide to take seriously the notion that Asian Americans, like other racial minorities, are central, not marginal, to the evolving history of the United States.

The relevant point for Chicano/a criticism, I believe, is Wong's argument that a "multiplicity of opinions [about Asian American literature] is not an embarrassing symptom of confused thinking or mere factionalism on the part of scholars and critics" (8). This multiplicity is itself a vital marker of how an "Asian American work may allude to Asian classics or folklore, draw upon an oral tradition maintained by immigrant forebears, participate in dominant Western genres like the realist novel or movements like postmodernism, serve class interests, engage in gender politics, and do a host of other things that multiply-situated texts do" [8]. Interpretation of these works must likewise be able to negotiate "the centrifugal and centripetal, the heterogenizing and homogenizing, tendencies inherent in the term *Asian American literature*" (8–9, Wong's emphasis). In the end, she advocates relying on the historical evolution of the term "Asian American" as a guide to interpretation. This concept of historically evolving terms presents an interesting potential for Chicano/a studies now that a recovery of Spanish Mexican colonial histories is under way.

As has been similarly true of Chicano/a scholars, Wong finds "Asian American critics have always had choices to make: notably between tracing Asian influence in the texts and demonstrating their grounding in American historical experiences; between accentuating their universal accessibility and uncovering their particular preoccupations" (9). Her choice is in the latter, since the former has always been "vulnerable to exoticization" (9) and since Asian American history is, in part, a history of being socially constructed as absent. To remedy this absence and address writers always multiply-positioned, she turns to a plural use of context since "there is no single, conclusive version of Asian American history to anchor their works and safeguard 'correct' readings" (10). A major reason for this reliance on historical context is that readings are themselves unnatural. Wong quotes Diana Fuss: "ways of reading are historically specific and culturally variable, and reading positions are always constructed, assigned, or mapped" (8). Wong's use of historical contexts would go far in historicizing Chicano/a writers' figurations of race, class, national affinity, and so on at different periods.

To historical context, Wong adds Kristeva's concept of intertextuality–the acknowledgment that any text embodies the "quoting" of other texts, the "absorbing" of other texts, and the "transforming" of other texts. Wong's "intertexts" avoids both high-theory abstraction and a break with New Historicist praxis by highlighting the specificity of the range of texts involved and by foregrounding all readings as ideologically constructed. Aware of the current privileging of the margin/center split as the means to identify ethnic literature, Wong observes:

While a dominant literary tradition may be conveniently reified, so that intertextuality within it appears to map the intrinsic or the self–evident, the reading of "minority" texts like Asian American ones demands the much more fundamental (and conscious) operation of determining appropriate intertexts for them. Without such a deliberation, any analysis that aspires beyond the boundaries of the single text would, by default, be governed by monocultural notions of canonicity. The resulting intercourse between the selected texts, then, would simply replicate the asymmetrical sociopolitical relationships in the extratextual realm, and the task of deepening one's understanding of an Asian American literary tradition is brought up short. (10–11)

In other words, by not conceding that minority texts sometimes interact textually with texts that are typically defined as part of the dominant, critics unintentionally give truth to the lie that minorities in the United States do not participate in the making of "American" culture, much less American literature. Rigidly insisting on an ethnic identity in literary criticism thus ironically reinscribes marginality in the social realm. For Asian American and Chicano/a literatures alike, this is a compelling reason to move beyond separatist treatments of ethnic writers.

Many exciting texts will soon resurface as writers and texts since the colonial period are recovered by scholars working in the Recovery Project. Indeed, the early efforts of Chicano/a scholars have made this latest phase in Chicano/a letters possible. Together with the increasing public exposure of Chicano/a writers in mainstream markets and universities, a new Chicano/a Renaissance would seem to be upon us. Like Wong, Gonzales–Berry and Tatum conclude that the current analytical retooling forced by the Recovery Project "is at once centripetal and centrifugal; the inward–flowing reverberations caused by calling attention to difference with the culturally specific space of literary production turn back upon themselves and spread outward, making their presence felt in ever concentric circles. Thus, the internal difference of local expression makes itself felt, aggregates to and expands further the contours of the American literary canon" (II:19).

Because the affixing of a political character to marginalized literature is ultimately an incomplete register of any author's or text's relationship to the world, the study of ethnic literature in the United States needs to account for that literature's dynamic relationship to the dominant. In the hands of the marginalized writer, the distinctions of margin and center, its social, historical, and economic meanings, are always already fluid. Our critical job is to attend to this fluidity with the broadest historical and theoretical methods available, while simultaneously being true to our own social moments. As critics and teachers, we should always ask ourselves what is it we want to teach and why. We should be aware of our role in the social construction of literature, yet we should not be stymied, by the theories we generate, in our efforts to uncover the richness of ethnic literature in the United States.

Thus, the comparative approach I advocate, here and throughout this book, combines Wong's model of intertextual reading with Kolodny's proposal for expanding our knowledge of non–Puritan colonial histories. In addition, Lauter's sensitivity to the changing demographics of our classrooms has a practical and experimental analogue in the successes and failures of the Recovery Project. Together these models of reading literature and history illustrate how the literary canon can come to grips with the ever–increasing multiplicity of differing readers and writers of American literature. More importantly, this approach emphasizes the pedagogic benefits for minority students when authors who reflect more of their own experiences are integrated with writers more historically and culturally removed even if considered "dominant." The lessons drawn from the obvious differences will empower students to ask more about literature and history. The succeeding chapters point to a day when American literature is no longer inordinately valued for its allegiance to a Puritan past, but instead for belonging to all those who desire to read about themselves–the hope that a future Sandra Cisneros and her Esperanza might find the road between home and the world a little less hazardous, a little less compromised.

PART II

Nuestra Literatura Americana

Toward an Integrated Literary History

All Strangers in a Strange Land

When Anglo and Mexican Histories Collide

In 1898, the year of the Spanish American War–ostensibly the last colonial war fought in North America–Mary C. Morse read at a gathering of
the Ladies' Pioneer Society an account of her memories of San Diego
when she arrived in 1865.[1] Then she was known as Mary C. Walker. Miss
Walker had been sent by the state superintendent of schools in San
Francisco to be San Diego County's official and only schoolteacher. In her
story, not unlike that of Richard Henry Dana's *Two Years before the Mast*
(1840), she finds a landscape that is desolate and barren. Nowhere does
she see green. Like many of her New England compatriots between 1848
and 1880, Mary C. Walker felt she had stepped into an alien world. She
writes of "wild looking horsemen, flourishing their riatas," dilapidated
buildings made of adobe, braying donkeys, and fearsome mosquitoes.
Of her school, she remembers that it "was composed mostly of Spanish and half-breed children, with a few English and several Americans.
Many American soldiers and some sailors had come to San Diego in the
early days, and married pretty señoritas. Hence the half-breed children"
(258–59). What made San Diego alien to this northeastern schoolmarm
was ultimately less the landscape than how the region itself retained the
cultures that had existed before the war.[2]

What really caught her attention, what she remembers most vividly,
are what she saw as the exotic gatherings of Californios, Native Americans, and their children, at dances, weddings, bullfights, and the seasonal
circus. Muchachos lassoing pigs are recalled alongside the elite Califor-
nianas. At a wedding, a bride is "surrounded by her lady friends, each

with a cigarita between her white gloved fingers." At circus performances of "trapeze and tight rope [that] looked especially weird and fantastic in the smoky light of those primitive lanterns," the "Americans and Span-ish" watched from one side of the corral, while "the Indians squatted on the ground on the other" (259). She adds: "The dinners to which I was invited by the Spanish were to me a novelty and very enjoyable. The table was spread in the garden under the trees, and outside was an oven in which was roasted a pig, a sheep, or a kid whole and served with a dressing composed largely of olives, red peppers and various savory herbs, also a sauce of tomatoes and [c]hili peppers, half and half. A small quantity of this would bring tears to the most stony eyes" (259–60). Within two years of her arrival, Mary C. Walker would marry E. W. Morse, known in 1898, and now, as one of the cofounders of modern San Diego. Except for noting this brief moment among the Ladies' Pioneer Society, regional historians relegate Mary C. Walker to the role of wifely appendage to E. W. Morse. Morse is widely credited, along with Alonzo E. Horton, with having transformed San Diego from its "sleepy Mexican origins" into its turn–of–the–century status as an oasis for Easterners seeking the salubrious climate of southern California.

The story of Mary C. Walker dramatizes the degree to which social relationships, racial hierarchies, and political structures in California had changed in the fifty years following the Mexican–American War. With-out an iota of irony, Walker confidently tells her audience: "The Old Town of today is quite a modern town compared with the Old Town of thirty–three years ago" (257). I purposely have begun this chapter with this "insider's" sense of change so as to contextualize processes that for-ever after marked the lives of people of Mexican descent in California. In particular, I start with Walker's memory of San Diego in 1865 because it relates both culturally and biographically to the primary interest of this chapter: the life and writings of María Amparo Ruiz de Burton. Ruiz de Burton knew both Mary C. Walker and E. W. Morse. In fact, Morse han-dled some of her legal matters in the 1870s, and very badly in her estima-tion. Furthermore, Morse was instrumental in helping to edge promi-nent Californios, like Ruiz de Burton, out of their land–grant claims even to the extent of supporting squatters. In this regard, E. W. Morse shows an uncanny resemblance to the thieving lawyer Peter Roper represented in Ruiz de Burton's 1885 novel, *The Squatter and the Don*. Roper makes his livelihood through ruthless exploitation of the law.

Walker's story thus provides a convenient entry point by which we can measure the collisions between Anglo and Mexican histories at a crucial moment: when the United States began to reemplot the social relations of the newly won territories away from those more characteristic of their previous colonial masters. In reconstructing the life and writings of María Amparo Ruiz de Burton in the following pages, I attempt to recover the worldview of one Californiana whom Walker would rather remember as "Spanish," not Mexican, a woman who in fact married an Anglo soldier, and subsequently gave birth to "half-breeds." Significantly, she wrote plays and novels, and during the Civil War befriended such diverse public figures as Abraham and Mary Todd Lincoln and Jefferson and Varina Davis. While these facts alone might interest historians and literary critics alike, the real potential of the cultural biography of Ruiz de Burton lies in revisiting the historical terrain traversed by Californios during the Mexican–American War and its aftermath.

Ruiz de Burton's life and writings vividly bridge and incorporate the two colonial histories that anchored, often for the worse, the social fabric of her generation. To clarify the profound cultural and political upheaval she experienced, this chapter provides an extended biography, much of which comes from my research on her extended New England in-laws and the other relationships she forged while living on the East Coast. I examine the fluidity of nationalist loyalties during and immediately after the Mexican–American War, and finally I offer a reading of Ruiz de Burton's 1872 satire of New England society, *Who Would Have Thought It?* Altogether, I demonstrate the role that history, biography, and culture might play in analyses of Mexican American texts that preceded the political ethos of the Chicano/a Movement.

Given the social and legal consequences of the Treaty of Guadalupe Hidalgo, Chicano/a scholars like Rosaura Sanchez and Genaro Padilla generally employ postcolonial criticism when studying the lives and writings of the Californios of Alta California.[3] For them, the Californios are to be considered "subalterns." While the concept of the subaltern may be applicable in instances, by and large its usefulness/appropriateness is directly linked to how one interprets individuals' and groups' relationships to Mexican colonialism. For example, Rosaura Sánchez interprets the oral voices, transcribed in the Bancroft Collection of early California histories, as linguistic vestiges of subalterns. But what is striking to me is that these voices remember and reconstruct their subject positions via narratives that portray their own colonial domination of California. That there's a contradiction between the theoretical valence of the word "subaltern" and the political and historical record of the Californio as an imperial colonizer, is, I am sure, not lost upon Sánchez. What's at issue for her and other like-minded Chicano/a scholars is the theory of historical agency best suited to promote a sociopolitical agenda for today's Mexican American community.

In other words, like many U.S. historiographers in the twentieth century, Chicano/a scholars have sought a "usable past" in the historical record. That usable past has been deployed as a corrective to the ethnocentric bias and racist portrayals in American culture of people of Mexican descent. Elsewhere, that usable past has been used to intervene on the low voting practices of twentieth-century Mexican Americans that imply, wrongly, disinterested citizenship. As I argued in chapter 1, a nostalgic and celebratory vision of the multiracial pasts of indigenous, Spanish, and Mexican peoples was fused in Chicano/a studies to create an alternative nationalism and sense of direction for contemporary Mexican American political life. Significantly, this fusion was itself articulated through and legitimized by linking Mexican American history to a highly visible national ideology that affirms immigration as a fundamental feature of nation formation. Like its counterpart in a Puritan myth of origins, the usable past constructed by Chicano/a studies invoked a progressive sense of history that had much in common with many other narratives of immigration to North America since 1620. More will be said on this topic in chapter 4, but what's important to reiterate is that the usefulness of this past was tied to its perceived differences from and opposition to U.S. history.

Yet the historic record that remains in archives, published materials, and even oral records from the nineteenth century suggests a more complicated story. Chicano/a historians, especially those involved in New Western History, have delved into the colonial record of a Mexican American past for some time now. Their findings suggest that by 1846 Mexican society in the northern territories was clearly stratified into racial and economic classes, the legacy of three hundred years of Spanish colonial policy and social practices. Violence against Native Americans was still common in 1846, as was racial discrimination–although Mexico had abolished slavery by 1826. Attempts to colonize the northern territories continued after Mexican independence. And some of the policies actually encouraged Anglo settlement. For their part, longtime northern inhabitants had developed longstanding economic relations with Anglo traders from Texas to California. Historian David Weber cites established economic relations as a contributing factor to what he calls "the Americanization of the North," a social and economic transformation of the northern territories that actually paved the way for U.S. domination of the area.[4] All this would suggest that among northern peoples there exists a more complex history than that of simple victimization. From time to time, these northern Mexicans exercised the kind of agency normally attributed to Anglo Americans. While Chicano/a historians have begun to work out the comparative aspects, literary critics have yet to venture onto this terrain.

In favor of more complex models of historical agency, I argue against Rosaura Sánchez's and Beatrice Pita's construction of María Amparo Ruiz de Burton as a "subaltern" and her biography as an unproblematized counterimperialist history.[5] I prefer not to identify her as a "subaltern." I am more comfortable with historicizing her, and her Californio peers, as products of competing colonial enterprises in Alta California. The critiques and contradictions that surface from the writings of these Californios about U.S. colonialism do so not from new subordinated subject positions but rather from enraged and embittered equals, who in losing the cultural and material privileges of elite society resort to "words"–literature, letters, diaries, histories–to set the record straight about the American invasion. Precisely because in the course of her life Ruiz de Burton comes to prefer her prior identity as a white Mexican colonialist, despite all its compromises and failures, we come to understand the subtle dimensions of two colonialisms, not just one, and importantly how they do and do not overlap with each other.

Overall, the goal here, and in the chapters to follow, is to offer a case study of how we might renarrate American literary history from the vantage point of New Chicano/a Studies. In this literary history, Mexican Americans, far from being marginalized entities, are also figures who have played a historic role in producing U.S. culture and literature since 1848. Ruiz de Burton's life and writings, for example, document a much more broad–based and lively engagement of Mexican Americans with discourses linking literature, aesthetics, and the nation than was previously assumed. Until the advent of the Recovery Project, these discourses about national formation were believed to be the exclusive purview of nineteenth-century Anglo and African American writers. Like those of many of her Californio peers, Ruiz de Burton's observations and judgments about New England society and U.S. politics are informed by her prior status as a Mexican citizen. Few canonical writers of this century share such a distinction. Whereas many U.S. writers have critiqued the nation by means of various strategies of distancing (Hawthorne through the Puritans, Melville through South Sea Islanders, Thoreau through even the Mexican–American War), Ruiz de Burton relies on her own memories of a Spanish Mexican colonial tradition to fathom her alienation from the culture and society that dominated her worldview after 1848. This alienation grounds her critiques of the United States in terms that are not instantly recognizable; in effect, she comes at her subject matter directly, and from the "outside," in contrast to those writers working indirectly from "inside." Yet at the same time, Ruiz de Burton's life and writings disallow any naively conceived hero worship of her. At times she was all too much a product of her century.

A Short Biography of María Amparo Ruiz de Burton[6]

The moon shone but dimly
Beyond the battle plain
A gentle breeze fanned softly
O'er the features of the slain
The guns had hushed their thunder
The guns in silence lay
Then came the señorita
The Maid of Monterey.

She cast a look of anguish
On the dying and the dead
And made her lap a pillow
For those who mourned and bled
Now here's to that bright beauty
Who drives death's pangs away
The meek-eyed señorita
The Maid of Monterey.

Although she loved her country
And prayed that it might live
Yet for the foreign soldier
She had a tear to give
And when the dying soldier
In her bright gleam did pray
He blessed this señorita
The Maid of Monterey.

She gave the thirsty water
And dressed each bleeding wound
A fervent prayer she uttered
For those whom death had doomed
And where the bugle sounded
Just at the dawn of day
They blessed this señorita
The Maid of Monterey.[7]

A short time after the Mexican–American War, the above verses were composed and sung as a ballad in honor of María Amparo Ruiz de Burton. According to turn–of–the–century historian Winifred Davidson, Ruiz de Burton's winsome ways inspired broad admiration from everyone.[8] Ruiz de Burton's first residence in Alta California was Monterey, California, where Henry S. Burton, her husband, was posted. Soldiers under his command were the likely composers of this ballad. There is no evidence yet to determine whether she was pleased by their tribute. But the ballad tells us a lot about how the Anglo American soldiers of the war wished to see her. Again, whether she mirrored this wish in any substantial way, apart from her marriage to Henry S. Burton, is not yet known. By the end of her life, the one–time Maid of Monterey would come to rue the events and forces that ceded Alta California to the United States and reduced her to a second–class citizen. Yet, if these changes caused her to grow bitter over time, they were also responsible for her move to Alta California, her marriage to an Anglo American West Point officer, the birth of their two children, and her maturity as a political commentator.

Ruiz de Burton's life and writings bear witness to an incredibly complicated time in Mexican American history. Born a Mexican citizen, heir to Mexico's particular and influential colonial history in the Americas,

Ruiz de Burton's life is a glimpse into the tremendous changes that occurred when Mexican citizens, like her, were suddenly beholden to an entirely different nation grounded in a non-Mexican colonial past. To make matters worse, the elitist privileges of her past slowly gave way to a demotion in class and social status that rendered her indistinguishable from lower-class Mexican Americans. In sharp contrast to her influential Anglo friends and acquaintances, Ruiz de Burton slipped into anonymity soon after her death.

Fortunately, Ruiz de Burton's novels were recovered through the impressive detective work of Rosaura Sánchez and Beatrice Pita. Together, they have firmly established a place for Mexican American authors within studies of nineteenth-century American literature. Before too long, other scholars will join Sánchez and Pita in redrawing the racial map of U.S. literary history, by calling attention to the writings of Hispanics who were the contemporaries of authors such as Nathaniel Hawthorne, Harriet Beecher Stowe, Harriet Jacobs, and W. E. B. DuBois. In a feat not to be underestimated, Ruiz de Burton's recoverers have disrupted the tendency to view the nineteenth century exclusively within white/black racial histories, and thus have expanded literary studies beyond the authors featured in F. O. Matthiessen's *American Renaissance* on the one hand and the feminist recovery of Anglo and African American women writers on the other. This diversification of racial binaries alone makes Ruiz de Burton an important figure in the evolution of American literary history and criticism.

Eleven years after the Treaty of Córdoba and sixteen years before the Treaty of Guadalupe Hidalgo, María Amparo Ruiz de Burton was born on July 3, 1832, in Loreto, Baja California, to an aristocratic family. According to Sánchez and Pita, her maternal grandfather, Don José Manuel Ruiz, was a military commander of Baja California's northern frontier and governor of the territory from 1822 to 1825. Because of his military service and familial connections, Don José would come to own ranch lands in Baja California. Though these same connections would later help Ruiz de Burton relocate to Alta California in 1848, overall, according to Sánchez and Pita, the family's aristocratic and military affiliations did not translate into economic prosperity. This discrepancy between economic prosperity and noble lineage would haunt Ruiz de Burton, at times overtaking her own ambitions and overshadowing her accomplishments.

Having successfully manufactured a military confrontation with Mexico, President James Polk asked for a declaration of war from the U.S. Congress on May 11, 1846. Congress declared war on Mexico by the end of that same day, putting into motion a series of national events that would forever transform Ruiz de Burton's life. Far from the more devastating theaters of war, Baja California was nevertheless invaded and occupied by U.S. military forces. Among the officers occupying La Paz was Captain Henry S. Burton of Norwich, Vermont.[9] Captain Burton was one of several officers ordered in late spring of 1847 to quell an armed resistance in Baja California. Successful in his mission, Captain Burton and María Amparo Ruiz apparently met and fell in love during his tour of duty. The citizens of Baja California showed little resistance to their new invaders. This was probably due to their small population, their distance from the political and military leadership of Mexico City, and the fact that the U.S. navy effectively controlled all the navigable harbors. Given the unlikelihood of the Mexican military coming to their rescue, Ruiz de Burton's family must have sought out, as did other families, cordial relations with Anglo American officers.

After the Battle of Cerro Gordo on April 18, 1847, a long period passed before a treaty was drawn up and signed. During that period, it was not clear what would happen to Baja California. This uncertainty came as a surprise because President Polk, prior to 1846, declared his intentions to make Alta California part of the United States in any conflict with Mexico. When the Treaty of Guadalupe Hidalgo was signed on February 2, 1848, it became shockingly clear that Baja California would not become part of the United States. For some of the elite citizenry in La Paz who had been supportive of the American invasion, this was a dangerous setback. Captain Burton and his fellow officers petitioned their superiors to evacuate these individuals and their families to protect them from Mexican government reprisals and to repay their loyalties during the war. United States authorities in Monterey, California, granted the petition. Over 350 residents of Baja California were relocated to Monterey, California, on two transport ships. The military commander at Monterey welcomed these Baja residents as individuals who had aided the cause of the United States during the war. By provisions of the peace treaty, Mexican citizens who remained or took up residency in newly conquered territories would be deemed to have elected U.S. citizenship.

María Amparo Ruiz and her immediate family—mother Doña Isabel,

brother Federico, sister Manuela, and Pablo de la Toba, her sister's husband–were among the several hundred who left for Alta California.
Eventually, some of this group returned to Baja California. Others, including María Amparo Ruiz and her family, stayed and took up residence in Monterey as new U.S. citizens. The courtship between María
Amparo Ruiz and Captain Burton that began in La Paz soon turned to
marriage plans. Following the news of their engagement, however, controversy erupted over religious differences and nationalist sentiments. A
jealous suitor of María Amparo Ruiz protested to Catholic authorities
that marriage was out of the question because Burton was not Catholic. In turn, according to historian Frederick Oden, California Governor
Richard B. Mason forbade state authorities from recognizing any marriage that joined a Catholic to a non–Catholic. In the end, María Amparo
Ruiz and Henry S. Burton were married secretly by Reverend Samuel H.
Willey at the home of Captain E. R. S. Canby on July 9, 1849.

Married just six days after her seventeenth birthday, María Amparo
Ruiz de Burton began a new life, with a West Point officer, in a rapidly
changing U.S. territory. The discovery of gold in 1849 at Sutter's Mill
accelerated not only internal emigration from Anglo America, but also
California's petition for statehood and entry into the Union. The California Convention of 1849 created a mixture of excitement and dread
among longtime Californios, who had much at stake in the proceedings.
As the convention drew to a close, it was apparent that race would become a defining feature of the laws that protected property and ensured
civil rights. Contemporaneously, abolitionists and anti–abolitionists in
the eastern states were debating the expansion of slavery to the newly
acquired western territories. The Missouri Compromise of 1850 led to
an accommodation of slavery, but it could not ameliorate the moral
and political differences of opinion that existed between the North and
South. By the end of the Civil War, the Californios would come to understand firsthand the consequences of racial and ethnic discrimination in
the United States through the loss of their lands, social standing, and
political representation.

But during the early period of the state, Ruiz de Burton and the
Captain settled down into family life. Ruiz de Burton gave birth to their
first child, Nellie, on July 4, 1850. Two years later, in 1852, Captain Burton was posted in San Diego. Their second child, Henry Halleck Burton,
named after Captain Burton's friend and comrade–in–arms Henry Wager

Halleck, was born on November 24, 1852, in the New Town section of San Diego. In 1853, the Burtons purchased land from Pío Pico's Jamul land grant—no doubt facilitated by Ruiz de Burton's kinship ties to the Pico family. It may have been during this period that Ruiz de Burton began to reveal herself publicly as a writer. Oden relates that while she lived at Mission San Diego in 1855, Ruiz de Burton seems to have written some of the more popular productions for Mission Theatre. Ruiz de Burton's social standing as a Californio and her marriage to Captain Burton surely made her literary debut a grand affair locally. She was well suited to this role. She had a French tutor as a child, and read with vigor the passionate novels of Victor Hugo.

Ruiz de Burton was particularly well connected among other Californios and was a great letter writer in Spanish as well as English, keeping up extended correspondence with relatives and friends throughout her life. As for the Captain, he was treated like a war hero and a favorite son of the new state. He was apparently well known for his avid, if not excessive, hunting of quail in the region. The only real shadow that plagued the family was the Captain's penchant for extravagant spending and a tendency not to pay his bills. After his death, Ruiz de Burton would have to contend with a number of lawsuits deriving from his spending habits and poor judgment in business dealings.

In 1859, Ruiz de Burton uprooted her family when the Captain was ordered to return east. She would stay on the Atlantic coast for ten years, following her husband through various assignments. The Burtons ended up making homes in several states: Rhode Island, New York, Washington, D.C., Delaware, and Virginia. With civil war imminent, these were heady but fearful times for Ruiz de Burton. According to historian Kathleen Crawford, Ruiz de Burton and the Captain attended Lincoln's inaugural ball, meeting the president and First Lady.[10] As in California, Ruiz de Burton circulated within the most prominent social and political circles. In fact, during the Civil War she had an audience with President Lincoln, making the case that her husband should be promoted. He was promoted to colonel after that meeting. After the war, Ruiz de Burton would become very good friends with Varina Davis, the wife of Jefferson Davis. The former president of the Confederacy was a prisoner of war at Fort Monroe in Virginia. Henry Burton became commandant of the fort and Davis's warden in late 1865. Varina Davis wrote that she and Ruiz de Burton would drink tea and talk badly about the Yankees.[11]

Throughout her life, Ruiz de Burton often held contradictory political loyalties that did not necessarily impede her personal relationships with individuals. Despite being married to a Union officer, Ruiz de Burton was not unusual in her sympathies for the South. Early in the war effort, Mary Todd Lincoln, the First Lady, was often vilified by pro–Union journalists and politicians as a Southern sympathizer. As a matter of public record, she did have friends in the South, but so did many Northerners, if not most people in Washington. The war fueled a hysteria hard to combat. In fact, all members of the Democratic Party, from the North as well as the South, were periodically harassed throughout the war even if they publicly supported the Union. Such were the cultural politics of the war that even President Lincoln's loyalties were questioned from time to time. Ruiz de Burton's own political affiliations and how she negotiated her political friendships during the Civil War should be viewed in the context of this suspicious climate.

Although the family survived the military campaigns and the politics that came with it, the war inevitably took its toll. Although breveted brigadier general for his efforts to capture Petersburg, Virginia, Henry Burton had also contracted malaria there. His health would never be the same. Moved to lighter duties whenever possible for health reasons, Henry Burton nevertheless died from complications due to malaria and hepatitis on April 4, 1869, at Fort Adams, Newport, Rhode Island. At his death, Ruiz de Burton was three months shy of her thirty–seventh birthday. His death was devastating to her: her romance with the Captain, nourished during a time of war, was a central part of her identity. Yet, such was Ruiz de Burton's own pride and personal resourcefulness that she lost little time in recognizing that she was the only person who could provide for her family. Ruiz de Burton and her children, Nellie and Harry, returned to San Diego in 1870, desirous of taking up residence again at the Jamul ranch, which she had left in the care of her brother and mother. Except to attend to one of the suits against her that reached the U.S. Supreme Court, Ruiz de Burton would never return east again.

The Jamul ranch, which originally comprised over half a million acres, had deteriorated badly in their absence. Complicating matters were the auctions held in the family's absence to pay off debts from before the war. From then on, Ruiz de Burton seems to have devoted herself to securing the family's livelihood; according to Sánchez and Pita, she was involved in "the large scale cultivation of castor beans and . . .

the building of a water reservoir at Jamul. . . [and finally] establishing a Cement Company to exploit the Jamul limestone deposits that her husband had first used in 1856 to make lime." Most of these ventures ended badly, costing her more money than she had, especially given that she executed her own suits to secure title to the Jamul ranch and Rancho Ensenada de Todos Santos in Baja California. Unfortunately, both ranches would be a source of lasting legal troubles for the family. In the case of the Jamul ranch, the promise of a major railroad line passing through the property on its way to San Diego motivated Ruiz de Burton's economic interests. Hampering her legal efforts were the laws that did not recognize women as owners of property, or as citizens due equitable legal representation. Interestingly, Mexican laws at the time offered her more protection, both as a female citizen and as a property owner.

Ruiz de Burton's Jamul title came under question when various Anglo homesteaders in the 1870s sued, claiming the land fell within the public domain. Eventually, Pío Pico's own title to the land was rejected by the infamous Land Commission that judged land disputes in the years following the Treaty of Guadalupe Hidalgo. Sánchez and Pita note that Ruiz de Burton's legal troubles with the Jamul ranch took odd twists and turns. She secured title from the state in 1870, only to fend off a series of lawsuits by illegal squatters. In October 1872, Ruiz de Burton scored a tremendous victory when her political friends persuaded the Supreme Court to dismiss an appeal that sought to overturn the 1870 ruling in her favor. Afterward, in order to save a fraction of the original ranch, she applied for a homestead, which the California Supreme Court belatedly granted in 1889. However, by 1889 Ruiz de Burton had incurred numerous legal costs and, at various points, had mortgaged parcels of land in order to finance her family's livelihood, as well as her legal suits and business ventures. In 1893, Harry, Ruiz de Burton's son, was forced to sell the remaining portion of the ranch in order to pay off a variety of family debts.

Despite all her financial woes and court battles, Ruiz de Burton found enough time to seriously pursue a literary career beginning in the 1870s. In doing so, she joined countless other women writers of the nineteenth century who took to writing to support their families. Instrumental in helping to secure publication for her first novel was a well-known New York lawyer, Samuel L. M. Barlow.[12] Like many of her friends and acquaintances, Barlow was an ironic choice for Ruiz de Burton. He had made his initial fortune and fame by settling a number of cases over land disputes that resulted from the Treaty of Guadalupe Hidalgo. He went on to become a nationally and internationally sought-after lawyer because of his ability to settle disputes out of court. Barlow's abilities typically placed him in the middle of national controversies, as in the 1857 Supreme Court case of *Scott v. Sanford* (*Dred Scott Case*). According to historian Richard M. Garten, he was the executor of the will of Charles P. Chouteau that listed Scott as a slave.[13] He made a memento of a copy of the Supreme Court decision that ruled against Scott's suit. On this copy, Barlow wrote: "At the time of this decision Dred Scott belonged to me." This very complex man was a major collector of Americana relating to the European discovery of the Americas, not unlike the more famous John Carter Brown or James Lenox.[14] Not surprisingly, Barlow was also a major political player in the election of James Buchanan as president of the United States in 1856. It was Barlow who put Ruiz de Burton in contact with her first publisher, J. B. Lippincott of Philadelphia.

In 1872, J. B. Lippincott published Ruiz de Burton's *Who Would Have Thought It?* The novel, a biting satire, is based heavily on her experiences in New England and her dealings with her husband's relatives and neighbors. In the course of the novel, Ruiz de Burton takes on what she judges as the sanctimonious righteousness of New England culture. New England clergy, the institution of republican motherhood, abolitionism, and the gap between the rhetoric of democracy and the corruption of government all come under severe scrutiny and criticism because of their blatant hypocrisy. Despite her own positive dealings with Lincoln, even the president is ridiculed and censured. Throughout this satire, there is nevertheless a belief in the perfectibility of government, and not just that of the United States. The novel provides evidence that Ruiz de Burton might have seen herself as an early Pan Americanist, interested in just government throughout the Americas. That her novel was published in Philadelphia, where the Declaration of Independence was penned and signed, that Lippincott was the most successful publisher of his time (by 1876, Lippincott was the largest distributor of books in the United States), testifies to the cultural authority Ruiz de Burton's very first novel wielded.[15]

As a playwright, Ruiz de Burton wrote *Don Quixote de la Mancha* (1876), a comedy in five acts, based on Miguel de Cervantes's 1605 novel. This play was published by J. H. Carmany & Co. in San Francisco. Carmany was an interesting figure in the early Anglo publishing history of the state of California. He bought the magazine *The Overland Monthly*, which Bret Harte as editor and contributor had made famous to readers on both coasts. When Harte left to pursue more lucrative offers, the magazine's popularity quickly faded. Given the literary company she kept with Carmany and his Anglo western readers, one wonders what cultural politics were at stake for Ruiz de Burton in presenting Cervantes during a period that idolized Shakespeare in everything from the theater to vaudeville acts. (The Duke and the Dauphin in Mark Twain's *Huckleberry Finn* [1885] represent a good example of Shakespeare's cultural capital in this period.) One might read Ruiz de Burton's *Don Quixote* as purposely written to forward a Spanish alternative. Coincidentally, Bret Harte was also very good friends with Samuel Barlow.[16] It is unknown whether Ruiz de Burton had any contact with Bret Harte. However, it is known that Bret Harte, as critic Raymund Paredes has noted, parodied Cervantes's *Don Quixote de la Mancha* when depicting the old Californio world, as in the short story "The Devotion of Enriquez" (1894).

The Squatter and the Don was published in 1885. As in her first novel, Ruiz de Burton converts autobiographical elements of her life into fiction—in this case her troubles with the Jamul ranch. The novel also criticizes the effects of transportation monopolies on the local regional economy as well as the illegal dispossession of Californios of their land. Again as with *Who Would Have Thought It?*, this novel contains fictionalized versions of people Ruiz de Burton knew personally, as well as public figures. For example, Ruiz de Burton holds railroad magnates Leland Stanford, Collis P. Huntington, Charles Crocker, and Mark Hopkins—California's Big Four—ethically and morally accountable for their questionable business practices and their corrupting influence on society. Because of the book's content, and unlike her first novel, *The Squatter and the Don* was published under the pen name C. Loyal. Sánchez and Pita note that C. Loyal was an ironic pseudonym, given that it was common usage at the time in Mexico to close a letter with *Ciudadano Leal*, which means loyal citizen. They suggest that C. Loyal is Ruiz de Burton's symbolic attempt to claim for herself a social creditability that she lacked in daily life. According to Oden, the novel was probably financed in part by Ruiz de Burton herself, or a friend, William Winder, in order to avoid publisher's fees and thus secure better profits from the book's sales. Sánchez and Pita also note that the novel was copyrighted by Ruiz de Burton and published by S. Carson and Company in San Francisco in the same year. She borrowed money from longtime friend George Davidson to finance the publication.

Numerous letters and documents of Ruiz de Burton are held in archives in California. Among them is an unpublished biography that Ruiz de Burton wrote of her maternal grandfather, Don José Manuel Ruiz (1878). In the 1870s, Hubert Howe Bancroft, the collection's namesake, began what is today a well-known project to compile a history of California, from its Spanish period to the early days of territory and then statehood. Oden writes that Ruiz de Burton was excited about the project and saw it as an opportunity for the Californios to narrativize their own histories and presence in the country. On Bancroft's behalf, she solicited contributions from her own Californio friends. However, in a letter to Bancroft, she lamented that many of her peers did not share her enthusiasm, or take the opportunity to record the injustices suffered by Californios.

Questionable Differences:
Mexicanos y Anglos in Baja California, 1848

I want to explore further a little-known historic event briefly mentioned above: the transportation of Mexican refugees from Baja California to Monterey, California, in 1848. Among the refugees were María Amparo Ruiz de Burton and her immediate family. In addition to speaking about this event and its relationship to the Mexican–American War, I will endeavor to establish a set of common terms that might link the Recovery Project to the ongoing efforts of Chicano/a historians and New Western historians and help us to understand the racial and nationalist discourses that framed the war and the Treaty of Guadalupe Hidalgo. What is intriguing about this episode is twofold: One, the U.S. military leadership in Baja California convinced its government to reward local Mexican citizens who aided in the pacification of the region with monetary compensation and U.S. citizenship. Two, prominent Baja Californios registered their sense of betrayal and demanded some form of redress for their loyalty when the Treaty of Guadalupe Hidalgo did not include U.S. annexation of Baja California.

By highlighting this episode, I emphasize the need for a model of historical agency that can more carefully explain the competing colonial discourses inhabiting North America in the nineteenth century. A closer examination of these refugees from Baja California destabilizes easy notions of nineteenth-century political, cultural, and military hegemony in North America. Thus, a more differentiated model of historical agency would address why certain peoples of Mexican descent opted to align themselves with Anglo Americans, while others did not. Equally important, under this revised model, is to understand anew those moments during which Anglo Americans recorded either their ambivalence about Manifest Destiny or their admiration for the different colonial project they encountered in both Alta and Baja California. In both regions, Anglo Americans evidenced a willingness to realign their own nationalist loyalties during a political period otherwise dedicated to the consolidation of a continental United States.

According to historian Doyce B. Nunis, Jr., when President James K. Polk assured Congress on December 7, 1847, that both Alta and Baja California were under firm U.S. control, he was grossly mistaken.[17] While both Californias succumbed early in the war to U.S. military rule, guerilla-style attacks throughout 1847 by Mexican forces in Baja California ended the cordial occupation that had been brokered through the efforts of elite Baja Californios in La Paz and San José del Cabo and Anglo military officers. Though wrong in his assessment, President Polk had little to worry about Baja California, because he never envisioned lower California as part of the United States anyway. His public statements to the contrary were mere rhetoric deployed in advance of negotiations with the Mexican government over territory. Unfortunately, Polk's military and some cabinet members took it as policy that Baja California would one day become American soil.[18]

This misunderstanding or confusion, as Nunis puts it, placed the Anglo invaders and the pro-American faction in Baja California in a serious quandary at the end of the war. Not only had some of the Americans fallen in love with the country, like William R. Ryan who remarked that La Paz offered more culture and elegance than Monterey (Nunis, 50), but some, such as Lieutenant Colonel Henry S. Burton of the New York Volunteers, had fallen in love with the country's people, in his case with fifteen-year-old María Amparo Ruiz of La Paz. Further, prominent officials like Governor Francisco Palacio Miranda and individuals like Padre

Ignacio Ramirez y Arollona of La Paz had gone out of their way to welcome the Americans and publicly support the U.S. annexation of Baja California.

When details of the Treaty of Guadalupe Hidalgo reached La Paz, the reaction was severe. Anglos and their Baja Californio friends felt betrayed that the United States had not insisted on the annexation of Baja California. Henry Burton spoke for many of his peers when he wrote to Governor Richard B. Mason in Monterey on June 27, 1848, requesting that something be done to protect these Mexican citizens who sided with the American cause (Nunis, 60). In turn, Baja Californios took up their grievances with Commodore Thomas Catesby Jones. While they found in Commodore Jones a sympathetic audience, they also knew these were times that required definitive action. On July 5, 1848, rebellious Baja Californios established a junta, with the expressed purpose of securing annexation to either the United States or Great Britain. Though serious about their goals, these Baja Californios hoped more to impress upon Commodore Jones their fear of retribution from Mexico. They succeeded.

Anxious for their safety, Commodore Jones intervened and convinced Secretary of the Navy John Y. Mason to grant political asylum to Baja Californios who feared reprisal from guerilla leaders like Manuel Pineda and the priest Gabriel Gonzalez (Nunis, 70). In the end, over 350 refugees were transported to Monterey, California, and were fed and housed at the military's expense. When they began to arrive, Governor Richard B. Mason issued the following order: "Justice and humanity alike require that they should be sheltered and fed, and their sick provided for at the public expense until they are enabled to look around and provide for themselves" (Nunis, 149–50). Additionally, Commodore Jones authorized the payment of war reparations in the amount of $37,698. Risking charges of insubordination by their superiors in Washington, these Anglo officers and officials did their best to help their wartime friends.

How do we make sense of this historic moment? Traditionally, the Anglo view was that such Mexican citizens as these supportive refugees from Baja California were few and far between. The vast majority of Mexican citizenry were obstinate, according to general Anglo opinion, in refusing to recognize the superior gifts of civilization that the United States offered the continent. Like their counterparts in Alta California, these Baja Californio refugees were viewed positively as taking advantage of the ideals of liberty and property espoused in the United States. Theirs was a faith in the democratic system of checks and balances. In other words, because these refugees were well aware of the deficiencies of Mexico, they chose pragmatically to acknowledge the inevitable hegemony of the United States.[19]

A related explanation of the new loyalties of these refugees lies in the ethnocentric observations about the Californios that clustered around stereotypes assigned to Mexicans in general.[20] In the nineteenth century, Anglo Americans commonly believed that Mexicans were lazy, illiterate, overly fond of music and dance, prone to alcoholism and bad tempers, reckless with money and resources, untrustworthy, incompetent administrators, thieves, and morally unfit as citizens. This view framed Baja Californios, like their counterparts in Alta California, as calculating opportunists who cared little for the day-to-day governance of nations; they welcomed the American invasion because they had little or no stomach to realize the potential of the region. In short, Baja Californios preferred to import a successful colonialism rather than to work among themselves to reform the underlying structures of their own government, society, and culture.

Surprisingly, despite the critiques of Chicano/a and non-Chicano/a historians since the 1970s, a dichotomy continues in historical analysis in which the Californios are viewed either as unique in recognizing the benefits of Manifest Destiny or as simply dilettantes at governance. As late as 1989, John S. D. Eisenhower writes: "The Californios, as a group, exhibited the Mexican proclivity to be easygoing, fun-loving, and extraordinarily hospitable. It was said that, along with the all-night fandango, the California man loved his horse above all else, and he was, truly, an unparalleled horseman. But being such an individualist, the Californio was not a good civic participant. He was not overly concerned as to who ruled him, so long as his own rights and religion were not disturbed."[21] While Eisenhower does make use of David Weber's thesis in *The Mexican Frontier* (1982)—that geography, demography, and economic interests played an uneven role in whether Mexican citizens would come to view the American army as friend or foe—he does so only to focus on the growing influence of Anglo settlers on longtime Californios. In other words, Eisenhower precludes any consideration of the reverse: of Californio influence on Americans like Thomas O. Larkin or European immigrants like John A. Sutter, or the possibility that Californios in both Alta and Baja California had been developing a colonial culture and philosophy that actually invited American curiosity.

I'll come back to American curiosity shortly, but for now the point is to emphasize general consensus among Chicano/a historians of this period. With respect to the Californios, Nuevo Mexicanos, and others who welcomed the American invasion, Alex M. Saragoza summed up the situation nicely for Chicano historians in a 1987 review essay.[22] During the height of the Chicano/a Movement, one would have been hard-pressed to find a Chicano/a historian laboring to unravel the ironies and contradictions of the Californio. The cultural context of the Chicano/a Movement, the Vietnam War, and the general fight for civil rights required a clear rhetorical split between the oppressed and the oppressor. This "'them versus us' perspective of Chicano–Anglo relations," according to Saragoza, centered much of the ideological force behind landmark texts like Rodolfo F. Acuña's *Occupied America* (1972). As a paradigmatic frame for Chicano/a historiography, this model lingered well into the late 1970s. But by 1978, Chicano historians such as Richard Griswold del Castillo, Albert Camarillo, Mario T. Garcia, and Juan Gómez–Quiñones were producing detailed labor histories that followed up David Weber's economic analyses of the Mexican frontier prior to 1846. While histories of racism and civic disfranchisement continued to provide the philosophical infrastructure for these new studies, the goal was now to document and theorize the "differences that marked the historical experience of Chicanos" (Saragoza, 28).

This shift in emphasis among Chicano/a labor historians had the effect of validating the material culture found in the historical record, no matter if unrelated to the ethos of the Chicano/a Movement. When it came to the nineteenth century, narratives of resistance and conflict gave way to narratives of complex racial and economic compromises. Even class analyses of pre–1846 Mexican communities revealed a rigid feudal structure that separated elites–*gente de razón*–from the lower classes, mestizos, and Native peoples–*gente sin razón*. More intriguing, as David Weber has shown, were Mexican communities that registered a growing affinity for Anglo–style capitalism long before 1846.[23] We can see, thus, that the refugees from Baja California were part of larger cultural processes that affected all of Mexico's northern territories, especially their elite citizenry.[24]

Having set out this complicated history of the northern frontier, I would like to put further pressure on analyses of the colonial process to question how cohesive and hegemonic Anglo American nationalism was in fact during westward expansion.[25] For it seems to me that there has been a long and misleading habit of collapsing American expatriates with American travelers, like Richard Henry Dana, or with explorers commissioned by the U.S. government, like Zebulon Montgomery Pike or John Charles Frémont, and even with short-term residents, like Walter Colton, author of *Three Years in California* (1851).[26] Misleadingly included in this "westward vanguard" have been longtime Anglo residents like Thomas O. Larkin of Monterey, California, or Stephen F. Austin, Jr., of Texas, who no doubt participated in their respective wars against the Republic of Mexico. Yet the historical record shows the intense degree to which some men, like Larkin and Austin, had assimilated into and embraced Spanish Mexican societies. One wonders what Texas would have been like in 1836 *without* the political influence of more recent immigrants like Sam Houston, or supporters of Texas independence like Davy Crockett, both of whom were more likely to share with each other a Jacksonian politics than was Austin—a man often criticized by other Anglo Texans for liking Mexicans too much.

Interestingly, recent scholarship on Anglo participants in the Mexican-American War emphasizes the alternative nationalisms at work in attitudes of officers and soldiers about the moral righteousness of the war. Contrary to historical treatment of U.S. army officers as largely self-interested expansionists, Samuel J. Watson argues that "officers [during the territorial expansions of 1815 and 1846] came to serve the nation-state not as individual free agents and loose cannons like Andrew Jackson, nor as ad hoc enforcement officers and diplomats like Winfield Scott . . . but ultimately as the politically accountable military agents of an empire that many of them (like Zachary Taylor, commander of the Army of Occupation in Texas) were privately reluctant to see absorbed into the United States."[27] In general, professionalism became the standard of officer conduct and decorum after 1815. According to Watson, professional officers saw themselves as an "accountable instrument of U.S. foreign and national security policy" (70). Their identification with foreign policy created an avenue for class mobility into elite circles. Watson writes: "Like other Americans among the nation's elite and aspirants to that status, officers sought authority and prestige by identifying their values with those of the Old World and its elites, including European military officers" (73). By the eve of the Mexican–American War, the officer corps had developed a "careerist neutrality," writes Watson (98). Officers greeted the Mexican–American War with a sense of duty and honor, but otherwise they were unenthusiastic about the specific expansionist goals of the war.[28]

In contrast to the insulated culture of these elite U.S. officers is that of the controversial Mexican battalion known as St. Patrick's Battalion. Michael Hogan finds that the participation of battalion members in the war revealed other common rifts in national identity among noncommissioned U.S. soldiers. Although many believed at the time that the battalion was mainly composed of Irish deserters from the United States, defectors were less than half of the group's total number. Hogan writes: "Critical to the issue of desertions from the American Army (which were higher in the Mexican War than in any other in United States history) was the lack of a sense of national identity. Americanism was a concept that had not yet been concretized by the majority of the inhabitants of the United States. There was little real sense of national unity, of cohesion. Loyalties tended to be personal, local, or at best regional."[29] According to Hogan, less than one percent of these deserters were apprehended or prosecuted, because xenophobia and the discourse of white racial superiority otherwise maintained the soldiers' focus on defeating the Mexican army (93). Ironically, winning the war produced for the United States the national identity it had sorely needed to sustain the conflict in the first place (Hogan, 113).

What emerges from Watson's and Hogan's treatment of the Mexican–American War is a more subtle understanding of the colonizing mentality that advanced the military confrontation on behalf of the United States.[30] When applied to the refugee incident in Baja California, their studies explain why Anglo officers became fast friends with the educated and aristocratic elite of the region. It explains in part why Henry Burton, for example, fell in love with María Amparo Ruiz. She came from a military family of aristocratic origins; she was, in short, an eligible and appropriate romantic prospect. Watson's and Hogan's analyses of alternative nationalisms also shed light on why Anglo veterans of the war immortalized Ruiz de Burton in their ballad "The Maid of Monterey." Unlike the majority of the war fought elsewhere in Mexico, the battles in Alta and Baja California were less brutal, took fewer lives, destroyed less property, and involved a much smaller percentage of the lower classes on both sides. These differences allowed for a cordiality that was nurtured by Anglo and Baja Californio alike.

Having focused on the colonial mentality of the aggressor, I return now to the culture of colonialism that Anglo Americans encountered in Alta and Baja California. Obviously much has happened within Chicano/a historiography since the publication of Ramón Gutiérrez's *When Jesus Came, the Corn Mothers Went Away* (1991). There are now a number of studies that look more closely at the cultures of colonialism produced in the northern frontier of New Spain and Mexico before 1846: Tomás Almaguer's *Racial Fault Lines: The Historical Origins of White Supremacy* (1994), Lisbeth Haas's *Conquests and Historical Identities in California, 1769–1936* (1995), Martha Menchaca's *The Mexican Outsiders: A Community History of Marginalization and Discrimination in California* (1995), Deena J. González's *Refusing the Favor: The Spanish-Mexican Women of Santa Fe, 1820–1880*, and Albert L. Hurtado's *Intimate Frontiers: Sex, Gender, and Culture in Old California* (1999). But much remains to be done. This is where the Recovery Project provides more than a helpful hand. If Lisbeth Haas's use of Californio *testimonios* and Ruiz de Burton novels are any indication, western and Chicano/a historians will find, in Recovery Project materials, yet another way to measure the material culture of these communities, as well as the differences between them. But unlike labor histories that conceive of labor only in terms of products of husbandry, agriculture, or industry, the Recovery Project will make the case that cultural production–novels, poetry, diaries, memoirs, and newspapers–enrich the historical record in original and efficacious ways.

How might a Recovery Project–inspired study shed new historical insight on the refugee incident? It would begin, as I have suggested, with marking the behavior of these Baja Californios, not as aberrant and isolated behavior, but as part of a deliberate, well thought out, and sophisticated political philosophy that had its origins in the establishment of the mission system throughout the Californias in the late eighteenth century. In reading the novels of Baja Californio Ruiz de Burton or the memoirs of her close friend Californio Guadalupe Vallejo, what one finds striking is their level of engagement with history, Pan American politics, and competing economic philosophies. One finds that even the anti–American Californio faction in Alta California, like their counterparts in Baja California, proceeded less on some romantic notion of

Mexican nationalism—though it existed—and more on a *regional* nationalism that was reasonably unsure of the trustworthiness of the U.S. political process. The recent translation of Antonio María Osio's *La Historia de Alta California* (originally published 1851) documents how Californios agreed to despise the central government of Mexico and therefore pursue secessionist dreams, but disagreed when it came to the American invasion. Despite the kind of opposition Osio's narrative exemplifies, one can read in Spanish-language newspapers of the 1860s, like *El Nuevo Mundo*, a belief in the pluralist possibilities of a U.S. society that included people of Mexican descent.[31] Altogether, the political beliefs of these Californios provide a unique way to appreciate the "structures of feeling" of a group of people who endured tremendous changes to their way of life after 1848. Understanding their role in the transformation of Mexican California is one aspect of the Recovery Project's offerings to historians.

Elsewhere in North America, similarly elastic nationalist loyalties were to be found among Anglo Americans who ventured west from the 1800s on, and often "went native." Captivity narratives, diaries, travel narratives all attest to the seduction of abandoning the cultural and nationalist traits of the young nation, even as expeditions, like Lewis and Clark's, busily mapped the path for future westward expansion. Along the old Spanish borderlands, commercial contact with Mexico encouraged many an Anglo American to adopt Spanish customs, language, dress, and Catholicism. Rather than seeing these Anglo Americans as mere opportunists, we should take more seriously when such individuals took oaths of allegiance to be citizens of Mexico, as in the case of Stephen F. Austin, Jr., in Texas, and countless others throughout the West. One final conclusion to be drawn from these observations is that colonial discourse in the nineteenth century is much more fluid and contradictory than previously imagined, a discourse deployed by Mexican and Anglo governments and citizens alike, but to different ends because of different colonial histories, cultures, and perceived futures. Given this, the refugees of Baja California and their Anglo American benefactors demonstrate the power of colonial discourse in the nineteenth century to override any single rhetorical referent: be it American or Mexican. Not even the intense Anglo-Saxonism of John L. O'Sullivan's Manifest Destiny could dissuade all Anglo Americans from becoming intimately involved in the lives of the people they just conquered, or vice versa.

Civil War and the Absence of Thanksgiving in Who Would Have Thought It?

Between 1848 and the publication of her first novel, the fluidity of Ruiz de Burton's nationalist loyalties slowly faded. She had gone east, experienced the trauma of the Civil War. During this period, she contradictorily assimilated and refuted the New England way that had survived and evolved in the figure of her husband, his family, and the culture at large. Even when she was still in California, the centrality of New England in the national culture reasserted itself. Henry S. Burton, for example, was a founding member of the New England Club in San Diego.[32] There were many such clubs and associations throughout California. When E. W. Morse first arrived in San Diego, he and his partner opened a boarding house called the Boston House.[33] Indeed, much of the newly settled West espoused some New England connection or "founder" in a relatively short amount of time. Because of New England's cultural and political status, it makes sense that Ruiz de Burton would feature New England and New England characters to varying degrees in her novels.

In *Who Would Have Thought It?*, Ruiz de Burton focuses on the crisis, occasioned by the Civil War, in the rhetorical and symbolic cohesion of the nation.[34] She confirms, as Harriet Beecher Stowe had dramatized earlier in *Uncle Tom's Cabin* (1852), that the heart of the conflict for the United States was its status as the most virtuous, if not most Christian, nation in the world. But unlike Stowe, Ruiz de Burton pinpoints the cause of the crisis not in slavery—for her, slavery was an ongoing symptom of a larger phenomenon—but in the unfolding rifts of national belonging itself, rifts dormant since the signing of the U.S. Constitution (1787), but exaggerated and unleashed explosively during the war. Ruiz de Burton judges that the fault lines in American society have to do with origins myths that overzealously celebrate New England as foundation of the United States. In *Who Would Have Thought It?* Ruiz de Burton encourages her readers to see the Civil War as not just about slavery, states' rights, or saving the Union, but more precisely about saving New England as the symbolic birthplace of America.

Ruiz de Burton underwrites her satire of New England's "errand in the wilderness" by taking deliberate rhetorical, literary, and biographical steps that refuse the subordinate, neocolonial identity forced upon her by Anglo–Saxon Manifest Destiny. In other words, she articulates herself in opposition to "the subaltern." To do so, she reclaims, albeit selectively and strategically, an eighteenth–century Enlightenment liberal ideology that affirms her as an aristocratic, white Mexican, and also as a rightful heir to a proud Spanish Mexican colonial past. Ruiz de Burton's displacement from her own "native" colonial identity thus fuels her indictment of U.S. culture as corrupt, and in so doing, reveals the extent to which competing colonial projects had existed in North America during the late nineteenth century and could survive, at least in narrative form, to contest the ongoing demotion of Spanish Mexican colonial subjects and culture.

Indeed, her novel's satire of Manifest Destiny should be seen in the larger context of the range of colonial enterprises operating in North America since 1492. Her repudiation of colonial/imperial intents is therefore not a condemnation of colonialism per se, but rather a rejection of the national political and moral power that had accrued to the region of New England by 1872. While not oblivious to the evils of slavery, Ruiz de Burton charges that doubts about the sacred direction of the nation stemmed equally from the moral and political deficiencies inherent in American–style Manifest Destiny. In a subtle manner, then, Ruiz de Burton proposes that New England needed the war in order to consolidate its moral authority and to extend and finalize the colonization of the West and the nation–on terms that prohibited slavery. Ironically, Ruiz de Burton's novel suggests that the Civil War was nothing less than Manifest Destiny aimed at the South, and the prize was a New England hegemony from coast to coast.

It should come then as no surprise that the novel assiduously avoids any representation of New England's most sacred ritual of nation-building, namely Thanksgiving. This is noteworthy, especially when read in conjunction with the narrator's litany of complaints about the denizens of New England and their symbolic standing as the first people of the nation. Ruiz de Burton's erasure of Thanksgiving as a symbol of the sacred history of the United States is no accident. Nor is Thanksgiving's absence a matter of sour grapes. With much cause to see the United States as her sworn enemy–as a victim of the Mexican–American War of 1846 and a target of nativist racism–Ruiz de Burton, the individual, nonetheless married into an old New England family. As the wife of a celebrated U.S. officer who helped in the military capture of Alta California, Ruiz de

Burton traveled far and wide in East Coast circles. In time, Ruiz de Burton could have easily gathered around her own Thanksgiving dinner table a crowd of dignitaries that included the Lincolns, the Hammonds, the Sumners, the Grants, and even their enemies, such as Jefferson and Varina Davis. Why then is there no Thanksgiving in her first novel? To answer this, we must delve into her biography once again.

The clear resolutions of *Who Would Have Thought It?* belie some of the tensions the novel opens up quite dramatically elsewhere. Burton's time among the New England family she married into is the probable source of the satiric anger expressed in the novel and the erasure of Thanksgiving—both as a regional colonial ritual and as a day of national reconciliation that Lincoln had intended would heal the costly Union victory at Gettysburg (1863). Given the cherished position of Thanksgiving as an American holiday, one wonders at the kind of anger Ruiz de Burton held for her in-laws. One wonders all the more, given that the notion of "thanksgiving" as a communal reckoning of the year's blessings was not unfamiliar among Catholics in Spanish colonial history, nor among Catholics in Mexican colonial history. Indeed, California history records Spanish colonialists celebrating a thanksgiving in 1769 after a year of much trial and tribulation. In the early American period of California, a Thanksgiving dinner was held at Portsmouth House, San Francisco, in 1848, according to Jane Hatch.[35] A year later, on the eve of statehood, a larger Thanksgiving celebration was held on October 24, 1849. Having relocated to Monterey, California, in 1848, before her marriage to the West Point officer from New England, Ruiz de Burton would have been quite aware of the cultural and social significance of such a celebration. And as an officer's wife, with her own family's elite military legacy as a guide to protocol, Ruiz de Burton would have been loathe to commit any obvious faux pas at her husband's expense. No, Thanksgiving, in itself, was not anathema to Ruiz de Burton. The telling change came after living among her New England in-laws from 1859 to 1869.

Her husband's relations were among the elite of New England. Henry S. Burton, her husband, was born at West Point on May 9, 1819. He was the son of Oliver G. Burton, West Point officer, and Almira Partridge of Norwich, Vermont. In fact, both the Burtons and the Partridges hailed from the same town. In 1839, Henry Burton married his first wife, Elizabeth Ferguson Smith, who died in 1841. Together, they had a daughter, who later married and had two children—these grandchildren of Burton would later (1894) claim, unsuccessfully, an inheritance from Ruiz de Burton. Ruiz de Burton went to live in Norwich, Vermont, for a while during her family's stay in the East, and this is probably where she gained a bird's-eye view of New England culture.

The Burtons and the Partridges are most likely the families fictionalized in her first novel. The Burton family likely produced models for the novel's corrupt clergy. Henry Burton was probably related to Asa Burton, a famous Congregational clergyman, who wrote, besides sermons, on a variety of topics including metaphysics, and is thought to have anticipated theories of psychology and evolution.[36] He was an educator, having founded his own academy, as well as one of the founders of the University of Vermont, and a corporate member of Middlebury College. Asa Burton died childless when Henry was a boy, but because becoming a clergyman ran in some families, there is a good chance that other Burton relatives followed the vocation of becoming a clergyman.

There seem to have been further family military connections on the Partridge side. Almira Burton, Henry's mother, likely was related to Alden Partridge, as either sister or cousin. Alden Partridge had been a captain in the corps of engineers at West Point, and his time there overlapped with that of Oliver Burton.[37] He would go on to a successful career as an educator, military theorist, and historian, specializing in artillery science. He would also establish a very important military academy in Vermont, from which evolved Norwich University. Henry Burton would attend both as a young man. In all likelihood, Alden Partridge was responsible for Henry's career as an artillery officer. In fact, Partridge trained a number of individuals who would later serve with distinction in the Civil War. Henry Burton would be posted at Fort Monroe before, during, and after the Civil War, because the fort was the U.S. Army's first school of artillery.[38] This is precisely why Fort Monroe enters the novel. Ruiz de Burton would have known it very well—because of the Partridge connection, and because at the conclusion of the war Henry Burton was commandant of the fort when it held the country's most notorious prisoner of war, Jefferson Davis.

Rounding out Ruiz de Burton's family in Vermont were the Willistons. After Oliver Burton's death in 1821, Almira Burton married Ebenezer Bancroft Williston, who taught Greek and Latin in Alden Partridge's academy.[39] This erudite man, who published an edition of works by the ancient Roman historian Tacitus, might have been a partial model for Dr. Norval. Although Williston died in 1837, family stories must have circulated to Ruiz de Burton about the only father Henry Burton ever really knew. In addition, Henry Burton had three step–siblings from his mother's second marriage. The most famous was E. B. Williston, who, like his older brother, became an artillery officer and was also a breveted brigadier general during the Civil War. Further complicating the picture for Ruiz de Burton, or at least adding new depths of irony, was the fact that Henry's stepfather had a cousin by the name of George Bancroft, the famous historian and author of the multivolume *History of the United States: From the Discovery of the Continent* (1834–74). He is also remembered as the secretary of the Navy in the Polk administration who gave the only official order to seize California "in the event of war with Mexico." It was Bancroft who, as secretary of war pro tem, ordered General Zachary Taylor in 1846 to occupy contested territory in Texas.[40] This is the extended family Ruiz de Burton came to know.

Ruiz de Burton reconceives her New England family history for her first novel, in which Lola Medina struggles to make a life for herself in an alien culture and environment. Lola's displacement from Mexican culture, Roman Catholicism, and aristocratic lineage symbolically unites author with character. It is through Lola that Ruiz de Burton manages to convey her initial cultural shock upon meeting Henry Burton's extended family. She no doubt experienced what Lola suffers in the novel: the pain of discrimination, ethnic and racial, even though she was "white"; attacks on her Catholicism as the reputed whore of Babylon; attacks on Mexican culture and society as backward and animalistic; and finally the insults of a regional chauvinism that empowered New Englanders to believe in the morality of Manifest Destiny. Curiously, Lola, as the main provocateur of the plot, is conspicuously absent for most of the novel. Her absence is filled by a narrator who speaks on Lola's behalf and takes revenge on her attackers. The narrator thus serves as mother figure and protectress to two orphans: Lola Medina, the character, and María Amparo Ruiz de Burton, orphaned by the vagaries of the political landscape surrounding the Mexican–American War. We can understand Lola's future marriage to Julian at the novel's end as Ruiz de Burton's desire to revisit the romance she once imagined possible with Henry Burton, a romance that would also help resolve her nationalist anger. This ending alerts us to the creativity and imagination of its writer, and, more poignantly, to the longing for a cultural reckoning that remained suspended with Henry Burton's death.

Yet, if most of Henry Burton's family relations and New England neighbors enter the novel as satiric fodder, there is good reason to see that at least some family members shouldered the legacy of an earnest, moral, and honorable vision of the nation. In fact, Ruiz de Burton demonstrates her appreciation for a certain brand of New England moral authority when she quotes abolitionist and political reformer John Greenleaf Whittier on the title page of the novel:

> But by all thy nature's weakness,
> Hidden faults and follies known,
> Be thou, in rebuking evil,
> Conscious of thine own.

Whittier's aphorism on the limits of censuring others finds its way into the characterization of Dr. Norval, Julian Norval, and Isaac and Lavinia Sprig. These characters anchor the novel's indictment of the political failings of a country waging a so-called holy war against the South. If there's a moral lesson to be learned in this novel, it is partly about the future of the United States as an ethical nation. This ethical nation surfaces from time to time through the various circumstances the above characters negotiate during the Civil War. Foremost in these negotiations are the actions and philosophies of Dr. Norval. Though a Democrat, Dr. Norval believes the South's secession from the Union disastrous, since it will most surely provoke a costly war. Nevertheless, his reluctance to join the popular support among New Englanders to quell the rebellion in the South makes him a pariah. Even his neighbors, the Cackle family, take advantage of the Doctor's low repute by accepting his money to raise troops for the Union but also capitalizing on available misinformation that frames the Doctor as a traitor to the country.

Ruiz de Burton's characterization of the politically and domestically besieged Dr. Norval becomes the means of establishing the moral wit of the narrator. Through Dr. Norval, the narrator is able to uphold the virtues of certain New Englanders while simultaneously revealing the hypocrisy of the majority. Nowhere is this dichotomous representation more clear than in the "election day" celebration Ruiz de Burton transcribes in chapter 14, entitled "The Doctor Was Rewarded for Listening to Mr. Hackwell's Sermon." The episode begins with the narrator's critical disdain for Puritan history: "It was the anniversary of some great day in New England when the Misses Norval were to make their farewell appearance in church before leaving for Europe—some great day in which the Pilgrim fathers had done one of their wonderful deeds. They had either embarked, or landed, or burnt a witch, or whipped a woman at the pillory, on such a day" (62). The cynicism expressed here and the understanding of the patriarchal nature of European colonialism and its explicit power over women hyperbolize the hypocrisy that sustains Reverend Hackwell's sermon on New England's contribution to liberty. Beginning with the Pilgrims' sacrifice of "home, civilization, and friends" (63), Hackwell ties the Puritans landing in New England with a defense of religious freedom itself, a principle these forefathers took comfort in when they encountered "horrible savages and privations of all kinds" (63). This meditation on religious freedom becomes "Freedom of Opinion" (63), which in turn becomes "the individual liberty of the soul" (63) and from there the basis for condemning the rebellious South. The South, according to Hackwell, has clearly rejected the manifest sacred history of the nation, favoring the role of Beelzebub and Judas Iscariot in contrast to New England's "City on a Hill" and New Englanders as the "chosen elect." Dr. Norval's response to Hackwell's evolving sacred history of the United States is to declare to Mrs. Norval that Hackwell's sermon on freedom of conscience has made plain his duty to have Lola Medina properly raised in her faith—Catholicism.

After this stunning moment, the novel proceeds deliberately to redirect the principles of eighteenth-century liberal ideology away from a Puritan historiography. Ruiz de Burton separates, or deregionalizes, various ideals about government, liberty, and the civic role of the individual in society.[41] She will not allow narratives of the nation to be unproblematically centered upon New England. She thus aims to uncollapse the events—the advent of circumstance, folklore, and Whig politics earlier in the nineteenth century, as Nina Baym shows—that supported dominant representations of the nation. For this distillation, Ruiz de Burton focuses on the plight of Julian Norval, son of Dr. Norval, who in the midst of war is accused of wrongdoing. Despite having been decorated for valor in the field, Julian Norval is dismissed from active duty on suspicion of treason. His dismissal comes without formal charges or the requisite military court–martial. The grave injustice of the dismissal and its air of conspiracy convince Julian that he must seek out President Lincoln himself before the dismissal is made public. What angers Julian more than the lie of the accusation is the public shame that the dismissal will invite. He goes to Washington convinced that his rights as citizen give him access to the president.

Julian's initial conference with the president occurs accidentally when the president is away from his political handlers. Julian, upset over the obstacles that bureaucracy and influence peddling have created between "the people" and their elected officials, stumbles into the president as the latter listens to a Marine band playing before a crowd. Ruiz de Burton's representation of Lincoln is of a piece with her overall critique of a democracy she believes is held hostage by regional and monied interests. Although Lincoln comes off badly in her satiric rendering, Ruiz de Burton's point is not to draw some easy caricature of the president, but rather to expose the scandalous suspension of legal due process during the Civil War. Lincoln confirms for Julian that his dismissal is based on accusations that the young officer has spoken critically of the president and is therefore deemed a Southern sympathizer. The Lincoln character explains: " 'Yes—something, too, about your saying that I had no right to issue the Emancipation Proclamation and that I am usurping powers, and that some members of my cabinet tyrannize over the people, and I let them do it, and I don't know what else' " (213).

Ruiz de Burton's ironic use of Lincoln for her novel is twofold: For one, Lincoln inadvertently gives credence to charges his Republican and Democratic opponents had publicized for years. Second, Ruiz de Burton's own personal dealings with Lincoln—she successfully petitioned the president to promote Henry Burton to colonel during the war—would suggest an opportunistic streak in her, "biting the hand that fed her." If the first irony plays into the overall satiric structure of the novel, the second irony is not lost upon Ruiz de Burton, because ultimately she has, or had, no problem with Lincoln the person. Rather, Julian's troubles with Washington represent Ruiz de Burton's legitimate concerns that during the war a "shadow government" threatened to undo the constitutional liberties of all Americans, even as the Union waged a rhetorical and military war to secure the future freedoms of the nation. The narrator signals her contempt for this "shadow government" by referring to Lincoln's handlers as his "high officials" (238). Indeed, the narrator insinuates that

Lincoln is overly dependent on these nonelected officials, and that their presence in the White House bodes ill for representative government, and more importantly undermines the connection between "the people" and their elected officials. According to the narrator, the Civil War has destabilized the American populace's faith in government despite its overall zealousness for the Union. These rifts are most apparent in the executive branch, which takes advantage of the war to break with tradition about the customary separation of powers. Overall, the novel reveals how dangerously close the Union comes to actualizing the kind of centrist tyranny the South had been arguing against through its insistence on states' rights.

Like many other characters, Julian might have been modeled after historical figures. A close friend, and crucial to the publication of *Who Would Have Thought It?* was Samuel L. M. Barlow. Not only did he help Ruiz de Burton secure a book contract with J. P. Lippincott, he was also an important Northern Democrat. He is credited by some with having engineered the eventual presidential election of James Buchanan in 1856. During the Civil War, this highly visible broker for the Democratic Party was caught up in a web of intrigue that figured him as a traitor to the Union. Richard M. Garten writes: "On every side he was branded as a disloyal copperhead who was an apologist for slavery to the extent of active participation in extensive disunion machinations. It is in these libelous terms that Barlow survives in the literature of the Civil War period" (44). Garten further describes Barlow as being the target of a media smear campaign throughout most the war, and even considered a threat to the Union by some members of Lincoln's cabinet. The kind of suspicion leveled at Barlow was fairly common in the context of the war and Washington politics. The war in fact fueled a hysteria over patriotism. At the outset of the war, Mary Todd Lincoln's loyalty was scathingly questioned because of her personal ties to the South. Even Abraham Lincoln did not escape a charge of treason or two.

Closer to the Burtons was the treason case of Claggett D. Fitzhugh.[42] He was a prisoner of war, captured on September 14, 1862. At Fort Delaware, he was charged with being a spy for the Confederacy. Fitzhugh protested the charge for months, claiming that he was a private in the First Virginia Cavalry, and therefore eligible for an exchange of prisoners between combatants. Having languished for eight months under these false charges, Fitzhugh wrote Colonel W. Hoffman, Commissary General of Prisoners: "I demanded a hearing upon this charge [of spying] three different times but received no answer to any of my communications. After the expiration of three weeks I was released from close confinement and placed among the officers at Fort Delaware, not, however, because I was an officer but only through the kindness of my friend Major Burton, then in command" (629). Fitzhugh goes on to explain that Major Burton informed him that he was on parole and ordered to report to Washington to petition his exchange. Yet, as Fitzhugh's letter makes clear, having visited the very same commissary to whom the letter is addressed, there is little or no desire among Union officials to resolve the matter. Fitzhugh sums up his situation as a travesty of due process, noting that the charges against him require a trial. In conclusion, he pleads: "I know I have no right to ask this favor of you, but knowing you have the power to exchange me if you please, and believing you to be a just and upright gentleman, I trust you will take the matter in hand and permit me to leave with the next exchange" (630). Fitzhugh's unlawful detention seems a model not only for Julian Norval's desire for a trial that will clear his name, but for the tragic fate of Isaac Sprig, who in the novel is victimized by a vengeful Union official when he is passed up numerous times in prisoner-of-war exchanges.

By contrast, what saves Julian's military career and his reputation is Lincoln's personal intervention. Once he hears that the accusations are partly based on public statements made by Dr. Norval and not by his son Julian, Lincoln concedes the whole matter a gross exaggeration of the facts (240). Indeed, Julian's anonymous accusers, these "high officials," are finally cowed into retreat by Julian's principled and eloquent protests. In order to avoid more trouble from a regional delegation that would profit from Julian's maltreatment, Lincoln resolves the matter in a handwritten note to the War Office (243). The ordeal over, the pettiness of this case of injustice nevertheless lingers in the narrative, calling into question the ability of government to represent adequately "the people." There is no Thanksgiving ritual in *Who Would Have Thought It?* because it is not clear whether the people of the United States will actually benefit from the Civil War, and therefore be in a position to be thankful. There is even less certainty over what conclusions to draw about a successful war effort so steeped in greed, regional partisan politics, hypocrisy, and suspension of civil liberties. Slavery as a social issue plays only a small role in this novel. It is not clear what position Ruiz de Burton took on this

issue, although I would venture that she shared a number of racist ideologies common to both Anglo and Californio elites. What is clearer is
that Ruiz de Burton denies New England culture and regional politics
the kind of unqualified respect that it demands of the nation as a whole.
For Ruiz de Burton, an invitation to a New England Thanksgiving dinner
is always more than just a family ritual, especially when no New Englander could be bothered to imagine what an accomplished woman
from a Californio colonial heritage could bring to the table.

In the end, Ruiz de Burton satirizes New England's national status in
order to question the symbolic foundations of Manifest Destiny. Her
novel directly links the territorial expansion of the United States, including that accomplished by the Civil War, to a teleology that mythologizes
a Puritan past in order to justify as destiny New England's governance of
North America. Thus, this novel sets up a critical representation of New
England as the cultural, political, and moral center of the country even as
the nation is narrated elsewhere in terms that obscure and complicate its
own constructed origins. By emphasizing the moral decay and corruption prevalent among descendants of the Puritan experiment, Ruiz de
Burton deromanticizes the ideology that would claim the United States
is heir to a legacy of progressive sacred history. Moreover, Ruiz de Burton's damning portrayals of New England clergy, abolitionists, Republican mothers, and electoral politics mark a crisis in the production of a
nationalist narrative during the Civil War. In winning, the Union survives the regional threat posed by the South, but in *Who Would Have
Thought It?* Ruiz de Burton reenacts the conflict to ensure that the spoils
of war do not include amnesia about the shortcomings of New England
and its native sons and daughters. Despite her great love for her New
England husband and their children, in her act of remembrance she
resists the totalizing effect of living in the shadow of Manifest Destiny,
which was an imperialist philosophy squarely bent on obscuring her
own preferred Spanish Mexican colonial traditions and the dignities
they conferred upon her as a daughter of the Enlightenment. This was a
colonial project she could never countenance.

Recognized at Last

Despite all her efforts to restore and bequeath to her family an unspoiled
Californio legacy, María Amparo Ruiz de Burton died in 1895 in Chicago,

just having traveled to Mexico City where she was unsuccessful in regaining her claim on Rancho Ensenada de Todos Santos in Baja California. In this land dispute, according to Sánchez and Pita, Ruiz de Burton identified herself as Mexican in her legal contest against U.S. investors seeking "to colonize the Baja California area." Historian Lisbeth Haas elaborates on this episode: having won title to Rancho Ensenada in 1871 from the Mexican courts, she later suffered a setback when her claim was nullified in part by Mexico's 1883 Law of Colonization, which enabled an international land company to claim Rancho Ensenada. Through herculean efforts, she won the title back, only to have the decision reversed by the Supreme Court of Mexico in 1889. In her later years, without much money, Ruiz de Burton often acted as her own counsel and prepared her own court briefs. Regarding this land dispute, Oden argues that Ruiz de Burton was unaware that her maternal grandfather, José Manuel Ruiz, had long ago, 1824, sold the property to his son–in–law, Francisco Xavier Gastelum, who had in turn sold it to Pedro Gastelum, a cousin, who later sold it as well.

Like many of her Californio peers, Ruiz de Burton died in poverty. Of all of her immediate family who had followed her to Alta California, she was the last to die. Doña Isabel had died in 1893, at the age of eighty–six. Her brother, Federico, died of pneumonia at fifty–four years of age in 1884. At death, he was penniless. Manuela had died in 1880, at age fifty–two. Oden's research shows that Ruiz de Burton "died of gastric fever at the Sherman House on August 12, 1895" in Chicago, where she was soliciting new political support to continue litigation over Rancho Ensenada. After her death, her body was shipped home by rail to San Diego. She was buried in Calvary Catholic Cemetery in San Diego. Her funeral was apparently well attended and, as Oden notes, her casket was "showered with floral offerings."

Through all the hardship and disappointment, Ruiz de Burton's children were her joy. Nellie and Harry would eventually marry and settle in the San Diego area. Nellie married Miguel Pedrorena, a childhood friend from nearby Rancho Santa Monica, on December 27, 1875. Together, they had only one child, Eileen, who was born on May 24, 1877. Ruiz de Burton was forty–four years old when she became a grandmother. Harry Burton married Minnie Wilbur on April 27, 1882, at Jamul ranch, having originally met her, Oden speculates, when the family resided in the East. Later that year, on Christmas day, Miguel Pedrorena died of illness. The family's sorrow was softened when Minnie Burton gave birth to Henry Halleck Burton, Jr., the following spring, on March 24, 1883. Harry and Minnie would have another son, known as D. C., who died at three months. But Ruiz de Burton's final grandchild would be Harry's and Minnie's daughter Carrol, who was born on June 24, 1887. Nellie Burton de Pedrorena died February 5, 1910. Harry Sr. would live a long life, dying at age eighty-one in Culver City, California, on October 17, 1933.

To this day, Ruiz de Burton's family descendants make California their home.[43] Her Jamul ranch still stands just outside of San Diego. It is known regionally for stories about ghosts emanating from past owners and occupants. One story circulates about an Indian attack that left dead Pío Pico's majordomo, José Leiva, and his wife and son brutalized, while two of the family's daughters were kidnapped. The expedition sent to find the Leiva daughters was even more brutal in their retaliations against the suspected native culprits. The daughters were never rescued. After that, Antoinette May writes: "the rancho was the scene of blood feuds and a series of grisly unresolved murders—squatters found with their heads bashed in. According to one legend the murderer was discovered and immediately lynched by an angry mob. When the authorities arrived, the body had disappeared. It was never found."[44] The Native American descendants of the area, who continue to live in Jamul, California, are part of the Jamul Band of Mission Indians. Under sunnier skies, 4,800 acres of Jamul ranch became part the San Diego Wildlife Refuge in August of 1997. The press conference announcing the transfer of lands to the refuge was held on the grounds of the brick-making kiln that Ruiz de Burton had ordered built.[45]

These events in Jamul ranch history, like the complicated course of Ruiz de Burton's life, poignantly remind me of Mary C. Morse. Her story closes with a sense of how the passage of time makes all things seem natural: "My first impression of Old San Diego gradually wore away, and as winter approached and the hills were brown and barren no longer, I realized the advantages we had here over a bleak New England climate. Instead of leaving San Diego at the first opportunity, for a more congenial field, as I had intended, I am still here, proud of the beautiful bay and the city that surrounds it" (260). Long overdue and a hundred years after Mary C. Morse's reading for the Ladies' Pioneer Society, María Amparo Ruiz de Burton's life and writings have finally found a home among readers of American literature. She too was with us all this time. We just didn't know it. Ruiz de Burton would have agreed with Morse that New England was bleak and that San Diego offered much to make one proud. Had she been alive and invited to the Society that fateful day, she would have insisted on telling her story first, since it came first. She could have told it in Spanish, English, or French. Really, it would have been no trouble. In the decades to come, avid readers of American literature will undoubtedly secure for Ruiz de Burton the cultural prominence she so yearned for in life.

CHAPTER FOUR

One Nation under New England

Immigration, Citizenship,

and Representation

The story of the Mexican Revolution of 1910 has been told a thousand times. With no lack of storytellers, scholars, and mythologists, the socialist revolution continues to capture the imaginations of people of Mexican descent on both sides of the border. It lives today in cinematic renderings such as Gregory Nava's *Mi Familia* (1995), and in the many representations of events in Chiapas, Mexico–for some the birthplace of the original revolution. And it is no wonder. Between 1910 and 1919, the first modern socialist revolution in the world reorganized the Mexican state from top to bottom, and inevitably displaced people from all sectors of Mexican society. As all wars do, this one created refugees. Conservative estimates put the exodus of Mexican nationals to the United States at around a quarter of million people.[1] These refugees were readily absorbed by a U.S. agricultural and industrial economy hungry for cheap labor. According to Chicano historian Rodolfo Acuña, nativist national policies that significantly reduced European immigration at the turn of the century, coupled with the surge of industrial growth, served to draw attention to African Americans and Mexican Americans as internal sources of cheap labor. This was true especially during World War I. During the first three decades of the century, Acuña notes, "approximately one tenth of Mexico's population [one and half million people] shifted 'north from Mexico,' in one of the largest mass migrations of people in the history of the world."[2]

Just as the postmodern Mexican nation is compelled to relive and reinvent the significance of a revolution that ushered in the twentieth century, so too has Chicano/a studies found the revolution a meaningful focal point of discussion, debate, and consternation over such perennial issues as immigration, labor, discrimination, nativism, assimilation, and acculturation. The Mexican Revolution set the cultural stage for the construction of ethnic identities, gender relations, and local and national political affiliations—all of which cohered ultimately with the modernist aesthetics prevalent at the time. The narrative productions that emerged from this process would become the bedrock of Mexican American working- and middle-class identities in the decades before the Chicano/a Movement. If in that earlier period, the Mexican American community registered its response to the tumult in Mexico, it soon endured equally significant events that affected the United States as a whole: the growth of labor unions, World War I, Prohibition, the winning of voting rights for women, the stock market crash of 1929, followed by the Great Depression. All these events, of course, had major consequences for people of Mexican descent, consequences routinely chronicled in the Spanish reading press throughout the Southwest and West. Eventually these events became the basis of Mexican American literary production in this period.

In the above historical trajectory, which is fairly well established in Chicano/a studies, the role of New England in Mexican American ethnic and political formation is a nonissue. What may be intriguing, nevertheless, is to think about the ascendancy of Puritan studies in academic circles happening at the same historical moment as the cultural and political growth of the Mexican American community. If the dominant narrative of Mexican American experience concerns economic absorption, political disfranchisement, and ultimately civic participation from 1910 to 1946, does a Puritan ethos have any meaningful significance to people of Mexican descent? My answer is yes. To explore the complex connection, let us turn to an area of study in which Chicano/a studies commands unquestionable expertise: immigration.

I wish to raise the prospect that the parallel development of Puritan studies and the Mexican American community is no mere coincidence. Their mutual growth is underwritten by historic as well as material connections. Thus I begin with this century's construction of the Puritans as the ideal and archetypal immigrant community of the nation. Here, in discourses about the ideal immigrant, certain immigrant groups are identified as potential citizens while others seemed to fail the litmus tests of appropriate racial, religious, and prior colonial identities and history. One of the more painful popular perceptions endured by the Mexican American community of this period was its status as an "immigrant community"–and a disfavored one at that. The general notion of Mexican Americans as typically immigrant, although not an incorrect representation given the overall numbers of actual immigrants in the period, had the unsalutatory effect of dehistoricizing this community's presence in the United States before and immediately after the Treaty of Guadalupe Hidalgo. Furthermore, discourses of the ideal immigrant served to displace the more recent civic history of Mexican Americans–whether that includes, like the Otero family in New Mexico, lawmakers at the municipal and state level, or, like Ricardo Flores Magón, Elisa Alemán, and Lucy Eldine Gonzales Parsons, labor activists.[3] Also swept aside was Mexican American participation in national events such as the U.S. Civil War (1861), the Spanish–American War (1898), and World War I (1917). In all, discourses of the ideal immigrant produced a totalizing (and paralyzing) portrayal of Mexican Americans as a failed immigrant community. This portrait culminated in an anti–immigrant discourse, which has harassed and discriminated against Mexican Americans and Mexican nationals alike since the 1930s.

One of the reasons for this anti–immigrant sentiment is a national cultural imaginary rooted in an immigrant Puritan experience that was also championed by scholars. To say that Puritan scholars had as their primary object to vilify the Mexican American community would be utterly false. It would be truer to say that Puritan scholars acted, however unconsciously, as high cultural conduits for nativist impulses that ran strong elsewhere in the nation. These nativist impulses in turn consciously and deliberately barred people of Mexican descent from claiming a civic history in the United States. In this context, Puritan studies became complicit in perpetuating discourses that would represent Mexican Americans, immigrant or otherwise, as undesirable. To make my case I follow the lead of Chicano/a historians who have taken up the topic of immigration in great detail. I rely particularly on the works of Camille Guerin–Gonzales and David Gutiérrez, for their analyses often traverse social terrain sympathetic to cultural studies. My purpose in using these histories as a cultural fulcrum is to recover the nativist consequences apparent in the scholarly creation of Puritans as this country's ideal immigrant community. Between, on the one hand, an idealized Puritan community and, on the other, a representation of Mexican Americans as unworthy immigrants, I uncover a political unconscious not only centered in a Puritan myth of origins but that has real consequences for Mexican American culture and history. I conclude the chapter with an extended review of literature by Mexican Americans from 1900 to 1960. Under the rubric of immigration, I explicate a variety of political positions to suggest the range of gender, economic, cultural, and racial representations at work in the cultural production of writers who until recently were, to some serious degree, lost to history.

Land of Dreams, Land of Nativism, 1880–1920

Guerin-Gonzales's history, *Mexican Workers and American Dreams: Immigration, Repatriation, and California Farm Labor, 1900–1939* (1994), is important to my analysis of Puritan studies. As her book title suggests, Mexican Americans and Mexican nationals have historically been quite aware of the mythos that hails the United States as a land of opportunity. Simultaneously, they have been aware of themselves as subjects hailed by that same myth, despite not being of Anglo-Saxon descent. Guerin-Gonzales focuses on the combined reactions of Mexican immigrants, established Mexican American communities, and dominant Anglo communities to historic forces that precipitated and maintained agribusiness' dependence on migrant labor. Situated in the first four decades of this century, Guerin-Gonzales's history narrates the myth of the "American Dream" as it was translated into ideologies that empowered Anglo farmers and migrant workers alike, but to very different ends. Guerin-Gonzales writes:

> Although Mexican immigrants encountered and believed a variety of ideas about America, the language of the American Dream in particular shaped their expectations and behavior. The American Dream promised economic opportunity and security— which would free people to realize their intellectual, physical, and spiritual potential—as the foundation for basic rights of individual citizens. Implicit in this American Dream was a belief in the uniqueness of individuals. Uniqueness (or difference),

human potential, and inalienable rights gave meaning to the American Dream.[4]

Because of their shared, if uneven, aspirations toward the American Dream, conflict inevitably led Anglo farmers to self-advocate by invoking individual rights under the law, including rights to hire and fire at will, whereas Mexican migrant workers sought out self-advocacy through organized labor and collective bargaining. Guerin-Gonzales cites the contest over the American Dream as vital to Mexican American history, because the conflict revealed the malleable nature of the dream itself. These same immigrants, who had used the American Dream before to imagine their own civic futures in the United States, could now transform it. In other words, as much as the myth of the American Dream stood for an idealized, stable set of identities, it also empowered individuals to interpret it in terms suitable to themselves and to produce a counterdiscourse of alternative but parallel narratives of the American Dream. In the end, this process of contestation and interpretation led both Anglo farmer and Mexican worker to claim legitimacy for their differing interpretations. As Guerin-Gonzales argues: "The contest over legitimacy was also a struggle for domination—of who would have economic security, who would have freedom" (6).

I would expand Guerin-Gonzales's argument by suggesting that a similar analysis can be applied to entire communities of self-ascribing individuals. Astutely, Guerin-Gonzales observes two images dominating access to the American Dream—that of "a white, middle-class non-immigrant male," and that of a relatively diffused, anonymous, but nationally oriented immigrant male (4). Her discussion of a privileged white, male, Protestant civic identity opens up to a larger discussion of communities' bids for legitimacy under the sign of the nation. Individuals were and are at risk for expulsion and punishment when they do not embody the preferred image of the American Dream (5); at risk too, I contend, are communities that fail to uphold an image of community that harks back to the Puritans. Discrete, individual expressions of privilege, like those of the ranchers cited by Guerin-Gonzales, are sustained by this Puritan mythos, especially as that privilege is implicit in such naturalized, secularized, and male-gendered concepts as the American Dream, the American Mind, the American Century, American know-how, and so forth.

This expansion of Guerin–Gonzales's thesis is important because it enlarges the cultural terrain in which the American Dream operates and clarifies the more likely beneficiaries of the cultural imaginary produced by such a myth. Even if Guerin–Gonzales's study is focused on regional labor history, it also offers a cultural analysis that always points to the centrality of regional economics and politics in the overall narrative cohesion of the nation. Guerin–Gonzales alerts us to the transformative potential of the second image identified above, which includes "anyone living and working in the United States" who believes that their "economic, social, and political contributions" (5) have entitled them to legitimate civic representation. She provides the kind of theory I believe New Chicano/a Studies needs to explain the emergent bicultural, binational nature of Mexican American communities in the twentieth century.

Implicitly, Mexican immigrants become *cultural* citizens long before they are legal citizens (Guerin–Gonzales, 5). In this second image of the American dream, a non–Anglo Puritan version I argue, we see that civic participation defined more in cultural than legal terms often makes citizens out of Mexican Americans. On the symbolic terrain of the nation, cultural citizens take advantage of the empowering elasticity of the American Dream to transform and be transformed. Hence, Guerin–Gonzales's formulation highlights an internal and cultural mechanism of U.S. citizen formation—the potential of immigrants both to adopt and adapt the promises of America—that might go otherwise unnoticed for these less privileged aspirants to American citizenry. This last point is crucial. Without an understanding of the aggressive way Mexican Americans pursued citizenship in this period, we invariably overlook their investment, practical and symbolic, in a United States that upholds the promises of the American Dream. It is not the Dream but their access and right to interpret it that becomes an issue. But this understanding need not stop with ethnic groups of color.

The second image of the American Dream also sheds light on the role that white ethnics, non–Anglo Puritan immigrants, played in the reinvention of Puritan America during these same years. From the Irish and Italians to Russian Jews and eastern Europeans, white ethnics embarked on their own aggressive pursuits that eventually afforded them the American Dream, though for some more than others. Later in this chapter, I will point out the role of white ethnic scholars in the formation of a Puritan sensibility that, again on the terrain of culture, justified and affirmed their own citizenry by injecting into U.S. history and culture a tradition of dissent. This tradition of dissent became the metanarrative that symbolically linked the Puritan dissenters of King James and Charles I to the shores of New England, and from there to the legal foundations of the nation in the documents of the Declaration of Independence and the U.S. Constitution. But the real "jewel in the crown" was the link between Puritanism and the nineteenth century, and the posthumous validation of the dissenting voices found in Emerson, Thoreau, Hawthorne, Melville, and Whitman that prophesied the emergence of a white, male, pluralist America. Here, significantly, Puritan studies merged with American studies in confirmation of the American Century. The dynamic relationship between the first and second image that Guerin–Gonzales theorizes thus clarifies the logic encouraging white ethnics in the early twentieth century to fashion themselves culturally as Puritan descendants in order to be accorded legitimacy, citizenship, and a privileged nationalist role. Yet, self–fashioning cannot occur without the erection of barriers to others who perform the necessary role of antithesis; much like the cultural role that Native America played to English colonization, Mexican America became a necessary scapegoat for the ambivalences of white ethnicity in the United States.

One of the best analyses of the ambivalences surrounding new immigrant populations is David Gutiérrez's *Walls and Mirrors: Mexican Americans, Mexican Immigrants, and the Politics of Ethnicity* (1995). Like Guerin–Gonzales's history, Gutiérrez's analysis of the Mexican American community has a double resonance for my own study. It highlights the profundity of the issue of immigration to people of Mexican descent from 1890 to 1990 in the United States, but it also speaks to the unsettling fact that the formation of a mainstream ethnic identity has been dependent on a minority "other" to shore up its own fault lines. What is most startling about Gutiérrez's history is the divided premise that structures his argument. From personal, anecdotal, and archival evidence, Gutiérrez arrives at the provocative conclusion that Mexican immigration and Mexican immigrants have historically posed a problem to Mexican Americans.[5]

According to Gutiérrez, the historical record since 1890 documents a divided response from the Mexican American community on the issue of Mexican immigration. There are those who see Mexican immigrants as a threat to job security, in the form of competition for lower–paying jobs, for example, but also as a threat to their civic standing in the larger national community. Because of the border that stretches from Texas to California, contact with Mexico is inevitable and frequent, argues Gutiérrez; it makes geographic distance meaningless for the Mexican immigrant looking to sever ties with the "home" country. It is impossible not to be reminded of one's un–Americanness. For this and the negative attention they draw to themselves among Anglo Americans, the more recent arrivals shoulder the brunt of Mexican American ire and contempt.

On the other side of the divide are those Mexican Americans who sympathize with the travails of those recently arrived and seek to make their lives less onerous. After all, the understanding goes, they are compatriots, like us but a few years earlier. Gutiérrez writes: "Noting that Americans seem to discriminate against Mexicans whether they are U.S. citizens or not, Mexican Americans oriented in this way can see little difference between their position in American society and that of more recent immigrants. From their point of view, as one elderly Mexican American woman put it to the historian Albert Camarillo, 'We were all poor. We were all in the same situation'" (5). With this sympathy develops a common political cause that views the plight of the Mexican immigrant as not unlike the plight of Mexican Americans in a society bent on capitalizing on their labor, while eschewing them the privileges of citizenship. To champion the plight of the migrant worker is thus to advocate for the civil rights of U.S.–born Mexican Americans.

Gutiérrez argues that Mexican Americans' divided response to Mexican immigration is the manifestation of a cultural logic in which Mexican Americans attempt to secure civic legitimacy. In other words, Mexican immigration is not the real issue, but a pretext to negotiating the Mexican American community's relationship with the nation. Gutiérrez explains: "In short, for nearly a century the more–or–less constant pressure of large numbers of Mexican immigrants in Mexican American communities has forced Mexican Americans to come to daily decisions about who they are–politically, socially, and culturally–in comparison to more recent immigrants from Mexico. . . ." (6). Like Guerin–Gonzales's history, Gutiérrez's study of Mexican immigration reveals a transformative mechanism at work in Mexican American communities. Whereas Guerin–Gonzales talks about the "American Dream" as fundamentally mutable to immigrant experiences, Gutiérrez cites ethnicity and personal identity as the cultural site where daily decisions are made by community members struggling to imagine and perform an identity straddling two nations but occupying only one. Under these conditions, ethnicity for Mexican Americans is tremendously fluid and subject to change, while the category of Mexican immigrant is conceived as static, despite the immigrants' greater economic and political vulnerability.

The cultural lesson to be drawn, more generally, is that the relevance or salience of ethnic identification in the United States depends on the presence of immigrants. In other words, if Mexican immigration to the United States were to end measurably or altogether, the question of ethnicity for Mexican Americans would necessarily involve a different process of identification. Gone presumably would be this ambivalent view of the Mexican immigrant by Mexican Americans, and gone too would be the daily decisions based on the cultural presence of the "home" country. What trajectory would ethnic identification for Mexican Americans then follow in the absence of Mexican immigration? Presumably, Mexican Americans would more or less adhere to the nationalist, pluralist model of immigration held out as the standard in the twentieth century: that of white ethnics from Europe. But wait. What about race? What about the relevance of Gutiérrez's analysis to other immigrant histories, including white ethnics? Can we not say that, in general, individuals with an immigrant history in the United States have historically displayed a bifurcated view on the role of immigration and nation? Indeed, immigration in this country has been both celebrated and vilified. The Statue of Liberty stands as monument to the rhetorical power of the United States as the land of opportunity, but also as a symbol of the political limitations of a nation born out of an eighteenth-century liberal ideology linked to an emergent capitalist economic philosophy.[6] If we were to extrapolate broadly, Gutiérrez's analysis encourages us to understand that the ambivalence of Mexican Americans toward more recent Mexican immigrants was and is but a reflection of larger historic forces in North America. Ironically, these ambivalent Mexican Americans were no less and no more ambivalent than their more Anglo predecessors.

Again, like Guerin-Gonzales's study, Gutiérrez's analysis permits a view of mainstream culture as it pressures those who do not fit the profile of the ideal immigrant to provide legitimating credentials.[7] Ample examples of this phenomenon are found among European ethnics making their way up the social and economic ladders of the United States.

Whether we study closely the conclusions of now–classic texts such as Richard Hofstadter's *Social Darwinism in American Thought* (1944), or John Higham's *Strangers in the Land: Patterns of American Nativism, 1860–1925* (1955), or Edward G. Hartmann's *The Movement to Americanize the Immigrant* (1948), what we consistently find is an older generation of immigrants casting doubt on the civic legitimacy of newer arrivals.[8] The Puritan persecution of the Quakers of the seventeenth century is just one early example of this ongoing communal practice of converting majority-group anxiety over civic legitimacy into an exercise of power and violence over a minority group's more tenuous claim of belonging. While Native Americans may seem to stand apart in this cycle as the New World's original inhabitants, the consequences of military campaigns like the Pequod War or forced removals like the Cherokee's Trail of Tears were, in effect, to make immigrants of the indigenous, thereby furthering the aims of colonization by supplanting prior tribal claims on the land with an ideology of superior sacred immigration.

Though quite aware of the racism that motivated anti–immigrant sentiments among nativists from the 1880s through the 1920s, the above historians were unable to handle the kinds of nuances understood today as part and parcel of race studies. Now we can admit the degree to which "European whiteness" played figuratively and pragmatically in the Americanization movement, which Hartmann charts as "immediately preceding, accompanying, and succeeding World War I" (37). Though immigrants from eastern and southern Europe, like Slavic Jews and Sicilians, were often targeted as nonwhite racialized "others," these immigrants eventually acquired a white ethnic status that later enabled their cultural and political assimilation into the United States. The status of "colored" for these eastern and southern Europeans during the late nineteenth and early twentieth century was temporary and tied directly to their realization of an economic and political class upward mobility–in contrast to the experience of African Americans migrating to the industrial North and Midwest and Mexican men and women who crossed the border to work the mines, smelting plants, and agricultural fields from Texas to California. As was true for the Irish immigrants of the 1830s and 1840s before them, the racial "otherness" of these Europeans was due in part to their Old World affiliations and customs, which included language, food, religion, and education. As soon as Old World traits, icons, and habits retreated to a realm of cultural nostalgia, white ethnic immigrants could symbolically apply and reapply for citizenship despite the misgivings or hostilities of an older set of immigrants. Even if some organizations with New England/Anglo–Saxon ties, like the Restriction Immigration League (Hartmann, 20–21) opposed their civic inclusion, other organizations with a patriotic agenda welcomed the assimilated white ethnic immigrant with more or less open arms. And even if the first generation resisted Americanization, for the succeeding generations of white ethnics, born in the United States, there was none other than the New World. The "old country" of their parents became a point of departure from the past rather than a compass toward the future.

Constructing the Ideal Immigrant Community, 1920–1940

Nina Baym has made it clear how the American publishing industry participated in the political and economic assimilation of turn–of–the–century immigrants. On the whole, this industry published and recycled a literary history that privileged New England authors and literary traditions while also locating the democratic origins of the United States in the culture of an Anglo–Saxon Puritan people.[9] She demonstrates that the major textbook presses of this period, but especially between 1882 and 1912, consolidated a variety of cultural and scholarly ideas about U.S. literature that had been in circulation since the 1830s. More specifically, presses like Houghton Mifflin responded directly to educators who desired a more systematic approach to literary history, as well as a textbook that would lend itself to the civic goals of Americanization (463).

Baym's findings are important to my own argument because in them we see the construction of "real" Americans in literature and history, as opposed to those who merely assimilate. Baym's analysis suggests something of the process by which the New England Puritans became the ideal representatives of literature and nationhood in this period. Beginning with Moses Coit Tyler's notion in 1878 that New England was "a thinking community," Baym traces a political and cultural movement that constructs the Puritans as virtuous immigrants who were neither greedy adventurers nor faddish dilettantes, but spiritually and intellectually motivated founders of a New World civilization (466–67). Further, these immigrants are portrayed as exuding an attractive masculine aura, so much so that it becomes a key in linking regionally and historically diverse nineteenth–century writers, from Ralph Waldo

Emerson and Nathaniel Hawthorne, to Charles Brockden Brown and Edgar Allan Poe, to Bret Harte and Mark Twain, and so on (468–77). This combination of masculine, vigorous, spiritual intellectualism culminates in the 1920s, according to Baym, with the canonization of many a New England writer. As for the rest, "Non-Englanders were added to the canon only if they could be assimilated to this still New England center, still preferably as a matter of racial inheritance, but at least as a matter of shared ideology" (478).

Notwithstanding the prominent complaints of someone like H. L. Mencken (who faulted the Puritans and modern fetishizers of Puritans for the ills of society), and the lamentations of Puritan scholars in the next decade who moaned loudly about the Puritans being treated unfairly by critics like Mencken, the cultural capital and authority of the New England Puritans actually increased during the 1920s.[10] Their ascendancy was all but assured when historians began to treat them as the exceptional immigrants, from whom evolved the special character and institutions of the United States. Nowhere is this idea more pronounced than in the body of literature that treats the Puritan immigrants of the 1630s, especially the Bay Colony Puritans, as the historic members of the "Great Migration." According to Virginia D. Anderson, this term "was invented not by the founders of New England but by their descendants, who wished to celebrate the religious mission of their forefathers. . . . [Their forefathers] chose New England as their destination, a wilderness home where God's saving remnant could re-create the pure church of apostolic times. Though small in size, this migration was great in purpose."[11] Though this terminology had been in vogue since the eighteenth century to describe this early Anglo immigrant community, it acquired overt nationalist and Anglocentric meanings between 1880 and 1920. Moses Coit Tyler writes in 1878: "Yet so thrifty and teeming have been these New Englanders, that from that primal community of twenty-one thousand persons have descended the three and a half millions who compose the present population of New England; while of the entire population now spread over the United States probably every third person can read in the history of the first settlement of New England, the history of their own progenitors."[12] Paradoxically, the increasing centrality of the Great Migration tale in mainstream American immigration history paralleled the political narrowing of actual open immigration. In contrast to the changes in immigration policy that resulted from nativist victories in Congress–from the Chinese Exclusion Act of 1882 to laws passed in 1917, 1921, and 1924 that imposed severe literacy requirements and national–origin quotas–the Great Migration theory held undisputed sway among the premiere historians of the 1920s.[13]

The legacy of the Great Migration is profoundly evident throughout Puritans studies in the decades that follow, especially in the work of Perry Miller, who continued the Great Migration thesis in the post–World War II period.[14] Miller's loyalty to this thesis was no coincidence. In a book by his mentor, Kenneth Murdock, *Increase Mather: The Foremost American Puritan* (1926), one can see how the Great Migration tale might have been shaped for those of Miller's generation. Murdock writes passionately of the immigrant spirit that brought the father of Increase Mather to the Bay Colony in 1635:

> Few of us can create for ourselves an Almighty so stern and rigorous as Richard Mather's, or accept the doctrine that only a chosen few are God's elect, and by Him saved from hell. Each of us, aided by the accumulated experience of three hundred years, can pick flaws in the government and policy of the Puritans. But is there one of us who can resist men who served their faith with such deep earnestness? They were radicals when it was far easier to be reactionaries; they were pioneers when the wilderness held unusual dangers; they were state–builders in spite of every material difficulty; they were church–builders unaided by the force of tradition; and they were, above all, sincere and single-minded in word and act. Grant them admiration for what they achieved, share their spirit for one moment, and the task of forgetting the twentieth century for the seventeenth is done, and with clear consciences and stout hearts we may land in Boston with Richard Mather. With him, we shall be ready to meet and face unafraid what the morrow may bring forth.[15]

Murdock's deeply sympathetic boosterism captures the intellectual spirit in which his generation of Puritan scholars pursued their objects of study; secondly, Murdock fashions a romantic cultural imaginary whereby a reader might be transported not only into the seventeenth century but more importantly into the feelings, dangers, and exaltations of Richard Mather's immigrant experience. Though symbolic, and possible only for sympathetic, acculturated readers, this travel back in time speaks to the culturally privileged position the Puritans commanded as "model immigrants" in the 1920s. Given that the federal government, in this same decade, enacts and validates every nativist fear about foreigners and immigrants since the 1880s, this representation is highly ironic. In June 1924, the United States Immigration Border Patrol is created to police officially the outer boundaries of the country.[16] Thus with a stroke of pen, in a tradition of pens striking out for the cause of liberty, freedom, and the pursuit of happiness, the means to detect and detain illegal immigrants was put in motion. Was there any other history of immigration, beside the Puritan one, that could be considered "positive" for this generation of Puritan scholars?

A Community of Scholars, Harvard 1946

What are we to conclude about the coterie of scholars who institutionalized the Great Migration as the ideal tale of immigration to the United States? And what relationship do these same scholars have to the successive waves of immigrants who could never embody the totality of the ideal Puritan immigrant? Finally, how do we come to terms with the fact that this whole discourse of the ideal immigrant community comes at the cultural and political expense of erasing those one and half million Mexicans who migrated to the United States in the early twentieth century? What keeps this Mexican migration from being considered great too?[17] Or Asian immigration for that matter? The Great Migration was numerically small by comparison to either–just over 13,000 between 1630 and 1640 (Anderson, 15).

Of course values and ideas, like people themselves, are products of their times. The faults and virtues of cultural productions such as the myth of Puritan origins cannot be divorced from the environment that encouraged their creation or from the nation's political contours between World War I and the Cold War that guaranteed their maintenance. The best we can do is to take seriously what history and reflection offer us now, and to view the past not as organic or a dead issue, but as a place in which to seek answers for difficult and compromising questions. In this spirit, I turn to that group of Harvard scholars who were instrumental in the birth of American studies in the post–World War II period.

Along with the end of the Great Depression, the defeat of the Axis

Powers signaled not only a military and ideological victory over fascism, but for some, a validation of what was perceived to be the country's "native" artists, writers, intellectuals, and cultural history. At Harvard, scholars as politically different as Perry Miller and F. O. Matthiessen converged in their writings and pedagogy to solidify what we think of now as the traditional literary canon. This postwar frame might seem an odd way to introduce linkages between ethnicity and nationality in the construction of American literary canon, but the years immediately after the war consolidated some crucial trends in American literary criticism that international supremacy permitted. This consolidation was shaped in part by the returning veterans under the GI Bill, who, as part of a victorious army, came home excited to celebrate their nationality and shared national past. They also came home, I argue, anxious to secure a national future, and for some that translated into an unprecedented study of American literature.

As reviewed in chapter 2, Kermit Vanderbilt reads Robert E. Spiller's now famous editorial efforts to produce the *Literary History of the United States* (1948) as part of the "nationalistic sentiment and progressive thought that was succeeded by the heightened self-awareness and patriotic emotion that courses through a nation in wartime."[18] In similar fashion, Vanderbilt notes the patriotic efforts of scholars, both overseas and on the domestic front, to secure "President Roosevelt's challenge that our colleges should help preserve the culture that our soldiers were fighting for" (461). At the national level, Vanderbilt reminds us, in 1939 Archibald MacLeish, poet turned Librarian of Congress by Roosevelt, instigated through speeches and essays an intensive, often bitter debate among American scholars of all fields by insisting on the activist role of the scholar during a national crisis (463–65). While the ensuing controversy gripped colleges and universities to various degrees, at Harvard, interventionists and noninterventionists were equally equipped with idealism, patriotism, and a belief that scholarship should take into account the contemporary world. After the Stalin–Hitler pact and Pearl Harbor, the presence of military officers and the training of troops in Harvard Yard dictated the overall direction of the campus. Harvard scholars like Perry Miller entered the war as officers (464). Even F. O. Matthiessen, former president of the socialist–oriented Harvard Teachers Union, tried to follow his students into war but was deemed too short by recruiters (473).

David Levin's biographical essay "Perry Miller at Harvard" (1983) gives an insider view of this period as a returning GI. Professor Levin portrays a community shaped by war and guided by a confidence in themselves as scholars:

> To those of us who were still undergraduates concentrating in history and literature, the sense of community was intensified by the participation of several academic generations. Captain Samuel Eliot Morison, President Roosevelt's personal nominee to write the history of United States naval operations in World War II, and Major Perry Miller, who as an officer in the O.S.S. had accompanied the French hero General Leclerc in his triumphant sweep to liberate Alsace, were both lecturing on early American culture. . . . Our respect for the historical imagination of these great teachers, our belief in its relevance to modern American life, and our eagerness to join them in the common enterprise of scholarship were surely reinforced by our belief that they had participated with us in the war against the Axis. Because the war had cost us from two to five years, the mingling of students from different academic generations intensified our feeling that we formed a community of scholars.[19]

In these celebratory remarks, we see the formation of a fraternity, united and directed in their scholarly efforts because of the war. We also see in motion an intense process of male-bonding that entirely informs and is inseparable from the definition of this fraternity. Given the nationalist mood, it is not difficult to see how the pursuit of American literary scholarship was remasculinized because of the war and by the flood of (male) GIs who entered colleges and universities in record numbers.

But as Levin's essay reveals, the confluence of nationalism with scholarship, masculinity, and foreign policy also evidenced itself in more domestic rituals like sports. In what I think is an incredible anecdote, Levin tells of these Harvard students creating a fantasy baseball team from their professors:

> Remembering [Miller's classroom] allusions to Ted Williams, some of us invented a baseball team made up of professors to whom we assigned the nicknames of major league stars. One of the pitchers was Harry (the Cat) Levin, whose quiet approach to

literary prey and whose stress on the last syllable of his surname reminded us of the St. Louis Cardinals' quick-fielding southpaw, Harry (the Cat) Breechen. The center fielder was F. O. Matthiessen, who rumor said had been too short to qualify for service as an officer in the army. We named him for Dominic DiMaggio of the Red Sox, who was known as the Little Professor. Sam (Boo) Morison we named for a Boston pitcher, Dave (Boo) Ferris; William Yandall Elliot, a blustering professor of government, for Bobo Newsom, a big, flamboyant pitcher. And Perry Miller we unanimously acclaimed as the winner of Ted Williams' title, the Kid. (810)

What I find startling here is the degree to which these individuals imagined themselves and their scholarly pursuits as part of the national fabric of their country. Acting well within baseball's mystique as a male, national pastime, Levin and his fellow students confer upon Miller the status of cultural hero that Ted Williams had earned in Fenway Park. Miller kept war trophies in proud display in his office (804), and it seems likely that he would have encouraged a cult of heroism; invariably his students, like David Levin, recast Miller and others through a special form of hero worship that subtly informed the character of the next generation of Americanists.

But what would have happened to this cult of heroism, indeed to their shared jubilant nationalism, if the status of these men's white ethnic histories was more problematic? Although they were all scholars of American culture, some of their names alone—Levin and Matthiessen, for example—suggest they negotiated their non-English ancestries through their professional personas. Although anti-German sentiment was less prevalent than during War World I, German Americans like Matthiessen would still have been wary of making too much of their ancestry. And as for their own domestic heroes, what if they knew then what we know now, that Ted Williams's mother was of Mexican descent? These questions alert us to how ethnicity, and thus national status, was conferred on the basis of race. Among these U.S. veterans, whiteness, not whether one was Jewish, or Polish, or Italian, became the primary definition of Americanness. This was undoubtedly an unlooked-for consequence of the war: the suppression of white ethnic differences in favor of national solidarity as Americans.

Yet this same status of national subject was not extended to soldiers of color, even though returning Mexican American GIs had a right to expect as much. Chicano historian Rodolfo Acuña writes: "Many Chicanos believed the propaganda emanating from World War II about brotherhood and democracy in the United States. They thought they had won their rights as U.S. citizens."[20] Among nonwhite ethnic groups, Mexican Americans received the highest number of military medals and honors during World War II. But the national narrative about the war was simply not written to include ethnic histories whose colonial origins might pose a threat to the Anglo Puritan domination of national culture. Whether or not they perceived themselves as subordinating their white ethnic differences, the scholars Professor Levin remembers at Harvard did just that, and they constructed American literary history to represent their newly de-ethnicized selves: strictly Anglo and therefore unproblematically American.[21] In the end, despite the sacrifices of Mexican Americans, African Americans, and Japanese Americans, the representative war hero was someone like Audie Murphy, a decorated white Texan from humble beginnings who later became a movie star.

In retrospect, Professor Levin's 1946 spring semester at Harvard was truly remarkable for its "community of scholars." Besides taking courses with Perry Miller and F. O. Matthiessen, Professor Levin rubbed elbows with Leo Marx, Leslie Fiedler, and Harry Levin. Others present at Harvard during this period were Kenneth Murdock, Howard Jones, Bernard De Voto, and Wallace Stegner. These scholars would become "pioneers" in the study of American literature. David Levin's memories demonstrate that the post–1945 canon represented a worldview promoted by individuals who saw themselves not only as the world's protectors from fascists and later communists, but as the vanguard of American culture, morally obligated to usher in American literature as a world literature, especially at home.

At issue in the formation of the post–1945 canon is more than the institutional prestige of the Emersons, Hawthornes, and Melvilles. At issue is the effort to define national character, and to show how these authors embody it. This generation of critics valued writers like Whitman for their perceived devotion to democratic ideals. Never mind Melville's Dutch heritage, or the Jewish or German ethnic heritage of many postwar scholars. The new postwar Anglo nationalism had secured, for Levin's "community of scholars," a new sense of historic civic belonging that retrospectively also rewrote their patriotism before and during the war. Assured of their nationalist credentials, their Anglo nationalism would usher in a new era of American literary criticism. Thus the postwar generation of literary scholars elided multiple ethnicities in favor of a single representation of the Anglo national subject, and they claimed "masculine action" in American letters to be the literary precursor of GI know-how in the twentieth century. It would take the Civil Rights Movement, which deemed the worldview of the post-1945 canon-makers to be dated and politically reprehensible, to dislodge the promotion of New England Puritans as the progenitors of American democracy, culture, and literature.

The Immigrant Dilemma: Mexican American Literature, 1900–1960

The title of this section alludes to a well-known biography of a Puritan figure, *The Puritan Dilemma: The Story of John Winthrop* (1958). In it, renowned American historian Edmund S. Morgan makes a sympathetic case for understanding how Winthrop embraced the formidable task of creating civilization on the edge of the American wilderness. Morgan sees Winthrop's life as representative of a moral and ethical dilemma that living in the New World exposed. He writes: "It was the question of what responsibility a righteous man owes to society. If society follows a course that he considers morally wrong, should he withdraw and keep his principles intact, or should he stay?"[22] Morgan's "Puritan dilemma" centers on the internal conflicts of what we would today call the "humanist enterprise"–the inevitable conflict that arises when discourses of individuality and dissent must contend with the political authority of the majority or the status quo.

Writing at the end of the 1950s, Morgan's perspective on this dilemma typified a trend in academic circles to rescue Puritan colonial history from popular cliché and to forward instead that Puritan colonial history was something the nation should celebrate. For Morgan, to read about the Puritans was to read about the origins of American democracy and to find in that history a moral barometer for the United States in the twentieth century. Oscar Handlin, series editor of *The Puritan Dilemma*, and at the time regarded as the nation's premiere immigration historian, states a similar belief in his introduction to Morgan's biography: "From its first discovery, the emptiness of the New World made it the field for social experiment. Europeans, crowded in by their seeming lack of space and by a rigid social order, looked with longing across the ocean where space and opportunity abounded. Time and again, men critical of their society hoped by migration to find the scope for working out their visions of a better order" (ix). The irony that escapes Handlin, given his historical moment, is not lost on us. In the tale of social better-ment that confers moral authority upon European immigration, the New World is depopulated of its indigenous inhabitants and cultures. Centuries after conquest, the recent passage of California's Proposition 187, anti–immigrant legislation targeting illegal immigrants from Latin America, should remind us that a Puritan vision of a better order is a renewable source of cultural capital–at least for certain groups–a reposi-tory of those social and legal values that continue to frame discourses of *restricted* immigration to the United States.

In 1958, Professor Morgan's "dilemma" supported the dominant view that the New World was a tabula rasa, a place were social experiments could be worked out. By contrast, the "Immigrant Dilemma" I would like to investigate is the experience of people of Mexican descent as recorded in their literature, a "tabula raza" full of their reactions to living in a society that modeled itself culturally and nationally after a Puritan immi-grant history. Overall, those writing long before the Chicano/a Move-ment took up the Puritans as a dilemma. For them, the dilemma could not be resolved through a simple rejection of dominant narratives. The hu-manist discourse that shaped Handlin's idea of an empty New World also shaped the literary world that these early writers worked within. What Morgan said of "his" Puritans also could be said of many Mexican Ameri-can writers from 1900 to 1960. They too were concerned about how one responded to a society that followed a course they considered morally wrong. Unlike the Puritans, though, the Mexican American writers of this period could not relocate to a New World when their social criticisms were refuted. No earthly realm existed to which they might retreat and engage in alternative social experiment; in fact, collectively, their writing calls into question precisely such kinds of social experimentation.

All of the writers featured in the following pages wrote from 1900 to 1960. During their lifetimes, some of these authors found willing pub-lishers, while others had to content themselves with their own private efforts. Regardless, together these writers enjoyed very little if any na-tional recognition. Fortunately, their recovery has been in full swing since the early 1990s. In *A History of Hispanic Theatre in the United States: Origins to 1940* (1990), Nicolás Kanellos meticulously traces the development of professional Spanish–language theater in the West and Southwest from the mid–nineteenth century on, with recorded theatrical performances going as far back as 1789 in Monterey, California. Print culture in the form of Spanish–language newspapers also has a long and rich history in the United States, from New York City and Philadelphia to San Antonio and Los Angeles. In the old Spanish borderland, Spanish–language newspapers busily catered to subscribers beginning in the early 1800s. In *So All Is Not Lost: The Poetics of Print in Nuevomexicano Communities, 1834–1958* (1997), A. Gabriel Meléndez undertakes the study of a regional print culture that reflected the social, economic, and political transformations of the New Mexican reader well into the twentieth century. Elsewhere, the narrative constructions found in diaries, memoirs, letters, short stories, and novels from 1848 to 1960 have been the subject of full–length studies, beginning with Genaro M. Padilla's *My History, Not Yours: The Formation of Mexican American Autobiography* (1993). Rosaura Sánchez's *Telling Identities: The Californio Testimonios* and Tey Diana Rebolledo's *Singing in the Snow: A Cultural Analysis of Chicana Literature*, both published in 1995, together recover the general historical perimeters necessary to understand the prevailing gender, economic, and political conditions that affected Mexican American women's narrative production from 1848 to 1960.[23]

Prior to this moment, Américo Paredes's *With His Pistol in His Hand: A Border Ballad and Its Hero* (1958) had been for years the benchmark of scholarship measuring the cultural production of people of Mexican descent from 1900 to 1960.[24] In *With His Pistol in His Hand*, Paredes recovers the various variants of the "Ballad of Gregorio Cortez" and, with it, the cultural history of South Texas. Since Paredes's groundbreaking work, the Mexican *corrido* and its influence on other literary forms has been studied by a variety of people using methodologies as different as folklore studies and poststructuralist feminism.[25] The publication of *With His Pistol in His Hand* has been cited by many a Chicano/a scholar and artist as an influential precursor to the Chicano/a Renaissance of the 1960s and early 1970s. Since Chicano/a studies has covered this cultural form so well, I will only comment on the corrido as it pertains to immigration and as it sets up a general historical context for the prose writers that follow.

Corridos, usually in Spanish, have been the favorite means by which Chicano/a literary critics and labor historians assess the cultural "mood" of Mexican immigrants at different periods. A turn–of–the–century ballad, "El Corrido del Norte," exemplifies for David Gutiérrez the ambivalence the political border creates for local residents' national identity: "I was born on the border / though here on this side / I'm a pure Mexican / even though people / may think I'm Texan / I now assure you / that I'm all Mexican / from here on this side" (67). As Gutiérrez points out, the male speaker maintains this ambivalence only because he retains a choice in ethnic identity. By the end of the 1920s, explains Gutiérrez, such choices were curtailed in a political climate engulfed by nativist fears (68). The combination of the Great Depression and the growth of Mexican American communities narrow ethnic identity to that of "Mexican," no matter how long settled. The national crisis of unemployment effectively turns all Mexican Americans into deportable Mexican immigrants.

The 1930s thus witnessed a series of local and national efforts to deport Mexican immigrants from the United States–recorded in the corrido "Los Deportados." Between 1929 and 1937, Gutiérrez notes, 80,000 people of Mexican descent were deported, and most illegally. Overall, repatriation efforts succeeded in moving somewhere between 350,000 to 600,000 people during the depression. "Los Deportados" dramatizes the dehumanizing consequences of these deportations, as well as the communal psychic toll taken when Mexican Americans wondered if they could return to what they called home:

> The Anglos are very
> bad fellows
> They take advantage
> And to all the Mexicans
> They treat us without pity
>
> Today they bring great
> disturbance
> And without consideration
> Women, children, and old ones
> They take us to the border,
> They eject us from this country

Goodbye dear countrymen
They are going to deport us
But we are not bandits
We came to toil.
(73)

Gutiérrez points out that repatriation campaigns against Mexican Americans further divided community opinion about more recent immigrants (73–74). The failure of the culture at large to make distinctions between Mexican Americans and recently arrived Mexican nationals had practical and symbolic ramifications. As long as individuals could be illegally deported because they looked "Mexican," Mexican American communities had to be inventive about proving their Americanness, or at least their separateness from Mexican immigrants. The well-known corrido of this same period "The Mexico-Texan" points out that the Mexican Texan always has to be ready to seize the political moment. If the Anglo politician stretches out a hand come November elections, then the Mexican Texan must take advantage of the situation, knowing well that political support one moment can turn into a political liability in another. Because of the mercurial demands of racial politics, both within one's community and without, "The Mexico-Texan" wryly concludes: "For he has one advantage of all other men, / Though the Mexico-Texan he gotta no lan' / he can getta so drunk that he thinks he can fly, / Both September da Sixteen and the Fourth of July" (80).

Even among those who managed to avoid deportation, the bitterness and cynicism produced by policies of the 1920s and 1930s affected the cultural development of the Mexican American community. Apart from the ever-present divide between recent immigrants and all others, families began to experience troubling generational differences. Gutiérrez cites "El Enganchado" ("The Hooked One") for its references to the cultural exchanges occurring among the children of first-generation immigrant parents:

Many Mexicans don't care to speak
The language their mothers taught them
And go about saying they are "Spanish"
And deny their country's flag
Some are darker than *chapote* [tar]

But they pretend to be Saxon;
They go about powdered to the back of the neck
And wear skirts for trousers. (120)

The male speaker's focus on language, racial identities, and patriotism all reflect the inevitable attraction, if not necessity, for second-generation children to acculturate into U.S. society. Among the strategies for assimilation, one can embody false white European ethnicities, as well as "whiten" oneself with cosmetics. While all these things are of growing concern for the speaker, what he holds more in contempt are the changing gender roles among Mexican American women. American culture has given women access and a license to explore sexual identities beyond the control of the patriarchal "macho" typical of Mexican families. Not surprisingly, in light of his wife's favoring of silk dresses, his children speaking only perfect English, and a youth that dances the "Charleston," the male speaker threatens to return to Mexico.

Despite these emerging generational and gender conflicts, the constant threat of deportations, and the racist and discriminatory treatment of Mexican Americans throughout the Southwest, Mexican immigration would increase during the infamous Bracero Program of the 1940s and 1950s. Although not the only means or cause of Mexican immigration to the United States, the Bracero Program is widely acknowledged for having established a general pattern and social context for Mexican immigration until 1964 when the last vestiges of the program were dismantled.[26] Even so, perhaps the 1935 corrido "An Emigrant's Farewell" sets out better the basic rationale for understanding most Mexican immigration in the twentieth century.[27] The male speaker begins with the painful recognition of loss: "Goodbye, my beloved country, / Now I am going away; / I go the United States / where I intend to work. / Goodbye, my beloved mother, / the Virgin of Guadalupe; / goodbye, my beloved land, / my Mexican Republic." The speaker acknowledges that in leaving Mexico to make a living in the United States, the immigrant sacrifices dearly. Though he hopes to return, such is the pathos of the corrido that the reader/listener knows it won't be so. Though perhaps in vain, the speaker seeks the reader's/listener's sympathy and not judgment: "For I am not to blame / that I leave my country thus; / the fault is that of poverty, / which keeps us all in want." Once on the other side of the border, this poverty, while not as great as that of those who stayed in

Mexico, is replaced by a host of symbolic and political dilemmas that over time, we shall see, rivals even economic desperation.

Immigration and Xenophobia: María Cristina Mena (1893–1965)

In 1907 at the age of fourteen, María Cristina Mena immigrated to New York City, far from the migrant labor camps of the emerging agricultural industries in the Southwest and West. Born in Mexico City in 1893, she was sent by her family to live among friends.[28] Her parents hoped to spare their daughter the national crisis that loomed in the last years of Porfirio Díaz's dictatorship of Mexico. Her family's class status and commercial interests in the United States afforded Mena the means to escape the trauma that soon engulfed the country. In fact, many well-to-do Mexican families eventually found their way to the United States, living as expatriates in cities like Brownsville, Laredo, El Paso, San Antonio, and Los Angeles during the Mexican Revolution. These Mexican expatriates tended to choose U.S. locales with a Mexican past. The fact that she was at a distance from anything "Mexican" might begin to explain why Mena, armed with an upper-class education—which included Spanish, English, and French languages—soon found herself writing for publications such as *American Magazine* and *The Century Magazine.* These prominent magazines had a cosmopolitan Anglo American readership.

Like María Amparo Ruiz de Burton, Mena had personal attributes and artistic talent that attracted a host of individuals who, before knowing her, had scarcely associated with a person of Mexican descent in the United States. In 1916 she married Henry K. Chambers, a fairly successful playwright for the Broadway stage. She would develop a lifelong friendship with D. H. Lawrence. One of her short stories was even republished in the *Monthly Criterion* (1927), then edited by T. S. Eliot. Altogether, she wrote stories from 1913 to 1931, and children's literature from 1942 to 1953. And like those of Ruiz de Burton, her stories reflected the various class circles and political environments she traveled in and out of. But unlike those of Ruiz de Burton, Mena's stories almost always maintained Mexico and Mexican characters at their centers. While she populates her stories with the type of upper-class characters found in Ruiz de Burton's *The Squatter and the Don*, Mena gives ample and sympathetic attention to *indios, mestizos, y los pobres.* In further contrast to Ruiz de Burton's writings, Mena's stories about Mexico and Mexican traditions often create imaginative spaces where eighteenth–century liberal ideologies work out a more generous relationship with native peoples and their pre-Columbian traditions and mythologies.

Despite the conservative and, oftentimes, nativist leanings of magazines like *The Century Magazine* for which Mena wrote, Mena's work, argues Amy Doherty, used subtle strategies that successfully subverted the worst aspects of U.S. xenophobia. In addition, Doherty writes:

> In her fiction, Mena becomes increasingly critical of the United States and supportive of the Mexican revolutionaries who rebelled against [the injustices committed by Porfirio Díaz and his United States corporate allies]. After setting the stage with more stereotypical characters in her early stories in *American Magazine* and *Century*, she moves toward revolution with characters who reject their upper–class background to join the militant underclass. First, as a Mexican woman expected to produce exotic, picturesque stories of romance and intrigue, she attempted to present the Mexican Revolution to U.S. readers. Second, she wrote about Mexican revolutionaries and native Mexicans after having lived an elite childhood in Mexico City. (Mena, xi)

In the context of, first, the socialist idealism fueling the Mexican Revolution and, next, Mena's encounter with virulent U.S. xenophobia, we can appreciate her exotic renderings of the *indios, mestizos, y los pobres* as not only representing a (perhaps condescending) political sympathy, but also as questioning nativist tendencies to see Mexicans in the most pejorative of terms. Interestingly, Mena takes a different approach than does Willa Cather in *My Ántonia* (1918) or Anzia Yezierska in *Bread Givers* (1925). Both Cather and Yezierska dignified their immigrant characters by chronicling their hardships and eventual successes in their adopted new country. In contrast, Mena locates the dilemma for Mexican immigrants in the United States in their unavoidable proximity to Mexico and its political crises. Hence, the literary project Mena envisioned was in a sense counterintuitive but still culturally significant. She recognized early on what Chicano/a historians would validate only much later: that the plight of the Mexican immigrant was inextricably tied to the Anglo American view of Mexico and its citizens. To reform the stereotypes of one might reform the stereotypes of the other.

Mena goes about her cultural work to combat xenophobia in at least two major ways. In "The Gold Vanity Set" (1913) and "John of God, the Water-Carrier" (1913), Mena writes vigorously against the "picturesque" requirements of her Anglo American editors. As Doherty observes, she refuses a "racialized literary hierarchy" that conceived of native characters as "literary undesirables" (xxii). In both stories, Mexican-Indian characters occupy center stage, and in both stories the moral dilemma they face is witnessed by either an Anglo American character within the story or the presumed Anglo American reader. In either case, Mena carefully reverses the imperialist gaze or the Anglo American chauvinism that would see Mexicans as yet another example of a "white man's burden." Mena accomplishes this feat by forcing either an Anglo American character or the reader to acknowledge the innate goodness and morality of the Indian, however implicated such an acknowledgement is in Rousseau's noble savage tradition. Far from soulless beasts of burden, her protagonists enact a religious faith, bordering on the mystical, that calls attention to acts of kindness and self-sacrifice that were unlike anything one might hope to find in a socially anonymous city like New York City. In stories like these, Mena challenges her Anglo American readership to find anything negative about a people so obviously rich in history, tradition, failures yes, but also stories of human triumph.

Greenhorn Immigrants and the Debunking of America: Daniel Venegas (Dates Unknown)

Whereas the rebuttal of Mexican stereotypes is subtle in Mena's work, Daniel Venegas deploys an avenging satire in his 1928 novel, *Las Aventuras de Don Chipote: O, cuando los pericos mamen.*[29] Written in a mixture of Spanish, English slang, and caló, a border dialect, Venegas's novel has been identified by Nicolás Kanellos as the first immigrant novel in Chicano/a literature. Kanellos sees Venegas as a precursor to the writers of the Chicano/a Renaissance, because Venegas anticipates many of the literary themes and strategies that would emerge in the late 1960s and early 1970s. His novel, argues Kanellos, should be treated as a Chicano/a text. He notes that Venegas thoroughly identified with the cruel and unjust hardships faced by Mexican immigrants in the 1920s. His defense of their proletarian character was evidence of his class consciousness. Kanellos observes further that Venegas's novel, like his work in theater and the humorous weekly newspaper he published in the 1920s, represented an ideological break from his elite background and from the contempt that many upper-class Mexican expatriates often expressed, in public venues, for their working-class counterparts in the United States. Unlike these expatriates, Kanellos writes, Venegas wanted to celebrate Mexican laborers and their culture. In reforming Mexican stereotypes, then, Venegas echoes Mena's narrative strategy to reverse the racist attitudes of Anglo America. Significantly, however, he makes his case by setting his novel in U.S. cities such as El Paso and Los Angeles.

While the story of Don Chipote starts off on familiar terrain—a friend, Pitacio, just returned from the United States convinces him to leave for the land of milk and honey—the mythology of America as popularized in Horatio Alger novels is proven false almost immediately.[30] Venegas writes:

> The United States is full of these Pitacios. Allow me to take the place of that egotistical man and talk of all of his lies, in order to tell you that every fellow countryman experiences bad luck when going up North; but instead of returning to his own great land to tell the God's honest truth about what happened, he twists it around when he returns, recounting stories to others and riling up all those that will listen.
>
> Unfortunately, Chicanos appear to be born yesterday and enthusiastically believe everything one tells them about the North, and it is for this reason, more than the poor conditions in which the Revolution has left the country, that more and more people emigrate each day. (28)

Although overtly humorous, this tale of the trials and tribulations of Venegas's version of Everyman succeeds satirically because the element of harsh truth is only one step removed. Like the migrant laborers in Camille Guerin-Gonzales's history, the Mexican immigrants portrayed by Venegas are almost too willing to believe they can adopt and adapt the American Dream. Only after much painful perseverance can they acknowledge the harm being inflicted upon them as Mexican immigrants.

Don Chipote enters the United States, for example, by surreptitiously

wading across the Rio Grande to avoid the Border Patrol that was commissioned only a few years earlier. Venegas takes the occasion to reflect
on the disappointment Mexican immigrants quickly encounter:

> El Paso, the American city from which Mexican immigrants are
> able to see and pine for native soil (which they have found
> themselves obligated to leave due to its own disgracefulness as
> well as the ambitions of our revolutionaries), is one of the cor-
> ridors through which Mexico has lost most of its people. Don
> Chipote found himself in this city—where thousands of Mexican
> *braceros* come with the hope of putting an end to the anguish
> they have suffered back home—a city where so many proletar-
> ians have found protection against the persecution of Mexico's
> ruling party—in the company of other countrymen expatriated
> in the shame of not being able to make a living in their own
> land—who, lured by the luster of the dollar, abandoned their
> own land to come to suffer ever greater hardship. (43)

In El Paso, Don Chipote and a new friend are easily duped of their money
by the criminal element, Anglo and Mexican, that is ready to take advantage of the greenhorn border-crosser. Shortly thereafter, Don Chipote
learns that the land of milk and honey offers either low-paying, treach-
erous work for the railroad company, or stultifying and demeaning dish-
washing work for a restaurant. Though he comes to enjoy success in the
Mexican American vaudeville of Los Angeles, his new glamorous life-
style and his adultery threaten the stability of his family life. In a move
that Venegas has prepared the reader for, Don Chipote returns to Mexico.
Under the auspices of home, Don Chipote comes to rue his experiences
in the United States and to complain bitterly that "Mexicans will make it
big in the United States . . . WHEN PARROTS BREAST-FEED" (160). The off-
color nature of this joke underscores the hopelessness that Mexican
immigrants experienced when they could not imagine humane treatment in the United States. Contrary to most U.S. immigrant novels up to
1928, Venegas's *Adventures of Don Chipote* answers the dilemma of Mexican
immigration by discouraging it altogether, or at least debunking the
prevailing mythos of the United States as a land of equal opportunity,
freedom, and democracy.

Immigration and the Crisis of Identity: Américo Paredes (1915–1999)

The debunking of U.S. mythology also proves strategic for Américo Paredes in *George Washington Gómez: A Mexicotexan Novel*. Though published in 1990, the novel was actually written mostly in the late 1930s and finished by 1940.[31] This novel has been celebrated by most Chicano/a literary scholars as an early borderlands text that anticipates the more familiar resistant texts of Rolando Hinojosa, Tómas Rivera, John Rechy, Gloria Anzaldúa, and others.[32] It also recovers an important cultural and social moment in the Mexican American community prior to World War II. The novel certainly critiques and questions the Anglo American domination of South Texas from 1915 to 1940. The strong-arm tactics of the Texas Rangers against local militant dissent and the co-optation of the Mexican American vote through ward party politics are targets of this critique.

Yet, the novel is also a bildungsroman and a narrative of regional transformation. While the Anglo American infiltration in South Texas is evident everywhere, from the effects of Prohibition to a grade school curriculum that glorifies only the American Revolution, evident too are the consequences of the new influxes of immigrants from Mexico's interior. These immigrants have the profound effect of destabilizing the more-or-less homogeneous Mexican culture of South Texas. Inadvertently their growing numbers, coupled with the illegal tactics used by Anglo developers to steal land from Mexican Americans, threaten the status and survival of the old Spanish Mexican land-grant ranchero families. Within this context, the novel's protagonist is born into a family that is both long settled on his mother's side (los Garcías) and recently arrived on his father's (Gumersindo Gómez). The dilemma posed by the novel concerns which history of Mexican immigration, colonial or contemporary, will gain the cultural authority to contest the Anglo Americans. The victor will, ironically, police the other, alternative immigrant history.

This novel is thus a wonderful dramatization of the tensions between more established Mexican Americans and newly arrived Mexican immigrants documented by David Gutiérrez. This tension is played out early in the novel when the family struggles to find the right name for the only male child born to this temporally divided immigrant/settler family. The child's maternal grandmother prefers "José Angel," a name signifying peace or holiness, whereas the child's maternal uncle, Feliciano García, who represents the older Spanish Mexican colonial hierarchy, suggests naming him after revolutionaries Venustiano Carranza or Anacleto de la Peña. The child's mother, María García de Gómez, "would like him to have a great man's name. Because he's going to grow up to be a great man who will help his people" (15–16). This idea of helping his people, with its messianic connotations, affects the child's father, but he takes it in an unexpected direction. Himself part of the exodus caused by the civil wars of the Mexican Revolution, Gumersindo Gómez represents not only this newly emerging immigrant class to Texas and the United States, but also a modern Mexican citizenry that would like to believe in the mythos of America as an immigrant country. Gumersindo Gómez decides it is best to give the child a namesake that will enable him to become a bicultural leader—hence the name George Washington Gómez. Unfortunately, the father is too much of a greenhorn to realize the conflict in store for his son. Gumersindo Gómez bequeaths a bicultural identity that has no political or social viability. The novel thus records the traumatic upheavals of "Guálinto," a Spanish transliteration of "George Washington," as he is periodically forced to choose between a Mexican identity and an assimilated immigrant identity.

Foregrounded among the many interesting complications that Paredes presents about Mexican immigrants is the interplay between Anglo racist discourses since 1848 and the cultural memory of a prior Spanish Mexican heritage. All the novel's tensions come to a symbolic impasse when Guálinto returns home after years away getting an education and becoming a lawyer. Having always passed for "white," Guálinto, the narrative implies, settles for a deracinated, second-generation immigrant persona, marrying an Anglo American woman to complete the transformation. While his family and friends are happy with what they perceive to be his actualization, they are slowly but surely disappointed by Guálinto, who now goes by his legally changed name, George G. Gómez, and refuses to play a role in the politicization of the Mexican American community. His childhood desire to lead "his people" against Anglo American injustices and reconquer Texas for Mexicanos has been relegated to the realm of the unconscious, where it surfaces only in haunting dreams that figure him as the Mexican savior at the Battle of San Jacinto.

He defeats Sam Houston with soldiers armed with more modern weapons like revolvers and grenades.

But in fact, he has sold out his community for individual success. He begrudgingly reveals to his uncle that he works for the government and that he has been assigned to spy on the border. Fascism in Europe and the threat that the long border presents to U.S. defense strategies are the real reasons for his return home. After the novel's poignant portrayals of the plight of all people of Mexican descent from 1915 to 1940, the resolution of Guálinto's story fails to show him fulfilling any of the goals set at his birth. At the same time and importantly, the novel encourages a readerly disappointment in Gúalinto's choice to "sell out." Paredes produces this effect, as did Daniel Venegas before him, I believe, to counteract the available mainstream fantasies of immigrant life in the United States. Paredes posits the harsh reality of *George Washington Gómez* as a sobering cultural narrative that perhaps one day can enable more radical calls for the civil rights of Mexican Americans, including immigrants. Because the novel envisions a political response to the United States that makes use of an alternative cultural nationalism without solely depending upon it, one wonders what cultural work it might have accomplished between 1940 and 1960 if it had seen publication. The novel also forecasts the complex ways the Mexican American community comes to police itself, against Anglo America but also against Mexico and its immigrants, as the century progress.

One clue to this question of cultural work and to Guálinto's policing of the border is found in Paredes's more recently recovered novella, *The Shadow* (1998).[33] Written for a Texas fiction contest in the 1950s, this novel is set loosely in the 1930s and early 1940s, and set south of the border, in Mexico. Implicit in the narrative are most of the symbolic tensions found in *George Washington Gómez*, minus the overt presence of Anglo America. This novella often offers a bleaker portrayal of life along the United States–Mexico border, though it ends, significantly, just the same as *George Washington Gómez*. Echoing the existentialist philosophy and disenchantment with Mexican socialism found in Juan Rulfo's *Pedro Páramo* (1994), the novella provides Paredes the opportunity to ponder the collapse of the Mexican Revolution and the undermining of the cultural nationalism that promoted la raza, the proletariat majority of Mexico, as the revolution's primary benefactors.[34] The government's abandonment of its former soldiers, now turned campesinos, is at the center of this story.

Having fought a civil war to redistribute wealth and land in favor of the masses, these new campesinos are increasingly subject to a police state interested in protecting the ruling classes who have betrayed the socialist goals of the Mexican Revolution. The most insidious kind of betrayal, however, happens among their own ranks, suggesting that membership in the ruling classes invariably tempts men and women to sacrifice collective ends for individual advancement. If this can happen in Mexico where the war was fought and won, Paredes seems to ask, what possibility exists for a Mexican American–led revolution in the United States? While the body of his scholarly work, fiction, and folklore would suggest that Paredes believed passionately in Mexican American culture, both *George Washington Gómez* and *The Shadow* suggest that the limits of a socialist revolution strongly devoted to cultural nationalist ideals are bound to surface over time. These two works of Paredes strongly suggest that the limits of cultural nationalist revolution should be vigorously interrogated, especially in light of contemporary Mexican immigration to the United States. Had these texts been available at the time, such an interrogation, coupled with Paredes's savvy awareness of the dilemma of Mexican immigration for Mexican Americans, would have been a major contribution to the Chicano/a Movement.

Immigration and the Pursuit of Civil Rights: Jovita González (1904–1987)

Like the novels of Paredes, Jovita González's recovered novels, *Caballero* (1996) and *Dew on the Thorn* (1997), are conditioned by contemporaneous waves of Mexican immigration to Texas.[35] Unlike Paredes, González chose not to set her stories in the contemporary period but rather in the recent past. She responded to the dilemma of Mexican immigration by setting out to preserve, more directly than did Paredes in his fiction, the cultural memory of the Spanish Mexican colonial society that once controlled South Texas. She did so, I argue, in order to imagine a social order that would champion the full civil rights of Mexican Americans. Cowritten with Eve Raleigh in the late 1930s, *Caballero* is essentially a love story with a Romeo and Juliet plot. With the Mexican–American War as background, the novel is an epic–style historical romance like that of Margaret Mitchell's *Gone with the Wind* (1936).[36] Full of romantic and military intrigue, picturesque characters, and full–fledged heroics by the central female protagonist—all attributes that would have seemed to guarantee popularity–the novel never found a willing publisher, though González and her partner tried for several years. González noted that the rejections came despite their efforts not to simplify the historical record by portraying all Anglos in a bad light or all Mexicans in a good light.[37]

In writing *Caballero*, González made tremendous use of her training as a folklorist–she was protégé of J. Frank Dobie at the University of Texas, Austin–and of her scholarship on prominent Mexican ranchero families of South Texas.[38] As in Paredes, colonial history in González's hands becomes the means to offer an alternative narrative to Anglo nationalism. But her revisitation of the 1846–48 period of Anglo and Mexican conflict is also, as critic María Cotera argues, her opportunity to deconstruct within the Mexican American community "the myth of the warrior–hero while politicizing the domestic sphere."[39] Together, this decentering of Anglo American history and the deconstruction of Anglo and Mexican patriarchy launch a wide–scaled critique while also enhancing contemporary mainstream opinion about Mexican Texans in general. As such, González's folkloric research as well as her fiction parallels the work of New Mexican contemporaries such as Fabiola Cabeza de Baca, Nina Otero Warren, and Cleofas Jaramillo. These New Mexican women were also interested in cultural preservation of the past through stories. They also constructed a "usable past" that would counter the changing social terrain of their present by displacing Anglo American political domination.[40] Unlike in González, their displacement of the Anglos sometimes doubled as an indirect attack on recent Mexican immigrants, whose sheer numbers over time threatened the older colonial social order.

While *Caballero* offers no overt representation of immigration to Texas in the nineteenth century or later, it is nevertheless conscious of the cultural power that settler traditions exercise in claiming newly "found" territory. The novel opens with a foreword that features Don José Ramón de Mendoza y Robles on an exploratory mission ordered by the viceroy of New Spain to investigate lands north of the Rio Grande. While riding up the crest of a hill and gazing into the valley below, Don José has a vision of a great ranch on Palm Sunday of 1748. In no time, this soldier of the viceroy becomes the undisputed patriarch of Rancho La Palma de Cristo. The novel's intent, here and elsewhere, is to educate the reader about Spanish colonial tradition, of which Jovita González, like Paredes, is a descendant. Also like Paredes, González regularly reminds her Texan audiences of that colonial tradition's significance to the history of South Texas. In the context of the 1930s depression and the scapegoating of all Mexican Americans as "drains" on the national economy, this production of alternative colonial plots legitimizes historic claims on the land.

On the other hand, Don José's vision of 1748, a full one hundred years before the Treaty of Guadalupe Hidalgo, anticipates the mercurial relationship between territorial claims and nationalist identities. As the novel moves forward to represent the Mexican–American War, all contestants over land and nationalism–from the peons of Rancho La Palma, to Anglo squatters, to the Anglo and Mexican families who periodically form political mergers–become uprooted from their previous social and political moorings. Symbolically, most of the novel's characters become associated with immigrant discourses, whether by choice or not, because of the disruptions in time and space produced by the war. As the war concludes, the novel's protagonist family, descendants of Don José, must reach some accommodation with the Anglo Texas ruling class or risk further social and economic demotion. Those who cannot accommodate, or, more to the point, who are unwilling to restructure their previous colonial identity so that it mirrors the Anglo American immigration/colonization of South Texas, will not survive the postwar period. Instead of Romeo and Juliet dying, it is the holdout patriarch of the old ways, Don Santiago de Mendoza y Soría, who dies an ignominious death.

From González's vantage point as one of the very few educated Mexican Americans of her time, man or woman, it must have been supremely clear that only a renegotiation of masculine traditions in Mexican gender roles, history, and citizenship could advance the civil rights of Mexican Americans everywhere. A *mano a mano* contestation with Anglo America would inevitably fail, as the case of Don Santiago shows. What was needed, then and in the 1930s, was a broad social politic that made alliances with Anglos where possible, but otherwise sought to foster better social relations within the Mexican American community. For that to happen, especially between the elite and working–class members of the community, *Caballero* welcomes the end of the peon class under Texas Anglo rule, and earnestly supports the civic enfranchisement of this class. The peons of the novel stand in, I argue, for Mexican immigrants to Texas since 1910, who increasingly become migrant labor for agribusiness in the region and elsewhere. In a subtle manner, the novel hails the educated elite of the Mexican American community to recognize the needs of these workers and to see the workers' plight as not dissimilar from their own. In a significant evolution since the writings of María Cristina Mena, the novel suggests that to pursue the civil rights of the least protected is to ensure the advancement of the community as a whole.[41] In her own way, González anticipates the link Chicano/a activists make during the Movement between a history of twentieth-century Mexican immigration to the United States and the pursuance of the rights and obligations of citizenship.

The Fulfilled Immigrant: America, Land of Education: Luis Perez (1904–1962)

Unlike González and Paredes, whose novels languished without a publisher, Luis Perez managed to publish his fictional autobiography, *El Coyote: The Rebel*, in 1947. According to Lauro Flores, the novel's recoverer, *El Coyote* was positively reviewed by a number of people from east to west.[42] Despite these reviews and publishing with a good press like Henry Holt and Company, the text and the author did not enjoy public recognition for very long. In hindsight, we can see how in the postwar climate a picturesque novel that is a war memoir, bildungsroman, immigrant novel, and a portrait of a revolutionary turned artist could have attracted early positive attention. By the same token, it is instructive of the period that these attributes, so well received during a heightened sense of American nationalism, meant less as the wartime rhetoric of national unity faded.

Published in a moment of patriotic zeal, the novel can be read as celebrating immigration to the United States as individual fulfillment. In this light, the novel is a wonderful example of Guerin–Gonzales's thesis about the attractiveness of the American Dream during the period depicted in the novel, roughly from 1909 to 1934. Yet the manner in which Perez marks individual fulfillment can also be read, outside of a nationalist moment, as threatening to what goes for a normative American identity in peacetime. In this regard, the novel hints at the limits of the American Dream inversely by focusing on those characters who are more regularly recognized within the secular rituals of being American. In this novel, what grounds and energizes the tension between those recently arrived to claim the American Dream as their personal process of salvation and those who guard and police the process from the "barbarians at the gate" is the promise of an education.

As Flores notes, it is the protagonist's grandfather who sets in motion the idea that Little Luis should travel to the United States for the best education possible. Given the political worries at the time the novel opens in 1909, it is highly rational that the grandfather would wish to spare his grandchild the troubles ahead. Luis is after all an orphan. His Mexican mother died at childbirth, and his father, a French diplomat, was recalled to France, never once claiming his son. From this moment on, the novel chronicles a twenty–five–year quest to fulfill the grandfather's wishes. The vast majority of the narrative is devoted to the hair-raising experiences of Little Luis as his uncle and aunt fail miserably to take care him or fulfill the grandfather's request. Abandoned a third time in his life, Little Luis cannot resist being drafted into one of the rebel factions of the Mexican Revolution at age eleven! Off and on, for over two years, the battlefield, camp life, and the vagaries of civil war are Luis's principal education. It is not until 1918 that he firmly decides, at age fourteen, to pursue his grandfather's dream on his own.

Though less than one–fifth of the novel is devoted to the protagonist's acquisition of an education, it is in this section that the novel affirms education as the means by which one becomes an American citizen. Luis's education begins legalistically when his entry into the United States is officiated by the INS in accordance with a recent congressional suspension of immigration law meant to aid the Arizona Grower's Association and their need for cheap labor (Flores, xxi). Luis takes an oath to honor the terms of his temporary visa and return to Mexico at the end of one year. But at the end of his first contract with rancher Benson, Luis realizes that his wages have been unjustly garnered through the unscrupulous dealings of Benson's on–site company store. After months of backbreaking cotton picking, Luis leaves the ranch with ten dollars and few belongings. Like the ranchers in California described by Guerin-Gonzales, Benson feels perfectly entitled to petition the federal government to aid in his own pursuit of happiness. Without any sense of irony, Benson is equally happy when he curtails and obstructs the American Dream for his Mexican migrant workers, despite how they all agree on the principles of self–reliance, hard work, and faith in democracy.

Of course, other moments of disillusionment are in store for Luis after Benson. Though the narrative never flinches from registering a critique of discrimination based on race and ethnicity, unlike Don Chipote who wants nothing to do with the United States after awhile, Perez's protagonist stoically forges ahead with his grandfather's dream. When he realizes the advantages of becoming a naturalized U.S. citizen, graduation from high school and enrollment in a Los Angeles university to earn a degree in Spanish confirm for Luis his inevitable destiny in the United States. Luis has a remarkable sense of confidence despite the fact that he takes his oath of citizenship in the middle of the Great Depression, and despite, as Flores notes, the ominous ring to the courthouse guard's praise that Luis is "one of us" (xxiii). Because the guard is African American, it is not clear whether the guard means one of us *Americans*, or one of us *Americans of color*, or both. The indeterminacy of this praise does not contradict at all, I think, the confidence Luis has in the fruition of his grandfather's dream. Rather, the indeterminacy marks the vulnerability inherent for immigrants like Luis who are only modestly given permission to dream the American Dream. In some ways, El Coyote's fulfillment stands in dark contrast to the tens of thousands who also left Mexico during the Mexican Revolution but never found fulfillment or education in America. For these others, the dilemma of being Mexican immigrants always shadowed their experience.

Exodus and the Birth of the Pocho: José Antonio Villarreal (b. 1924)

The angst-filled dialogue between two cultures that unevenly straddle the same geopolitical space is the subject of the last text and writer reviewed in this chapter. The story of the Mexican Revolution and its consequential transformation of the thousands who fled to the United States is poignantly narrated in José Antonio Villarreal's *Pocho* (1959). In this fictional autobiography, Richard Rubio, the second-generation son of a Mexican family, tells the story of growing up in California in the wake of this massive movement of Mexican immigrants into the United States. Rubio is born in a migrant camp of agricultural laborers to parents who were refugees of the Revolution. *Pocho* is a stridently masculinist narrative. As Ramón Saldívar argues, Richard Rubio's painful acculturation into U.S. society is set in the context of his father's devolution as a patriarch, *machista*, and former soldier of the Revolution.[43] Unlike with El Coyote, the end of the Mexican Revolution signaled the end of Juan Rubio's accomplishments. His entry into the United States is marked by necessity, not desire. The dilemma for Juan Rubio and others is that their refugee status offers little or no viable national imaginary to carry over into the United States, nor a healthy nationalist nostalgia that might suture the violence that preceded their exodus.

Juan Rubio's narrative of failure in the United States becomes the contradictory ground upon which Richard develops a masculine identity capable of negotiating the discriminatory contours of American citizenship. Ramón Saldívar observes:

> In the course of the novel, Richard will freely accept the derogatory term pocho and transform it into a sign of his ambiguous status as a child of two cultures–Mexican and American–yet claimed by neither. His story is that of a sensitive young child struggling to create an acceptable identity for himself from the clash of these two cultures. . . . All the while as the young Richard matures, learns to live in an English–speaking American world, and realizes that he wishes to become a writer, we also see the gradual disintegration of this traditional Mexican family. (61 62)

As the father's reveries of a revolutionary past are critiqued and displaced, the novel also shows Richard groping for a better way to forward himself as an "authentic" citizen of the United States. The bombing of Pearl Harbor sets in motion the means to authenticate his civic identity. He enlists in the Navy, leaving behind his family to fend off the ethnic wars at home.

At war's end, Mexican American *veteranos*, like Richard Rubio, as well as survivors of the battles on the home front, confronted a postwar America transformed by their sacrifices. If ambivalence, discrimination, and oppression had before bracketed their collective identities as U.S. citizens, the war effort had the potential of transforming these negative experiences into something positive, namely, national belonging or respect. As a result, the Mexican American community became increasingly eager to put their citizenship on the line for a broader range of social causes. As was the case for Native Americans, African Americans, and Asian Americans, the experiences of the war had forever altered their sense of civic duty to family, race, and nation. Despite its internal ethnic and nationalist diversity, a bicultural Mexican American community had come of age. With still fresh memories of the illegal deportation of Mexican American citizens during the 1930s, Jim Crow laws fiercely defended throughout the Southwest, and the Zoot Suit Riots in Los Angeles (1943), a whole new leadership structure within Mexican American communities emerged.

By the 1950s, the archetypal Mexican family that had taken flight from the Revolution to settle, however precariously, in the United States was now gone but not forgotten. For this postwar generation, the future had a history. In the nurturing shade of their labors, the seeds of another revolution, the Chicano/a Movement, were slowly taking root among countless *pochos y pochas*.[44] In 1959, José Antonio Villarreal risked the unknown to become a published writer. He began a writing career never knowing there were many more writers like him waiting to be acknowledged, and hardly confident that there would be more like him in the decades to come. One can only wonder at the cultural work that could have been advanced by the authors studied in this chapter, or by the works of other writers not included here, such as Miguel Antonio Otero, Jr., Leonor Villegas de Magnón, Fray Angelico Chavez, Josephina Niggli, and many more, had society embraced their works. We can only speculate on the impact their work might have had upon Mexican American consciousness in the years leading up to the Chicano/a Movement and the Chicano/a artistic renaissance.[45]

CHAPTER FIVE

From Camelot to Barrio on a Hill

Contemporary Chicano/a Literature and

the Puritan Crucible

If, by 1945, the Great Depression and World War II set the stage for the nationalization of American literature, national events in the 1960s were no less important for the emergence of a Chicano/a Renaissance. This was the era of Kennedy's American Camelot, New Frontier, and the space program. It is also the time of the Bay of Pigs, the Cuban Missile Crisis, and the sending of military "advisers" to Vietnam. John F. Kennedy was an important political figure for Mexicans and Mexican Americans, as he was for other minority groups. This importance was made all the more clear with his assassination in November 1963. For Mexican Americans, the death of Kennedy signaled a poignant loss in perceived opportunities to rectify social, economic, and political inequalities. As Chicano historian Juan Gómez-Quiñones observes, Kennedy was the "first presidential candidate to address the Mexican American voter saliently." Kennedy's awareness of Mexican American issues ignited a deep response from a number of Mexican American political and social clubs that had been growing in number and regional influence since 1945.[1]

The Viva Kennedy clubs that sprang up throughout the Southwest and West as part of Kennedy's election campaign effort were instrumental in increasing Mexican American voter registration and turnout. Gómez-Quiñones writes: "In Texas, Kennedy won an extraordinary 91 percent of the Mexican American vote, 200,000 votes, which allowed him to win the state and hence the presidency" (91). In contrast to Anglo political pundits who claim that "Texas" won the presidency for Kennedy, Gómez-Quiñones argues persuasively that it was the Mexican American vote that gave Kennedy the presidency. Significantly, Kennedy's successful bid for the presidency proved to politicians everywhere that Mexican Americans were a growing political bloc. Also significantly, Kennedy's appeal to the Mexican American vote, I argue, fostered an ethnic identity among Mexican Americans not seen since World War II and, further, urged Mexican Americans to consider themselves as national subjects, that is, as not just Mexican Americans but as "Americans."[2] Perhaps it took a powerful Irish Catholic family from Boston with its own brand of New England cultural authority to redirect national politics toward Mexican Americans. This change would be important in the politically charged 1960s, and would be important for Chicano/a literature.

After this election, Mexican Americans would increasingly become a force in regional politics, despite the later loss of Kennedy. Some of this political activism would continue within a traditional Democratic Party framework, as in Lyndon B. Johnson's presidential campaign of 1964.[3] Other Mexican Americans would stake out alternative political directions as they became part of the growing Civil Rights Movement. These activists preferred the name "Chicano" to Mexican American. In 1962, one such activist, Cesar Chávez, began organizing migrant workers into what would become the United Farm Workers (UFW). Chávez's union efforts, with a focus on nonviolent, nationwide boycotts of growers, would galvanize the Chicano/a Movement and provide a national platform to address the problems affecting Mexican American people, a platform that had been missing in mainstream politics, missing even in the previous Viva Kennedy clubs.

Chicano/a scholars have long argued the importance of the UFW to the emergence of the Chicano/a Renaissance in the late 1960s. Chávez's championing of the plight of the migrant worker gave Chicanos/as, in urban and rural areas alike, a political sense of themselves as an ethnic, racial, and working-class people. In an era of social revolution, it was the role of Chicano/a artists and writers to reinforce UFW goals and create narratives that represented a broadly defined ethnic identity based on a shared embattled history in the United States. Fortified with an awakened political resolve to demand civil rights for people of Mexican descent, Chicano/a artist/activists ventured out in protest against the status quo. They depicted class and race warfare in murals from Los Angeles to Houston, unearthed forgotten cultural heroes like Joaquín Murrieta in California and Gregorio Cortez in Texas, and finally, through a savvy deployment of pre-Columbian cultural myths and symbols, created a usable past for contemporary Mexican Americans, which offered the added advantage of educating people about their Mexican heritage. As Kennedy inaugurated his presidency with the poetic blessings of Robert Frost, this generation of Chicano/a writers and activists were soon to draw sustenance from a history of neglect and oppression. In the re-kindling of Mexican culture, they found themselves in command of a means to produce a new national identity.

In the context of this political struggle, to compare Chicano/a and Puritan writers may seem irrelevant or, at least, insensitive to past sacri-fices. Yet, the point of this comparison is not to subordinate Mexican American writers to an Anglo Puritan interpretive paradigm, but rather to measure the historic effect of a modern Puritan ethos on Chicano/a literary culture. In the following pages, I argue that Chicano/a liter-ary history owes its construction and maintenance, in part, to a main-stream American critical tradition that presents Puritan writers as the original dissenters in American literary history. To say all models of re-sistance for Chicano/a writers come from the Taylors and Mathers would be ridiculous, for that would erase the social history so crucial to Mexi-can Americans in the figures of Cesar Chávez, Dolores Huerta, Américo Paredes, Luis Valdez, Alurista, Rosalío Muñoz, Celia Luna de Rodríguez, and others. And yet Chicano/a resistance to the mainstream canon could not have come without an appreciation and interrogation of its master-works, nor without some kind of dialogue with U.S. history and its pop-ular myths.

Certainly, the educational biographies of most Chicano/a writers speak to their relationships to canonical works. From Gary Soto's classes with Philip Levine, to Bernice Zamora's feminist revisions of Robinson Jeffers, to Reyes Cárdenas's angry rejection of what Robert Lowell's works have come to signify about American poetry, Chicano/a writers since the 1970s have been actively engaged in defining Chicano/a literature within the larger context of American literature. At times they clearly defy and resist the status quo through their choices of alternative literary subjects and voices, and at times they clearly write within more ca-nonical traditions of American letters. Nevertheless, this chapter does not propose absolute critical stances. Chicano/a writers are not Puritan clergy in disguise; nor should they be confused with Mexican writers such as Octavio Paz or Carlos Fuentes. In the end, Aztlán, the political and literary symbol of the Chicano/a Movement, exists within the geopolitical confines of the United States, and ultimately its literary significance lies not within the canon or literary history of Mexican literature, but in its complicated history with the American literary canon.

In "Myth and Comparative Cultural Nationalism: The Ideological Uses of Aztlán," Genaro M. Padilla observes a general "orphan complex" in the works of contemporary Chicano/a writers (126).[4] For Padilla, this "orphan complex" underscores the alienation experienced by Chicano/a authors in the United States and, through them, the severe forms of alienation endured by la raza. Padilla concludes that overall the adoption of "lo mexicano"–the essence of Mexicanness–has enabled a positive response against the dominant Anglo culture. Yet, he also admits that "Chicanos . . . have found it necessary to exorcise or divest themselves of those elements of the Mexican mythos, ancient or modern, that deflect from the reality of their situation in this country" (126). He cites the example of Tomás Rivera to draw out this point further. Once asked about the relationship of Chicano/a writers to Mexican literature, Rivera replied that in some cases, as in his, the relationship is a learned one.[5] Though he had read the Mexican classics, it was going to Mexico that helped him develop a better understanding of who he was:

> Then I began to realize that I'm not a Mexican. All these things I feel are a result of learning, not of growing up in Mexico with all its problems, its beauty and all its affinities. I thought, 'It's not really mine. I know it as mine, now, because I've learned it. I don't actually have it, nor have I lived it.' After that I had to come back and say this is reality right here. . . . The fact is that if I had not gotten a college education I would know very little about Mexico. O. K., I could go over and buy trinkets and look at the pyramids, but reality, ours, is not there; it's here. (153)

His identity was intimately bound up in what he had read and where he had lived. But Rivera's "orphan complex" wasn't solved by adopting Mexico as a true parent country. Seeking a resolution actually steered him back to "reality right here."

In calling attention to the "orphan complex" in Chicano/a writers such as Rivera, Padilla employs one of the most prevalent themes in Anglo American literary criticism. From this perspective, Rivera is no different from the Hawthornes or Melvilles who have dealt with "orphan complexes" through their creations. Pearl and Ishmael eventually find literal and figurative homes. And so does Rivera, but in the voices and hardships of the migrant workers whose homes are as transient as their hopes, grounded in a kind of second-class citizenship that Nathaniel Hawthorne or Herman Melville never knew. Padilla's "orphan complex" resonates with a host of other writers in American literary history. What thus starts off as a category of distinction also serves as a point of similarity between Chicano/a writers and canonical ones.

In the same interview referred to by Padilla above, Rivera speaks about the influential books of his formative years:

> Junior high school was lost; no reading that was worthwhile, pure mishmash. First of all, they didn't think you could read, *porque eras mexicano* [because you were Mexican] . . .
>
> In high school I got into American literature. I was really taken with the Graveyard Poets, which is natural for a fourteen-year-old; the age of reflection and all that. Steinbeck I liked very much. The movie *The Grapes of Wrath* led me to read all his novels. I got into Hemingway; read everything he had written. Walt Whitman became a very important source, not only of inspiration, but at one point he seemed like the only connection that made sense, in almost a religious way. I dropped out of the Catholic Church at about fourteen—not dropped out, really, I just didn't want to have anything to do with religion right then. By the time of high school graduation I was reading about religion and I became pretty cynical. Well, Walt Whitman was my replacement: "I sing the body electric." Powerful things like that. (144)

Rivera's decision to replace a religious worldview with that found in Walt Whitman epitomizes his evolution as a reader. Abandoned to ignorance because of racial prejudice, Rivera nevertheless reads what his immediate culture offers; he claims Whitman and his poetry, I would argue, for its dissenting, subversive, liberating elements. It influences his distance from Catholicism, a perspective that allows him to critique the role Christianity plays in the economic oppression of migrant workers.

What can we conclude from this? Rivera goes on to earn a B.A. in English but, because of discrimination, cannot find a teaching job (145). He eventually earns an M.A. in English and administration, but ends up earning a doctorate in Spanish, in part because he is told there are more jobs for him teaching Spanish. What we can thus conclude is that both formal education and biographical events have shaped Rivera's writing. His early attraction to literature via Whitman and twentieth-century American novelists was in time complemented by Spanish literary figures and forms. Add to this combination the political significance of the Chicano/a Movement and you have the basis for understanding his *chicanismo* in binational, bicultural terms. By placing Rivera's work within the larger social and political context of the traditional post-1945 canon, we do in fact retrieve important aspects of his writing that in the long run serve to identify Chicano/a literature, Chicano/a nationalism, and Chicanos/as within U.S. literary cultures.

Like Rivera, Chicano/a poets who came of artistic age in the 1970s inherited two sets of American narrative origins: one Puritan, via the post-1945 canon, and one in the Chicano/a Movement, with its eyes on Aztlán. Both narratives conditioned their development as students and writers of literature in the United States. This second generation of Chicano/a writers—Pat Mora, Lorna Dee Cervantes, and Gary Soto, as taken up in this chapter—articulate thus a binational experience that incorporates these two nationalist origins myths. Chicano poet Alberto Ríos, winner of the Walt Whitman Award (1981), comments that

> every good writer ignores nothing, so that Chicano literature, while filled with the concerns of Chicanos specifically, is also American literature. It is both things; it does not fit into either one of these labels so conveniently. This is one of the things that makes it exciting. This literature is like the Chicano language, neither Spanish nor English altogether, but something more central than that, something that derives from the lesson of using binoculars—we must use both eyes to see the one thing clearly.[6]

Chicana poet Pat Mora expands this argument by reminding us that the same politics of ethnicity that can empower a Chicana writer can also limit her:

I advocated the preservation of our stories, songs, customs, and values in my writing, as do many of my fellow writers who were and are termed *ethnic writers*, a term that falsely suggests that some of us have ethnicity and some of us don't. At its most dangerous level, this label perpetuates the false notion that Anglo American writers are the real writers, rather than one tradition in the evolving body of U.S. literature.[7]

If Mexican American literature were regularly integrated within a broadly revised American literary history, as I have shown in chapters 3 and 4, we would be better able to reveal and interpret the bicultural world of the Mexican American writer. To do so, critics must appreciate and develop the category of literary binationalism in order to account for the contemporary period and the literary borders Chicano/a writers frequently traverse. In effect, I argue we must invoke a literary binational framework when it comes to understanding Chicano/a literature since 1960–no single nationalist framework can adequately interpret literature written during the Civil Rights Movement, the Vietnam War, and postmodernity. Such development of literary binationalism would enable comparisons between Chicano/a and Puritan writers that avoid simple reification of an Anglo Puritan myth of origins. In the following pages, I am fully mindful of how the dominant U.S. literary culture has policed and discouraged comparisons that call into question the utility of a monocultural, national literary history. These comparisons are therefore all the more critical to revising American literary history.

Common Ground on Different Borders: A Comparative Approach

This section develops comparative links between Chicano/a writers and a New England myth of origins by strategically deploying Puritan texts to understand the critical and aesthetic categories that unconsciously structure contemporary Chicano/a writing. It assumes that Puritan scholars have erected cultural institutions and "American" experiences that challenge contemporary ethnic writers to either assimilate, accommodate, appropriate, or reject outright a national literature based on New England origins. Nowhere are these challenges more overt than in the construction of genres that are used to classify the masterworks of the traditional canon. With these genres, early Americanists have established a literary genealogy that invariably links contemporary poets to

Ralph Waldo Emerson and, before him, to Edward Taylor. To this day, the canonical evaluation of a minority poet often depends on his/her relationship to a genealogy ultimately defined in seventeenth-century New England contexts. The limitation of this genealogy is of course that it discounts works that depart from the form, meter, and subject matter of readily identifiable New England biographies, cultures, or literary predecessors. Nor, more importantly, does this genealogy concede that additional traditions may be at work other than those originating from New England.

My comparisons attempt to denaturalize this genealogy by emphasizing the importance of certain genres—like community histories, jeremiads, and the confessional poem—to the whole of American literature, including Chicano/a literature. At the same time, I see gestures by Chicano/a writers toward a New England Puritanism as inevitable vestiges of an educational system that traditionally has mirrored the politics and ideologies of an Anglo Protestant past. For example, poetry tends to be the genre most accessible to minority writers, even if its high art status makes it one of the most fiercely contested genres in debates about canonicity. This dynamic tension between accessibility and canonicity thus makes poetry an appropriate vehicle for testing what, in fact, can be read in the "tradition of American poetry"–a critical terrain often dear to Early Americanists. Further, this kind of evaluation reveals how the significance of a literary history or the contributions of a particular poet are largely shaped by the presence (or absence) of other poets and histories in scholarship and in the classroom.

Sau-ling Cynthia Wong's theory of *intertexts*, noted in chapter 2, provides a sophisticated understanding of the interplays between canonical and noncanonical texts in the context of specific ethnic histories. Her model of reading illustrates how critics might more expansively understand the literary influences of minority writers in the twentieth century. Wong's concept of intertexts can be adapted, I propose, so that it includes those discourses that intervene on the material and intellectual conditions of ethnic writers. From there, returning to R. C. De Prospo's contention that once we "theorize American literary history not as a diachronic passage from past to present . . . but as the synchronic differentiation of past from present," I can then present Early American literature, as De Prospo puts it, "no longer as the progenitor but as the necessary semiotic companion of modern American literature." The hope is that this kind of comparative theory would reverse the critical markers that long have identified an Edward Taylor as dominant and a Gary Soto as marginal.

In the comparisons that follow, I attend to each Puritan writer's critical status, and then, using that writer as a semiotic Other, I explore the intersections of ethnic writers with a Puritan–based American literary history. In effect, I enact De Prospo's "synchronic differentiation of past from present." By understanding the Puritan writer as a kind of ghostwriter or, in De Prospo's words, a "companion of modern American literature"–and, I would add, modern *ethnic* American literature–we can then historicize the binational character of Chicano/a literature, enabling a comparison between Chicano/a and Puritan writers that does not remarginalize Chicano/a literature. These comparisons reflect not only the literary histories internal, more or less exclusively, to each writer, but how such different writers can still share mutual interests in broad subjects like religion, immigration, and "America" as the "promised land." In short, the comparisons that follow pave the way for an integrated literary history that adds more substance to today's renovated canon.

Cotton Mather and Pat Mora: The People of the New World

In *The Puritan Origins of the American Self* (1975), Bercovitch begins the final chapter, "The Myth of America," conscious of the power of the United States. He writes: "In retrospect, it seems clear that the Puritan myth prepared for the re–vision of God's Country from the 'the New England of the type' into the United States of America" (136). Implicit in this claim is that "early New England rhetoric provided a ready framework for inverting later secular values–human perfectibility, technological progress, democracy, Christian socialism, or simply (and comprehensively) the American Way–into the mold of sacred teleology" (136). What he sees in Cotton Mather's *Magnalia Christi Americana*, for example, is a kind of rhetorical blueprint for a secularized Christian nation–state. As further evidence of this tradition, Bercovitch offers cultural figures, from Jonathan Edwards to Ralph Waldo Emerson, as latter–day Cotton Mathers: "Each of them, in his own way, responded to the problems of his times by recourse to what I have described (with reference to the *Magnalia*) as the genre of auto–American–biography: the celebration of the representative self as America, and of the American self as the embodiment of a prophetic universal design" (136). United States national identity is therefore intimately a product of New England Puritan writers' figuration of the New World as themselves, and vice versa. Importantly, this correlation between self and New World rests upon an unquestioning faith that America is the site of a sacred providential history and that every individual American is representative of this sacred history.

Quite aware of the different colonial histories of North America, Bercovitch's focus on Puritan origins is an attempt, I believe, to account for the most enduring characteristics of *the* hegemonic discourse in U.S. letters and culture. By having identified what he calls "auto–American-biography," Bercovitch has in fact characterized a paradigm that can be properly attributed not only to writers but to critics. When he writes that Mather advanced the concept "of the American who stands for the New World, in spite of, or beyond, the forces of secular time, [which consequently] justified the claims of a long procession of solitary keepers of the dream" (136), he implicitly includes the Perry Millers of the twentieth century. Yet, how might Bercovitch's model account for those whose national identity is questioned because of their racial, ethnic, and/or class status in the United States? For example, how might Pat Mora's "auto–American-biography" relate to Cotton Mather's archetypal definitions of America as the promised land, to America's national destiny, and to America's immigrants?

In the hands of poet and educator Pat Mora, the figurations of New World lands and indigenous peoples as antithetical to the Puritan mission continue to resonate. From her position as mestiza and Chicana, Mora uses poetry to take up her historic marginality as woman and person of color and turn on their heads the symbolic and linguistic terms of oppression deployed since Columbus sailed to the New World. Mora implicitly deconstructs Cotton Mather's ethos by denaturalizing his demonized New World, and taking up a subject central to Mather as Bercovitch understands him: that is, Mather's construction of an "American" identity through communal historical narratives such as found in *Magnalia Christi Americana* (1702). In Mora's careful attention to Chicana history and her conversion of misogynist pre–Columbian myths and symbols, such as La Malinche and the serpent, into feminist symbols of female endurance and power, she shows how alternative community histories are constructed that counter the dominant narratives of U.S. history and culture. Significantly, Mora's alternative communal histories are deeply and negatively affected by what Bercovitch argues is the Puritans' chief legacy: their evolving self-fashioning as America itself.[8]

Mora ends her first volume of published poetry, *Chants*, with a poem entitled "Legal Alien." Given that she is representative of a dual colonial history, Spanish and Anglo–Saxon, Mora's title signifies both the historic dispossession of Mexican Americans in the Americas and also contemporary U.S. definitions of legal residence for immigrants. From the title, Mora leaps to the other terms that identify the speaker's language and social relationships in the United States:

> Bi–lingual, Bi–cultural,
> able to slip from "How's life?"
> to *"Me 'stan volviendo loca,"*
> able to sit in a paneled office
> drafting memos in smooth English,
> able to order in fluent Spanish
> at a Mexican restaurant,
> American but hyphenated . . .

The ambivalence of the poem, like the anxiety over national identity, resides in this linguistic and cultural hyphenation of the speaker's self. Unlike Mather, Mora's speaker cannot claim herself as an undivided American. Indeed, there is a sense of fraudulence in Mora's speaker, a sense of illegitimacy in the face of otherwise public competency. Though the hyphen is a cultural and linguistic sign that confers the civic legitimacy historically denied to people of non–Anglo Puritan descent, a sense of unease remains. Mora's poem is representative of the racial and ethnic rhetoric of self that is in conversation with Bercovitch's "auto–American-biography." Mora's speaker articulates the individual/communal identity of a history of discontinuous and fractured subjectivity forged in resistance and survival ever since the United States won control of the Southwest in the Mexican American War of 1846.

Mora's resolution of "Legal Alien" typifies the experiences of Mexican immigrants and Mexican Americans who must engage, for better or worse, with the Puritan symbolism that figured North America as the site of Christ's second coming. She highlights the continual need to negotiate the discontinuities between U.S. citizenship and a non–Anglo Puritan ethnicity:

> viewed by Anglos as perhaps exotic,
> perhaps inferior, definitely different,

viewed by Mexicans as alien,
(their eyes say, "You may speak
Spanish but you're not like me")
an American to Mexicans
a Mexican to Americans
a handy token
sliding back and forth
between the fringes of both worlds
by smiling
by masking the discomfort
of being pre-judged
Bi-laterally.

While elsewhere, especially in her later poem "Immigrants," Mora acknowledges that Mexican immigration to the United States bears similarities to white ethnic experiences in the twentieth century, she points out that Mexican immigration is conditioned additionally by race and the proximity of Mexico as the "mother" country.[9] The speaker is the quintessential "other" in Anglo hegemonic discourses, a second-class citizen whose destiny in America is ancillary to the overall providential design of the United States, reserved for Anglo Americans. To Mexican nationals, the speaker represents the historical subjugation of their country to the United States. Via the speaker's literal body, past exceptionalist mandates aimed against Latin America—the Monroe Doctrine, Manifest Destiny, the Good Neighbor Policy, the Tortilla Curtain—merge in their contradictory ethnic and nationalist loyalties to create a bicultural liminal world. For Mora's speaker, like millions of people of Mexican descent, this is what it means to be a binational subject in an Anglo Puritan defined country.

Busy "sliding back and forth / between the fringes of both worlds," where can the Chicana subject reside more wholly? Where can a Chicana poet write her "auto-American-biography" without reifying Puritan colonialism? Interestingly, Mora turns to a key concept in the Puritan cosmology of North America, the land, for a psychological and spiritual grounding. In Puritan writings, the land is a valued vehicle, not for itself, but as the prophetic future of those who live upon it. In contrast, Mora turns, as a grateful supplicant, to the desert that surrounds her West Texas home in El Paso. This is in fact the subject of the poem "Bribe," which begins *Chants*:

I hear Indian women
chanting, chanting
I see them long ago bribing
the desert with turquoise threads,
in the silent morning coolness,
kneeling, digging, burying
their offering in the Land
chanting, chanting
Guide my hands, Mother,
to weave singing birds
flowers rocking in the wind, to trap
them on my cloth with a web of thin threads.

Secretly I scratch a hole in the desert
by my home. I bury a ballpoint pen
and lined yellowing paper. Like the Indians
I ask the Land to smile on me, to croon
softly, to help me catch her music with words.

Chicana critics emphasize that Mora foregrounds Native American and oral traditions as a way to reclaim a feminine muse often discredited in Western literary traditions. Her obvious kinship with the land counters typical Western binarisms that figure the land under patriarchal dominance. A product of Western education, Mora quiets the more obvious dissonance between her writing and the Indian women's blanket weaving and singing by reversing what Shakespeare's Prospero made so famous in *The Tempest*. The power of the text, for Mora, lies not in the book buried in the land but in the land that nurtures the subject who writes. Likewise, if for the Puritan clergy and magistrates the Bible became the single textual referent of epistemology and ontology in the New World, for Mora the American desert retains its own creative and procreative genius; it provides an alternative interpretive schema of the New World and a history particularly important to Native Americans and mestizas since 1492.[10]

In contrast to Mora, Mather draws specifically from the Bible in order to anchor, for his generation of Puritans, a spiritual and civic legitimacy in the New World. According to Bercovitch, Mather's biography of John Winthrop represents a rhetorical synthesis of Christology with civic behavior. Mather's Winthrop appears as an exemplary lawgiver, like the biblical Nehemiah, and also as "one of a *series* of magistrates and divines who contribute to a particular New World enterprise" with an emphasis on "the idea of the exemplary American" (35). Mather's conceptualization of the self with regard to the New World in *Magnalia Christi Americana* confirms a Puritan legitimacy in an alien land. The Puritans' alienation from the land is offset by their supreme confidence in their nationalistic identity as New Israelites. Despite their real distance from England theologically, politically, and geographically, their typological claim on America, of which Cotton Mather's writing is representative, resists fragmentation of their individual and communal identity. While it is generally true that Mather represents the indigenous population as American, that he upholds their historic relationships to the land, nonetheless, for him the future of the land lies with the latest Americans because they represent the *true* inheritors of a Christian cosmos.[11]

Given the Bible's obvious silence on the existence of the New World, the scriptural refiguration of the American landscape was an important part of Puritan cosmology. In Mather's introduction to *Magnalia Christi Americana*, the land of America represents "those ends of the earth" where God's "Divine Providence hath irradiated an Indian Wilderness" (25). Not only does America stand beyond the edge of Christian civilization, it lies outside of history itself until God reveals "wonderful displays of His infinite Power, Wisdom, Goodness, and Faithfulness" (25). It is through this theological context that Mather reminds his audience, on both sides of the Atlantic, that the Puritans were persecuted into leaving England for "the dark regions of America." Once there, Mather furthers his case by casting his Puritan forefathers as Old Testament Israelites. These cast-off Christians proved be "profitable sorts of creatures":

> But behold, ye European Churches, there are golden Candlesticks [more than twice seven times seven!] in the midst of this "outer darkness": unto the upright children of Abraham, here hath arisen *light in darkness*. And, let us humbly speak it, it shall be profitable for you to consider the *light* which, from the midst of this "outer darkness," is now to be darted over unto the other side of the Atlantick Ocean. (27)

Mather invokes the language of *"light in darkness"* quite consciously to establish a celebratory narrative of the reformed churches in America.

And consequently to insinuate that Europe's own present darkness will be alleviated in time by the example of the Puritan saints in America. Through all this Christian reformation, America as land appears as a ritual exercise of the biblical Canaan: incomplete, pagan, and inscrutable without the Christian God and the Christian English. For this reason, Mather's narrative line in the *Magnalia* is that he will set down a history of New England to prevent a loss to humanity: "but certainly one good way to save that *loss*, would be to do something that the memory of the *great things done for us by our God*, may not be lost, and that the story of the circumstances attending the *foundation* and *formation* of this country, and of its preservation hitherto, may be impartially handed unto posterity" (40). By "country," Mather means indisputably the nation of English Protestants that has colonized the New World. And it is to *their* posterity that he offers an *impartial* story of their special salvation in America. For those native nations in America, Mather's narrative represents the theological and rhetorical foundation of their "othering" and the loss of their power to define America.

To the extent that a recuperation of those "other" Americas is possible, Mora offers in her poem "Secrets" a glimpse of what has opened up since Martin Luther King, Jr., the Chicano/a Movement, and the Vietnam War:

His feet could read mountains,
dark, hard, bare feet, beating
a rhythm in the canyons,
season by season, feeling paths
no one else saw, leading
the weary judge up rock slopes,
senses bare to the whisper of smoke,
the scent of crushed herb,
classic guide to that mystery
world devoid of books, people,
my usual clues.[12]

Remembering a family story passed on to her about her great-grandfather, a judge, Mora rediscovers the vestiges of a post–Colombian moment, untarnished yet by the demonology of Christianity or the empiricism of Western science. Here the natural and human are presented as mutually accepting of each other. Here the Native American is knowing and whole without Western intellectual discourses. And significantly, here Mora finds the pulse of a different rhythm to appreciate.

The poem progresses in the second stanza to clarify that this "weary judge" is no Hernando Cortés in search of gold and dreaming of empires, and less a lawgiver like Mather's Winthrop, leading a flock of the faithful into the promised land. Instead, the great–grandfather appears as no "judge" of his surroundings, totally dependent on his guide for interpreting his experience:

> Felipe, the Tarahumara, guiding
> my great–grandfather, pointing;
> to the man hushing horses with hay,
> to the machete dark, dark in the sun,
> to his wife scrubbing blood stains
> in the arroyo.

What scene the Tarahumara points to we can only guess by what Mora has left us. There has been some bloodletting; whether or not it is the aftermath of a successful hunt or a sacred or female ritual is not clear. The horses are fed to quiet them. The man and woman are engaged in their respective gendered roles. What is clear is that Felipe actualizes its meaning for the judge and later his great–granddaughter. Like the horses and machete that occupy the same New World context, one a European import and the other an indigenous tool, the Tarahumara, with the Spanish Christian name of Felipe, stands at the crossroads of two worlds, balancing his bicultural status in relation to those, like the judge, that so clearly occupy just one.

In contrast to Mather, who creates an in memoriam to "the first Settlement of Colonies, which have been renowned for the degree of REFORMATION" (25), Mora memorializes a tale that has more to say to those like her who live the experiences of a binational subject in the United States. The poem encapsulates what Chicano novelist Rudolfo Anaya calls a "Chicano/a consciousness" of multiple histories, cultures, and languages. Anaya writes: "we are American Chicanos; we are inherently American, indigenous people. We are Hispanic from our European heritage, we are Native American from our American heritage. We are heirs to the mythologies and religions and philosophic thought of Western civilization, but we are also heirs to the mythologies, religions and thought of the Americas."[13] As an heir to these cultural and historical intersections, Mora is also an heir of the Chicano/a Movement. This poem, like those in *Chants*, traverses the landscape of the Southwest, both as a memory of those things lost to colonialism and a celebration of a mestizo heritage now recoupable. From the mythic homeland of Aztlán, the "psychological and spiritual center" of Chicanismo, Mora can sally forth, in Anaya's words, "to joust against [the legal, religious, and literary legacies of] King Arthur's knights" in the Americas (116–17). She ends this poem desirous of a more complete path for herself and others. This entails, I argue, shaping a community identity commensurate with a binational experience, one that would balance Mather's City on the Hill with the Chicano/a myth of Aztlán.

In the final stanza, such is the power of this Tarahumara's indigenous metrics to read the mountains with his un-Westernized bare feet (pun intended) and guide the uninitiated over a landscape devoid of books, that the speaker muses about the possibility of an equivalent feminine Felipe for herself:

> The old tale buzzes round
> my head till I wish
> for such a guide, a woman
> teaching me the art of bending
> close to the land,
> silent, listening, feeling the path.

Like other Chicano/a poets, Mora recognizes the need to retain an ethnic identity that can counter hegemonic discourses. And politically, her poetry echoes what Anaya sees as the task of Chicano/a artists in the post-Chicano/a Movement era: "to keep reminding each other that each cultural community has an inherent right to its own definition, and Aztlán does define us more accurately than Camelot" (117).

But at the same time, for Mora as a Chicana this identity must correct for patriarchal abuse of women whether Anglo, Spanish, or Native American in origin. Felipe, the Tarahumara, lives in her memory as a wonderful binational, bicultural guide, but obviously the gendered roles of the past have limited women's access to the world, its "secrets," and the ability to wield representations of themselves. In short, Mora's poem here, as elsewhere, demonstrates that she is also an heir of the feminist movement. While "Secrets" ends on a hopeful note, it remains to be seen whether or not the speaker will find or become her own guide to "the art of bending / close to the land, / silent, listening, feeling the path." In the meantime, Mora, like her other Chicana peers, must tread lightly between the various poles that make up today's Chicana feminism and simultaneously engage social issues, like poverty, child abuse, and male violence against women.

Michael Wigglesworth and Lorna Dee Cervantes: Jeremiads Then and Now

To explore further this meeting place between ethnic and feminist identities, especially as they are figured by colonialism and patriarchy, I turn to Lorna Dee Cervantes's poem "Uncle's First Rabbit," from *Emplumada* (1981), and read it in the context of the jeremiad tradition as popularized by Michael Wigglesworth's *Day of Doom* (1662).[14] A dominant American literary form since the seventeenth century, a jeremiad typically foretells a community's fall from God's favor, and its subsequent apocalypse. I invoke the jeremiad here to study a narrative legacy little explored for its influence in the twentieth century: the subjugation of the body or body politic for spiritual and/or nationalist ends. In this comparison, I argue that the jeremiad endures not only as a symbolic and semiotic text for writers and scholars who ultimately desire a reaffirmation of America's providential place in the world, but as a text equally suited to a narrative of the colonized, a narrative for those for whom the Puritan errand or American mission has been anything but a dream come true.

For Wigglesworth, the body is the site of contest between good and evil, where the Puritan mission meets its first and perhaps most meaningful confrontation. In a rhetorical leap, Wigglesworth shapes this battle for the Christian body as an allegory for what he perceives as the colony's backsliding ways. Wigglesworth's self-proclaimed mission as a Puritan minister is to step into the Old Testament role of Jeremiah and remind the Puritan nation of the crisis they have entered. To avoid the wrath of God for their sinful ways, they must rededicate themselves to the same contract that guided the first two generations in New England. Abdication of their errand will have disastrous consequences. Proof of their impending doom, argues Wigglesworth, is everywhere to be found. Wigglesworth found a ready audience for his warnings. The immediate publication success of *Day of Doom* helped to codify an orthodox consensus of a Puritan errand in New England after Charles II returned to the throne in 1660. Thus, ironically, the Puritan revolution in England continued in no small way in America, and contributed to a nation-building discourse that influenced the American Revolution a century later. The original jeremiad warned Israel about its impending conquest and enslavement at the hands of Babylon's Nebuchadnezzar. The legacy of Wigglesworth's New England narrative of a backsliding nation manifests itself even centuries later as a mythic rationale for the Anglo Puritan colonization of North America.

A focus on the body in Lorna Dee Cervantes's poetry expands what Chicano/a scholars have noted generally: that *Emplumada* is inhabited by constellations of binary oppositions. As in Mora's writings, Cervantes's mestiza body is reproduced in her poetic rendering of her experiences as a binational subject. While this might come as no surprise, what is surprising is the extent to which "Uncle's First Rabbit" behaves within a jeremiad tradition. Perhaps even more so than Wigglesworth, Cervantes echoes the scriptural Jeremiah in attempting to forewarn her people of the dangers inherent in colonization. Specifically, this poem articulates the apocalyptic fate for Chicanas if the socialization and gendering of men continues to reinforce violence and misogyny as "essential" categories of masculinity. In place of the vengeful God of the Old Testament, Cervantes presents her uncle as a figure of patriarchal authority, whose own tortured past cripples him emotionally and makes him worthy of sympathy. Yet his internalized hatred of himself and his conversion of his own vulnerability into violence against the women he loves bankrupt the reader's capacity to care. Much like Wigglesworth's *Day of Doom*, this introductory poem encourages us to embrace the uncle's narrative as a colonized and racialized subject as allegory, and as allegory find in it a call to reform the past and check future calamity. Like Mora, Cervantes is intimately concerned with building her ethnic body/community, but Cervantes is also ever alert to patriarchal violence.

In contrast to Cervantes's secularized moral tale of female oppression, Wigglesworth's battle of vices and virtues is more obviously Christian in context:

1
Still was the night, Serene and Bright,
　　when all Men sleeping lay;
Calm was the season, and carnal reason
　　thought so 'twould last for ay.
Soul, take thine ease, let sorrow cease,
　　much good thou hast in store:
This was their Song, their Cups among,
　　the Evening before.[15]

Here the evil portrayed is called "carnal reason," because it is a kind of logic that finds security and satisfaction in the earthly, corporeal, and human imagination. Unlike Milton's Satan in *Paradise Lost*, Wigglesworth's sinners are not in contest with the Christian God. Rather, their collective crime is their complacency with regard to divine retribution. Wigglesworth makes clear that on "judgment day" those who have made a temple of their bodies are to be punished precisely through their bodies. In contrast, the elect and faithful will enjoy a spiritual union with God; they will inherit a superior body bereft of mortal temptations. In short, the moral is that no one knows when "judgment day" will arrive; therefore one must be constantly on guard against "carnal reason." The body, and its affinity for worldly connection, must be feared and restrained.

While *Day of Doom* is directed to a defined community, as is Wigglesworth's other jeremiad, *God's Controversy with New England* (1662), it also is written toward the individual reader's own meditation and mediation. The action of *Day of Doom* concerns a debate between the unregenerative, arguing against divine retribution, and Christ, championing the righteousness of God's scriptures. Jeffrey Hammond writes: "By whittling away at the presumptions of carnal reason until only faith in Christ and the Word remained, the *Day of Doom* provides Puritan readers with a verbal parallel to doomsday itself. The association of inner conviction in sin with the broader conviction of the damned at the Judgment encouraged the reader to seek the humiliation of the self that was so conspicuously absent in the doomsday sinners."[16] However, the poem has more than the "homiletic strategy" Hammond points out. Wigglesworth's personal writings in his diary provide a glimpse into how psychological and sexual components of his poetry encouraged an internalized "warfare" with the spiritual self. Indeed, it is Walter Hughes's contention that "this spiritual record, so private that parts of it were written in code, describes in scandalous detail the religious and sexual predicament that secretly inspired Wigglesworth's public poetry."[17]

Hughes's main argument identifies the atypical and ambivalent use of eroticism in Puritan poetry to locate the homoerotic. Accordingly, *The Day of Doom* represents Wigglesworth's projection of the story of Sodom "onto the world at large and then describing God's fiery punishment in terrifying detail" (111). By adapting the story of Sodom, Wigglesworth simultaneously attends to his own need to repress his sexual desires and ambivalences and asserts his perception of the needs of the Puritan community. This "terrifying detail," I argue, gets redirected against the literal body of the author/reader in order to render it chastened and resigned to an angry but ultimately merciful Christ.

Despite its injunctions against the flesh, Wigglesworth's jeremiad, like sermons throughout the seventeenth century, is deeply invested in representing the unregenerative body in its unbridled, lustful state. Kathleen Verduin explains that "fear of punishment, often unspeakable punishment, drives discussions of sexual offenses in Puritan literature, and the rhetoric regarding deviance is often exaggerated, even hyperbolic."[18] Such is the case with Wigglesworth's *Day of Doom*. According to Verduin, sins of the flesh were connected in Puritan theology with idolatry and paganism, and thus at odds with a Puritan devotion to scripture (230). She writes: "Of special import was St. Paul's teaching, in a verse that made Wigglesworth [in his diary] anxious: because of the idolatry of the heathen, 'God gave them up to uncleanness . . . God gave them up unto vile affections . . . God gave them over to a reprobate mind' " (Rom. 1:24–28) (229). Verduin's focus on Scripture is important, because, as she notes, Puritan clergy went to the Bible for examples that supported "their correlation of unchecked sexuality and divine retribution"; as in the story of Sodom, "shameless sensuality was a hallmark of worlds God had in anger destroyed" (228). Thus, through these unregenerative bodies, evidence of eroticism, sensuality, and human ingenuity is simultaneously identified, decried, and then properly punished to make way for Christ's second coming.

Of course, the whole import of Wigglesworth's jeremiad is the greater confidence that the Puritan colonies will not be destroyed and that a heavenly Eden awaits the elect. The reason for this lies in the depictions of

Christ that run the gamut from the vengeful God of the Old Testament to the shepherd of his flock in the New Testament. Hammond writes:

> In its characteristically Puritan manner of providing simultaneously the problem and the solution, of balancing the fear of hell with the anticipation of bliss, *The Day of Doom* sounded the dual theme of castigation and reaffirmation which Sacvan Bercovitch has identified as a central trait of the jeremiad. Devout readers would welcome—even cherish—the lessons of doomsday, since reproofs from the Word were in themselves evidence that God still cared and that salvation was still within reach. (63)

The trade-off for this optimism was twofold: advocacy of patriarchal authority as control and the affirmation of intolerance toward individuals, groups, or religious ideas that threatened Puritan orthodoxy.[19] Not surprisingly, Wigglesworth's poem reaffirms the need for control against humanity's innate depravity. By reinventing the patriarchal figure of Christ as vengeful against sinners but merciful to the faithful, Wigglesworth naturalized theological structures that gave temporal authority and license to fathers as heads of households and to magistrates as male heads of states, and finally he naturalized the abdication of the body for reasons of religious orthodoxy and community unity. The resulting proscriptions against the body and sexuality reified Puritan theology, thereby ensuring a male-centered religion and society.

The second consequence of this optimism was, and here I expand on Verduin's thesis (237), the tendency in Puritan society to scapegoat and persecute individuals, such as Anne Hutchinson, or groups, such as the Pequods or Quakers, in terms that set their bodies against the elect and more significantly against themselves. In *The Day of Doom*, the initial experience of the revelers in the first stanza gives way slowly but surely to their bodily and spiritual demise:

205
They wring their hands, their caitiff-hands
    and gnash their teeth for terrour;
They cry, they roar for anguish sore,
    and gnaw their tongues for horrour.

But get away without delay,
   Christ pitties not your cry:
Depart to Hell, there may you yell,
   and roar Eternally.

And as the unregenerative are cast down into hell, their psychic and bodily punishment increases accordingly:

209
With Iron bands they bind their hands,
   and cursed feet together,
And cast them all, both great and small,
   into that Lake for ever.
Where day and night, without respite,
   they wail, and cry, and howl
For tort'ring pain, which they sustain
   in Body and in Soul.

Finally, the punishment inflicted on them reaches a crescendo that is psychosexual in character:

210
For day and night, in their despight,
   their torments smoak ascendeth.
Their pain and grief have no relief,
   their anguish never endeth.
There must they ly, and never dy,
   though dying every day:
There must they dying ever ly,
   and not consume away.

While Wigglesworth's jeremiad holds out the promise that the sinful will be punished, it also conveys the sense that sin, evil, deviance from religious orthodoxy, and "unrestrained" sexuality can be identified anthropomorphically and thus duly punished by the pious. The jeremiad thus serves as a blueprint not only for individual salvation but community salvation. It reinforces the Puritan distinction between the elect and the damned, thereby sacrificing ritualistically the unregenerative to hellish punishment.

Socially and legally, as Anne Kibbey has argued, such allegorical and figurative punishment of the sinful underwrote the discourse of persecution of women, Quakers, and natives in the seventeenth century.[20] Conditioned linguistically by such texts as sermons, those who saw themselves as part of the elect, Kibbey argues, took it upon themselves to evidence God's power against the sinful and heathen as a way to prove their own piety and reify their political and theological positions of power in the community. Likewise, I argue, Wigglesworth commits in his jeremiad a ritualistic punishment and killing off of those elements of society—behavioral, intellectual, and cultural—he found antithetical to a Puritan faith. As a linguistic model for judgment day, it served notice for himself and others how to control and limit bodily and worldly temptations. Furthermore, he converted what was essentially a biblical narrative (that of Jeremiah), which advocated against the religious and political colonization of a nation, into a proto–nationalist narrative that affirmed the Puritan errand in America.[21] In looking to reform his society, as scholars have noted, Wigglesworth certainly captured a sentiment already prevalent in New England. The popularity of the poem—in England as well—attests not only to the wide acceptance of its theology and belief in judgment day, but, as I have shown, to the less articulated anxiety to control the body. It is through this latter narrative of the body as innately antithetical to the Puritan mission in New England that I will continue the second half of this comparison.

In his seminal study *The American Jeremiad,* Sacvan Bercovitch has argued for the "persistence of the Puritan jeremiad throughout the eighteenth and nineteenth centuries, in all forms of the literature, including the literature of westward expansion."[22] What attracted him to the jeremiad was his "learning of the prophetic history of America . . . that, despite its arbitrary territorial limits, could read its destiny in its landscape, and a population that, despite its bewildering mixture of race and creed, could believe in something called an American mission, and could invest that patent fiction with all the emotion, spiritual, and intellectual appeal of a religious quest" (11). For Bercovitch these believers in a latter–day American mission include such luminaries as Thomas Jefferson, Henry David Thoreau, and Martin Luther King, Jr. I agree that these individuals followed a tradition begun in the seventeenth century of forecasting the country's decline as a measure of its deviance from its "founding principles." Invariably, Bercovitch believes, these later jeremiads "joined lament and celebration in reaffirming America's mission" (11).

In addition, I argue that the jeremiad manifests itself in twentieth-century discourses that pit race, class, the body, and sexuality against the future of America's destiny. Its most recent manifestations have singled out people of color, the poor, legal and illegal immigrants, pro-choice advocates, and those ill with AIDS. In spite of historic differences, a discursive structure, descended from the jeremiad, remains in all prophecies of American doom. As in other ideologically deployed symbols of the nation, the jeremiad has been and can be manipulated to serve contradictory political ends.

Despite the jeremiad tradition's typical alignment with the status quo, this tradition surfaces in Lorna Dee Cervantes's poetry as a narrative of reform for the underprivileged. As in much Christian allegory, Cervantes's "Uncle's First Rabbit" depends upon the dialectical relationships between opposites. Juan Bruce-Novoa identifies these oppositions in Cervantes's poetry—men vs. women, ethnic identity vs. male dominance, racism vs. U.S. society—as, in general, coming from the influence of Carlos Castaneda's *The Teaching of Don Juan: A Yaqui Way of Knowledge* (1968). According to Bruce-Novoa, Cervantes "sees life as a struggle with the enemy/guide, incarnations of the spiritual forces in Nature that can destroy if not brought into harmony and control, but once mastered, help one reach fulfillment."[23] Yet each poem leaves open the possibility of continued struggle. For John F. Crawford, Cervantes's *Emplumada* poems propose binary oppositions, "in which each new stage of dialectical development leads to a new proposition awaiting similar testing in the future."[24] Taken together, Bruce-Novoa and Crawford describe the formal and rhetorical structure of a modern confessional poem, but one that has its American roots in jeremiads such as Wigglesworth's. The importance of this jeremiad connection lies in the depiction of the mind and soul as either a heaven or hell depending on the symbolic value of the body. As in *Day of Doom*, it entails a narrative of the future, which is at once individual and communal, as well as regional and national. In short, Cervantes channels all that she sees as wrong with Chicano/a life in the United States through Uncle's body; it is here that her moral starts.

In "Uncle's First Rabbit," Cervantes takes advantage of the explicit hell vs. heaven dichotomy in the jeremiad to carve out a linguistic space for a better world for women. Chicana critic Marta Sánchez considers the testing of such utopian visions in the context of Cervantes's dual and sometimes conflicting poetic impulses: to write poetry that can envision a better life, a desirable utopia, as well as to vent revolutionary anger at the world's social problems.[25] This dualism is primarily concerned with depictions of patriarchal life in the United States. Bruce-Novoa writes: "Cervantes defines her terms through poems about male/female struggle within the context of class and cultural struggle. Men are trained to exploit their environment, which leads them to abuse women, a situation that forces women to become self-reliant" (3097). Indeed, in her much anthologized poem "Beneath the Shadow of the Freeway," Cervantes succeeds in holding back the menacing terrors of patriarchy and female silence. Critics largely agree that in this poem Cervantes proposes female solidarity and independence in the face of male violence, abandonment, and betrayal. Yet as "Beneath the Shadow of the Freeway" signals, heterosexual love in the end is possible as long as the speaker trusts what she has built with her own hands. How stable these personal constructions will ultimately be both plagues these hard-won resolutions and points to an overriding faith in some future imperious construction.

But how this poem enacts this confidence is conditioned initially by male-on-female violence in the volume's first poem, "Uncle's First Rabbit." Here the prospect of female/male resolution is far from certain. As Marta Sánchez writes: "The male has two options: to stay or leave. For the woman, it will be better if he leaves, for if he stays he will not change his [violent and misogynist] behavior. Yet he will not leave. The decision is up to the man for the women are completely passive and silent" (119). Sánchez's view is that Cervantes does not offer a real logic to her uncle's violence, except perhaps as an illustration of how male violence is interiorized and visited on women as part of a socially sanctioned ritual of partial cathartic relief (118). Viewed in light of a jeremiad tradition, the inarticulate logic serves notice that reason and rationality have been lost to a crisis that the present moment cannot fathom. The only thing left is to chronicle what has been lost and what will be further lost to invisible but real spiritual and political forces.

Note how in the first stanza phallocentrism defines masculinity as paternal obedience, violence, and familial responsibilities:

He was a good boy,
making his way through
the Santa Barbara pines,
sighting the blast of fluff
as he leveled the rifle,
and the terrible singing began.
He was ten years old,
hunting my grandpa's supper.
He had dreamed of running,
shouldering the rifle to town,
selling it, and taking the next
train out.[26]

Cervantes significantly singles out her uncle as the representative "everyman" of her female experience. He is the mestizo descendant of the Spanish and local Indians. He hunts through a land that was usurped and Christianized under the aegis of the Santa Barbara Roman Catholic mission. Its pastoral beginning is immediately marred by unredeeming violence. The uncle's pre–Columbian connection with the landscape is nowhere to be found. Equally lost is his own volition in this hunt. The hunt does not serve him. Rather, the uncle is the child providing food for a conspicuously absent father. The derelict father figure serves as a model for abandoning one's family; his father's dereliction encourages him to take the next train out, to take a chance on the promises of American capitalism the train has come to symbolize. But the uncle cannot leave. The psychic drama, combined with his ethnic identity, makes him a slave to his own fear and hatred of his father and ties him spatially to the scene of his family's tragedy.

What becomes apparent in the following lines is that the uncle's sanity begins to unravel as a direct result of not enacting his dreams, not taking that train out. The uncle's hunting of the rabbit begins the "terrible singing" that will haunt him for the rest of his life. From here on, he will constantly wage a battle with himself, between being "a good boy" and acknowledging his anger against his father:

Fifty years
have passed and he still hears
that rabbit "just like a baby."

He remembers how the rabbit
stopped keening under the butt
of his rifle, how he brought
it home with tears streaming
down his blood soaked jacket.
"That bastard. That bastard."
He cried all night and the week
after, remembering that voice
like his dead baby sister's,
remembering his father's drunken
kicking that had pushed her
into birth. She had a voice
like that, growing faint
at its end; his mother rocking,
softly, keening. He dreamed
of running, running
the bastard out of his life.
He would forget them, run down
the hill, leave his mother's
silent waters, and the sounds
of beating night after night.

The second stanza makes clear the basis for the uncle's childhood trauma: an abusive and alcoholic father responsible for the premature birth and death of his sister and the chronic battering of his mother. The moral tale that emerges is not only about the disintegration of her uncle but about the near inescapable male–on–female violence that is her and her aunt's legacy as Chicanas.

The third stanza chronicles the uncle's attempt to leave his family by entering the military during World War II. The uncle, like thousands of Mexican Americans of his generation, answered the national call for defense of the United States by taking up arms against the Axis powers. As mentioned earlier in this chapter, many Mexican American men and women joined the war effort believing that their patriotism would be rewarded with a recognition of their American citizenry. When this recognition was less than forthcoming, the war came to symbolize their continued second–class status in the United States:

When war came,
he took the man's vow. He was
finally leaving and taking
the bastard's last bloodline
with him. At war's end, he could
still hear her, her soft
body stiffening under water
like a shark's. The color
of the water, darkening, soakening,
as he clung to what was left
of a ship's gun. Ten long hours
off the coast of Okinawa, he sang
so he wouldn't hear them.
He pounded their voices out
of his head, and awakened
to find himself slugging the bloodied
face of his wife.

The death wish the uncle took with him to the war never materialized. Instead, his survival from a sinking ship added to the psychic wounds already endured. The sounds of his dying shipmates are associated with his "mother's silent waters," the passive tears cried in response to his father's physical abuse of her. These tears are shed in such volume that they change his mother's "soft body" into one that is stiff like shark's skin under water. These two memories are subsumed under a history of voices that denote dying: from the keening of the rabbit to the death throes of the sailors. These voices reemerge later in the uncle's battering of his own wife. The war he hoped would sever his father's legacy has instead revisited him in a fury of combat–fatigue syndrome and a survivor's complex.

His mock battle with his internalized demons, ghostly voices that no doubt blame him for their demise and for the killing of the rabbit, has real–life consequences. Unlike Wigglesworth, Cervantes does not offer a transcendent universe for the elect. Her jeremiad is about attending to the cultural, political, and gendered forces that have made the uncle's life possible and her aunt's impossible. In the last stanza, Cervantes is particularly clear that that other uncle, Uncle Sam, has not fulfilled his promises to either the uncle or his family:

Fifty years
have passed and he has not run
the way he dreamed. The Paradise
pines shadow the bleak hills
to his home. His hunting hounds,
dead now. His father, long dead.
His wife, dying, hacking in the bed
she has not let him enter for the last
thirty years. He stands looking,
he mouths the words, "Die you bitch.
I'll live to watch you die." He turns,
entering their moss-soft livingroom.
He watches out the picture window
and remembers running: how he'll
take the new pickup to town, sell it,
and get the next train out.

Cervantes's final picture of Uncle is emblematic of the social conditions that make up contemporary life for Chicanos and Chicanas in the 1970s. "The Paradise pines" of a wealthier neighborhood in Santa Barbara, like the new pickup, mask the different levels of poverty operative in the uncle's final phase of life. The promise of middle-class life in America is still elusive; it can offer a token here and there in the shape of material gain like a picture window, but it is stingy about bestowing a legitimate social identity; furthermore, it is a promise that perversely fuels a hostility toward one's own kind. While there is no way to read away the poem's indictment of the uncle's misogyny and violence–the poem holds him accountable for his actions–he remains a tragic figure. Cervantes leaves him running in his mind, seeking an escape, searching for meaning somewhere, on a train that by the 1970s probably no longer runs. This futility of effort signals the end of Cervantes's first poem in her first published volume of poems.

While this futility defines Uncle's life and certainly shapes the life of the speaker's aunt, the poem functions to disclaim the oppressive circularity entrapping this generation of Mexican Americans. By finishing the biography of Uncle, the speaker breaks from the most difficult of roles in patriarchy: that of the uncomplaining, dutiful daughter who sacrifices her life to her father's will, even in madness. This poem challenges all women not to embrace Cordelia's example, not to accept the dystopia that is the legacy of Shakespeare's Lear. The poem does not end with tragic, noble death. Instead, the silence by the speaker is answered by the myriad of female voices and lives in the poems that follow. In them, Chicanas survive and thrive in their relationships with the state and men. What emerges after "Uncle's First Rabbit" is a patchwork vision of a better life for Chicanas. Even when, as in "Lots: I," the choice is between rape and death, the protagonists of this new vision prefer wrestling with the enemy.[27] The overall challenge these poems present is the belief that Chicanas will have to help themselves long before anyone else will. The utopia painted is of the here and now. Unlike Wigglesworth's jeremiad, and latter-day versions like Allan Bloom's *Closing of the American Mind*, judgment day has already come and gone for millions of U.S. citizens. It's the second coming of more of the same that they're trying to avoid.

Edward Taylor and Gary Soto: Shaping Masculinity through Community

I turn, for my last comparison, to a wholly twentieth-century phenomenon. I take up Edward Taylor and compare him to Gary Soto. My intent in the previous two examples was to offer comparisons that explained the place of Puritanism in contemporary Chicano/a poetry and to illustrate how Chicano/a poetry reacts to the dominant Puritan imaginary. Here, at the end of this chapter and book, I take up a Chicano poet more clearly identified within an Anglo American confessional tradition.[28] My purpose is twofold: One, I argue for a reading of Soto that places him more in the center of an American poetic tradition. That is, I read Soto as fulfilling one of the major criteria of twentieth-century American confessional poetry: embracing the poetics of displacement. Second, by comparing Soto to Taylor, we see how the poetics of displacement has encouraged American male poets to appropriate the feminine to bridge the gap between the personal and public, the individual and community, and finally community and nation.

There are several literary trends afoot in the 1950s and early 1960s that connect Gary Soto, albeit indirectly, with this Puritan poet. Winner of several national awards, including the Academy of American Poets Prize (1975) and the American Book Award from the Before Columbus

Foundation (1985), Soto has always insisted, when asked, that he had two very decisive influences. One was taking a class at Fresno State with poet Philip Levine, and the other was Donald M. Allen's 1960 anthology *The New American Poetry: 1945–1960.*[29] Soto's relationship to canonical poets, like Edward Taylor, can thus be traced first through poetic mentoring and then through his own self-education.

In 1993, Levine wrote about his days at the Iowa Writers' Workshop in the early 1950s where he was taught by Robert Lowell and eventually mentored by John Berryman.[30] In addition to his own depictions of working–class Americans, Levine brought to Soto much he learned from Lowell and especially Berryman.[31] In both cases, a New England tradition figured greatly. Lowell came from a literary New England family whose past members included James Russell Lowell and Amy Lowell. Berryman thought the Puritan influence mattered enough to write "Homage to Mistress Bradstreet," a poem that became critically important to his career.

A second line of poets who influenced Soto emerge from Allen's anthology: Charles Olson, Denise Levertov, Robert Creeley, Jack Kerouac, Allen Ginsberg, Frank O'Hara, John Ashbery, Gary Snyder, and the list goes on. What's notable is Donald Allen's account of this generation of poets. He sees a poetic evolution stretching from modernists such as William Carlos Williams, Ezra Pound, H.D., e. e. cummings, Marianne Moore, and Wallace Stevens to a second generation that includes Elizabeth Bishop, Edwin Denby, Robert Lowell, Kenneth Rexroth, and Louis Zukofsky. All leading to what he identifies as the present generation of poets who have followed "the practice and precepts of Ezra Pound and William Carlos Williams [and] built on their achievements and gone on to evolve new conceptions of the poem."[32] Given Allen's reading of these poets and Soto's regard for this anthology, it is hard to imagine that Soto does not see himself within this evolving poetic tradition, even if he also might see himself as part of the Chicano/a Renaissance. In fact his initial reviewers read him in just such a national (not Chicano/a) literary context.

Born and raised in Fresno, California, the agricultural center of the San Joaquín Valley, Soto was undoubtedly influenced by the long presence of the UFW in the region. His first published volume of poetry, *The Elements of San Joaquin* (1977), reflects a social and political awareness of the migrant worker's daily struggle. Chicano/a critics such as Juan

Bruce–Novoa and Julian Olivares have observed that Soto's poetry reminds one of T. S. Eliot's *The Wasteland*. Indeed, this collection of poems depicts an apocalyptic vision of the universe, but with a signature Soto twist. Patricia de la Fuente writes: "Recurring images of loss, disintegration, decadence, demolition, solitude, terror and death create a desolate landscape in which the voice of the narrator is that of a passive, impotent observer, helplessly caught up in the inexorable destruction of human ties. Within this seemingly hopeless, profound grey world of Soto's poem, however, occasional affirmative images introduce muted, contrapuntual notes of something akin to hope."[33] Perhaps not so oddly after all, de la Fuente's critical language here suggests a bridge to Edward Taylor. For what has Taylor's poetry come to signify in the twentieth century but the attempt to give shape to a spiritual landscape always threatened from the outside by the figure of sin and human frailties? Here I should pause to recall that like T. S. Eliot, Edward Taylor's poetry and its critical significance is a twentieth–century creation. Thomas H. Johnson discovered Taylor's largely unread poetry in manuscript form at the Yale library, and only through his critical efforts was Taylor linked with metaphysical poets such as John Donne, who, I should also note, was brought back into critical favor by T. S. Eliot himself. As in Soto, Taylor's poetry, especially his preparatory meditations, often takes the potentiality of irreparable loss, in this case uncertainty over his electness as a Puritan saint, to its most poignant measure, before he retrieves loss through a metaphorical twist of language. Soto and Taylor are of course talking about different landscapes, but just as one can talk of Eliot and Taylor as stemming from similar traditions, one can talk of Soto and Taylor as occupying different but similar stances as poets in the New World.

This is especially true if we highlight one of the categories of analysis that has shaped American criticism of poetry by male writers in the twentieth century. Again, T. S. Eliot plays a role, as the premiere poet/critic of the modernist period. As Mutlu Blasing has argued, Eliot's "early work attests to a profound national, historical, and literary displacement, which would be 'corrected' only by his becoming the archetype of belonging—his somewhat anachronistic conversion to become a royalist, Anglo–Catholic, and classicist."[34] This displacement, argues Blasing, ironically identifies Eliot as American: "Eliot's 'fit' is always [as] a 'misfit,' whether in American, English, or European traditions. A poem like *The*

Waste Land, however un–American William Carlos Williams and others may have considered it, could not have been written by a legitimate heir to the English poetic tradition: it is the work of a poet overwhelmed by a past to which he has a less than direct connection" (17). Here, I would gloss what Blasing has already identified, that there is a cultural/critical perspective endemic not only to American male poets but to twentieth–century critics themselves. The old nineteenth–century argument that American writers were like orphans in search of their literary parents resolves itself in the acceptance of the poet as a self–made thing–in the reverence for a poetic parthenogenesis that transforms the poet into his own parent and child. This is certainly the tradition that Walt Whitman inaugurates in "Song of Myself." But Whitman's confidence in the stability of his "I" is an ideal harder and harder to achieve in the twentieth century. And hence critics, having less confidence, could never believe in the transformation from orphan to his own parent; the act of conversion itself attested to an extra–natural need to rectify what was deemed un–natural. Displacement, alienation, dislocation are constantly in need of renegotiation especially when the past looms as an irretrievable loss or unattainable goal, and when, as in the case of Eliot, it involves claiming a national identity that corresponds with a body of literary traditions.

Within this twentieth–century critical tradition, one can easily find in Soto and Taylor displacements and acts of conversion that have a social and historical significance because they occur in the New World. In both cases, a sense of historical displacement is both aggravated and relieved in their relationships with their respective communities. Taylor finds in New England a Puritan orthodoxy lately out of political fashion in England; unfortunately for him, this orthodoxy itself survives on the very edge of English colonialism. The presence of the "wilderness" and its natives dislocates his Puritan identity even as it sharpens a religious and ideological resolve. In comparison, Soto operates in a twofold historical displacement: as a descendant of those "natives" Taylor feared and repudiated, and as the inheritor of two colonial enterprises, one Spanish Mexican and the other Anglo Puritan. Thus, his poetry foregrounds a social and cultural experience that is the outcome of an intersection of these colonial histories. Soto's ethnic identity depends precariously upon the barrio's dual cultural significance: one, as the Spanish word for neighborhood, and two, as a linguistic marker for poverty in the United States. This dual significance in turn borders on the middle–class benefits that American culture does not readily extend to people of color. Soto's resolution of his various displacements is to adapt a model of poetic conversion that has cultural and political legitimacy in U.S. culture, thereby toying poetically with the various "borders" that constitute his subjectivity: Mexican/American, educated/uneducated, working-class subject/university professor. All the while, he maintains his ethnic identity by belonging to a community that he proudly claims. And this leads us back to Taylor, who becomes in twentieth-century American criticism the archetypal example of the displaced American poet/prophet, the poet from the wilderness, the prophet who is least known in his own town.

This connection between Soto and Taylor is found, in particular, in their gendered relationships to cultural and social institutions. Their privileges as men often mitigate the more uncertain aspects of their different subject positions, Taylor as a Puritan minister after a failed Puritan revolution, and Soto as a poet of color in the United States from a working-class background. In both cases, the certainty of their maleness grounds their otherwise discontinuous subject positions in their respective communities. In short, their reliance on maleness as an implicit trope negotiates the various displacements they are struggling to control. Hence, it is possible to read in their poetry instances when these poets commit themselves to some kind of poetic psychic conversion by momentarily releasing the forces of displacement, only to have those forces symbolically contained in favor of achieving a sense of belonging to a community larger than oneself.

To explore how this trope might exist culturally and how it might deploy itself as means of authenticating an individual or community, consider Gary Soto's "Black Hair," from his 1985 volume of that title. In this poem, the speaker recounts a critical childhood experience that functioned as the occasion for experiencing pride in his ethnic community. Recently fatherless, the young speaker hero-worships Hector Moreno—an accomplished baseball player at the local park. A baseball game comes to symbolize a rare moment when his racially marked community affirms its participation in the game as a positive link to cultural and social forces beyond the barrio. What Soto recounts from his childhood are not only the personal forces that drove him to the baseball diamond but also the communal impulse to identify one another, on and off the field, as familial members, as *authentic* within the bounds of the bilingual cultural matrix, the barrio. Finally, because baseball deseg-regated itself to admit athletes of color from the 1940s on, it emerges as one of the few cultural institutions that allow the expression of ethnic/racial pride within a national context.

The speaker comes to identify himself by his growing appreciation of the familiarity that marks the barrio community in the bleachers, a familiarity that emerges outward and against the discontinuities and inequalities leveled at the speaker and the Mexican American commu-nity to type them as necessarily different. This cultural "othering" is conducted and maintained through the overwhelming presence of a hegemonic discourse that does its best to deny a marginalized commu-nity the means of self-representation. To overcome this hegemonic force, the speaker must first confirm his own marginalization and then elevate the social status of a member of his raza. Through this apotheosis, he reclaims a previously silenced but authentic ontology that, in addition, projects itself onto "the arms of brown people" (l. 30).

By contrast, in Edward Taylor's "Huswifery" we see the interesting intersection of this trope of maleness with the trope of marriage. Though not specifically about marriage, the poem plays off the socially con-structed duty of housewife, in particular the spinning of cloth, which is the major conceit of the poem. Historian Laurel Ulrich defines the role of housewife in the following manner: "A *housewife* polished female spe-cialties. Her role was defined by a space (a house and its surrounding yards), a set of tasks (cooking, washing, sewing, milking, spinning, clean-ing, gardening), and a limited authority (the internal economy of a fam-ily)."[35] In using the term of huswifery Taylor invokes the role of the wife as analogous to his community position as Puritan minister. What the analogy affords him is a "homely" comparison to his own duties. As both representative of the congregation and "shepherd" to his "flock," he stands in a range of gender figurations from the feminine to masculine. He calls attention to both his status as "a bride of Christ" and as Christ-like. In the course of the poem, then, his initial identity with huswifery, which associates him with the feminine icon of a spinning wheel, will give way to adopting the masculine robes of Christ, which signify his entry into a priestly vocation.

Taylor accomplishes this movement to a masculinized figure by re-defining the various mechanical parts used in making cloth. Through supplication, he first asks to be made into "thy Spin[n]ing Wheele compleat" (l. 1).[36] Having transformed himself figuratively into a feminine icon, Taylor allows himself to be used by the male-gendered Lord. And thus the complete transformation of Taylor is ensured:

Thy Holy Worde my Distaff make for mee.
Make mine Affections thy Swift Flyers neate,
And make my Soule thy holy Spoole to bee.
My conversation make to be thy Reele,
And reele the yarn thereon spun of thy Wheele.
(ll. 2–6)

What also is ensured is a dual gender position of the Lord to Taylor. In a poem that seeks affirmation of his ministerial authority, Taylor succeeds in part by leveling the relative distance between divinity and humanity. Once the speaker is made into a spinning wheel, the Lord can work through the instrument that he has endowed with his own grace. By association, the Lord spins cloth from a feminine position. In a maternal sense, Taylor is reconceived; his affections, soul, and conversation, are quickly metamorphosed into the finished product of the yarn. The only gender that exists at this moment is feminine, which is more completely associated with human and divine conception.

Soto begins his conversion process by acknowledging the social conditions of his childhood. He titles his poem "Black Hair" to mark the Anglo cultural distinction given to his person via his body. He is not white; he is not blonde; he is not blue-eyed. Nevertheless, because he is given that negative representation, Soto is able to deconstruct it precisely at the place it most inaccurately reflects his experience: "At eight I was brilliant with my body" (l. 1).[37] Despite the absence of a father whose "face no longer / [Hangs] over the table or our sleep" (ll. 17–18) and the nearly indecipherable presence of a mother whose loss and pain translates into "the terror of mouths / Twisting hurt by butter knives" (ll. 19–20), this is a poem of celebration, of a victory over those social, economic, and political forces that deny marginal experience as "authentic." As if to awaken hegemonic discourse from its self-induced delusion of grandeur, the speaker reiterates: "In the bleachers I was brilliant with my body" (l. 21).

Both the cultural "othering" of the ethnic body and the potential escape from the marginalization of that body are articulated when the speaker acknowledges this dualism:

> I came here because I was Mexican, a stick
> Of brown light in love with those
> Who could do it–the triple and hard slide,
> The gloves eating balls into double plays.
> What could I do with 50 pounds, my shyness,
> My black torch of hair, about to go out?
> (ll. 11–16)

Soto's focus on the body is dual: it is the means by which the athletic body of Hector Moreno, the subject of the speaker's hero worship, can appropriate and control the cultural symbolism of playing "America's oldest pastime," and it is the means by which the young child at eight can access the nationalism and egalitarianism promoted through baseball cards and then appropriate it, through the prowess of Hector Moreno, for himself. In short, the speaker reveals how as a child he used his own relatively negated body as a vehicle for communal approval. In choral fashion, he joined the "presence of white shirts" (l. 23)–the other Mexican children, identified here economically through the T-shirts that their parents or guardians can afford–as they wave and stomp in adoration of Hector's performance.

Underlying this transformation of the speaker's child self is the relatively unproblematized alignment of the baseball diamond with the pastoral. Despite the diamond's manicured and geometric look, baseball has come to symbolize a "natural" escape from the increasingly industrialized and mechanized landscape of American capitalism. Baseball's lore of heroic players and statistics masks what otherwise is a redemptive playing surface where feminine attributes associated with the natural world can be appropriated to ease masculine anxieties about the marketplace. By extension, it is also a "playing surface" where, in this country's uneven racial politics, a select number of minorities have made inroads into mainstream society and economic power. For minority and nonminority alike, baseball embodies the American Dream. Thus, baseball holds out the promise of a simpler Edenic America, where heroic transformations occur within a celebration of malehood as nationhood, and vice versa.

In "Huswifery," the feminine world of nature/domesticity also provides a space for individual transformation. That this transformation must first trace out its alliance to feminine creativity through spinning cloth signals the importance of the trope of the feminine in the conversion of the unregenerative. Huswifery, understood here as the continuous renewal of the domestic realm, stands as an experience figuratively closer to an act of grace than any male activity, except perhaps for the role of priest and prophet. When compared to Soto's use of a baseball field, Taylor's appropriation of the feminine seems more dramatic, perhaps because there is no public field/discourse in Taylor's time that so willingly associates the regenerative processes of nature with male activity. This lack of a public field of experience where rebirth and masculinity are both literally and figuratively played out is also perhaps the reason Taylor's poem moves toward the acceptance of the priestly robes, leaving in its wake a discarded collection of feminine icons; no longer needed, they are once again relegated to inferior status.

Interestingly, once the cloth is endowed with "Understanding, Will, / Affections, Judgment, Conscience, Memory" (ll. 13–14), the poem quickly ends its feminine affiliations; and with that severance, the poetic voice that was once a spinning wheel, and then a loom, now becomes a public voice:

My Words and Actions, that their shine may fill
My wayes with glory and thee glorify.
Then mine apparell shall display before yee
That I am Cloathd in Holy robes for glory.
(ll. 15–18)

Instead of being an instrument in the hands of the Lord, the cloth is now liberated and independent. The creativity of the product speaks its own words and acts from its own volition, and because it is a product of the Lord it can only speak and act in recognition of its creator. But the birth of this spiritual identity is no longer gendered feminine, nor is the Lord positioned anymore as housewife. "Cloathd in Holy robes," the speaker is ready to commence a priestly vocation that defines itself as male and enters the world through public words and actions.

There's no less of a symbolic masculine reentry into the public in "Black Hair," though it is significantly different. Soto's child speaker has no "office" or "vocation" to assume once the anguish of metaphysics is resolved. If Taylor lacks Soto's public field of the masculine and feminine, Soto's speaker lacks the cultural ability to assume the robes of social importance without fear of racial discrimination and economic reprisal. What in Taylor's poem occurs privately, as an affirmation of his public role as minister, occurs publicly in Soto's poem: "The game before us was more than baseball" (ll. 6). It is a "game" to affirm the private dignity of ethnic solidarity that was so infrequently enjoyed in the racially segregated years of the 1950s and early 1960s.

Baseball as an American cultural institution is to Soto what Puritan theology and history in New England is to Taylor. Each is an institution infused with all the presence and force of America's political documents and predicated on a set of definable values, as well as a discourse for the deployment of those values. The mythological dimensions of baseball parallel and intersect with the mythic proportions of America as the "land of the free, home of the brave." How appropriate then that the local icon is named Hector Moreno. He is both reminiscent of the Trojan hero Hector and a linguistic sign for a race of people–*moreno* is Spanish for brown. If for Taylor the trope of marriage and domesticity provided the ground for his priestly transformation, for Soto baseball provides a heroic field that not only consolidates ethnic solidarity but provides the means to social transformation. Baseball's appropriation by the Hector Morenos of the barrios signals not a simple assimilation, but a masterful wielding of a game/discourse that has the potential to change the nationalist narrative baseball represents and produces.

Given what we know of Taylor's relationship to his poetry, it should not surprise us that "Huswifery" prepares him to be a minister. Indeed, we can see how this poem functions very similarly to poems that are more obviously about his doubts before a sermon–the main motivation behind his sacred meditations. What is of interest, though, are the final attributes that irrevocably gender the speaker. Until the last stanza, the feminine figuration of the Lord and speaker stand equally for a poet of either gender. But the series of attributes–"Understanding, Will, / Affections, Judgment, Conscience, Memory"–can only be associated with ministers, because they actually refer to concepts crucial to Puritan preaching.[38] That these attributes are gendered male is certain and consequential. In an otherwise feminized realm, they "enter" in a phallic manner, displacing feminine icons that have sewn the robe. In fact, the gendered and priestly quality of these attributes is understood to have entered the very fabric of the cloth. And in the poem's final transformation, the robe figures not only the priestly vocation of the speaker but his new masculinized authority to reveal God's glory. By contrast, the feminine realm that made the robe possible cannot participate in this public vocation. The priestly role is vehemently reserved for men. As the controversy surrounding Anne Hutchinson shows, feminine incursions into preaching in the seventeenth century were widely, even brutally, discouraged.

"Huswifery" demonstrates how gender could be appropriated by theology and ministers such as Taylor to serve some spiritual end. By the same token, it illustrates how gender, in the service of spiritual matters, could have a real impact on the status of an individual. By the end of the poem, Taylor is confirmed both as a minister and as a male; a great deal of social entitlement is collapsed into this moment. Nevertheless, in spite of itself, Taylor's poem attests to the currency and affirmation of the feminine in a Puritan culture. To be a regenerative Puritan woman entitled such an individual to a social standing and respect rarely found elsewhere. The choice of huswifery by a male minister to semiotically center his poem might be an indication of the favored social place of women with regard to theological issues. Except for the last stanza, the poem in fact approves of "feminine" activity in the service of religion. It would not be unusual—given such affirmation and the fact that Puritan theology promoted a spiritual equality among the sexes—for a woman to eventually see herself as conducting her life in a ministerial manner.

In comparison to Taylor, Soto reinvests in Hector Moreno what the speaker–as–child once sought in the deck of baseball cards: an identity commensurate with his male experience in the 1950s and early 1960s via the pastoral/feminine realm of baseball:

> It was a figure—Hector Moreno
> Quick and hard with turned muscles,
> His crouch the one I assumed before an altar
> Of worn baseball cards, in my room.
> (ll. 7–10)

No longer satisfied with the cultural heroes bequeathed to him by hegemonic discourse, he demotes the worn cards and prefers the living exemplum of Hector Moreno. He assumes the "crouch"; he mimics the readiness of Hector to play the game; he vicariously appropriates the institution and remakes it into his own. Reversing the Catholic rite of transubstantiation, where bread and wine are transformed into the body and blood of Jesus Christ, the child rejects the deification of those other cards in favor of, in this context, the more pagan attributes of this Hector. This Hector stands outside the usual constraints of hegemonic discourse, and is therefore a more appropriate model for resistance and bilingual cultural identity. And because this act of iconoclasm, the fracturing of hegemonic discourse, occurs in the privacy of his own room, the child is better able to internalize the liberating experience of creating and controlling the production of a representation—here an ironic and iconoclastic shaping of a playground member as icon—that speaks to him as individual and, as we already seen, as a member of a community.

In the final lines, Soto reiterates this liberating experience by elevating this figure, Hector Moreno, to the position of a trope, whereby the whole community can possess it:

> When Hector lined balls into deep
> Center, in my mind I rounded the bases
> With him, my faced flared, my hair lifting
> Beautifully, because we were coming home
> To the arms of brown people.
> (ll. 26–30)

Through the phrase "in my mind I," the speaker reverses the transference that occurred in the first stanza; instead of assuming the "crouch"–momentarily substituting his subjectivity for Hector's public and performative figure–he transports himself into the body of Hector–"With him, my face flared, my hair lifting"; Hector ceases to be only Hector Moreno. In the act of stomping and waving–public signs of affection and celebration–Soto locates this reconfiguration of bodies and selves in the most liberating, as well as incarcerating, of all "places," the imagination. When Hector lines balls deep into center field, he not only hits successfully on the baseball diamond, he also breaches profoundly into the maturation of the child, and, by extension, the social formation of the community of youths in the bleachers. The child can thus imagine a self freed from the constraints of his personal family history and liberated from the negation of hegemonic discourse.

From the striking athletic figure that Hector assumes on the field to the literary figure of the Trojan Hector, Soto turns this "figure" further by expanding its perimeters to be inclusive of a systemic signification that binds the barrio not in denial of but beyond race, ethnicity, and class. As the child/Hector rounds the bases, the position of the speaker shifts from "I" to "we." Thus, past and present are conjoined; this "we" includes the child at eight, the older speaker of the poem, Gary Soto as poet, the barrio, perhaps finally all readers who identify with "coming home." Having started with the *familiar difference* that marked the child as a social construction of the barrio and that allowed for the hero worship of Hector Moreno, Soto modifies this trope, this systemic signification, so that it is more reassuring, more comforting, and culturally more responsive. A new trope emerges, "because we were coming home / To the arms of brown people." Basically orphaned, the child finds a home in the larger context of the barrio. Thus, the trope of home, which shapes the language and hence culture of the barrio, nurtures an ontology located in and expressive through community; and in this manner, the trope of home as barrio conditions his historic and epistemological grasp of the world. Finally at the end, the speaker/child is ready to embody his subjectivity in the "real" world and, like Taylor's speaker, reenters the public with a renewed confidence in himself to mediate between the personal and communal.

In closing, let me say that what I find most exciting about this kind of comparative study is the possibility of making old things seem new and new things seem old. As the Taylor/Soto comparison reveals, confidence in the self and one's people, like confidence in the nation as a whole, is the product of narratives that seek not only hope but pride. I have focused on literary binationalism to advance our understanding of Chicano/a writers as late twentieth-century participants in and producers of U.S. literary culture. That the Puritan myth of origins survives today should no longer surprise us. What is a surprise is how it survives, changed and adapted by the non-Puritan descendants of this country. With the right kind of binoculars, to borrow Alberto Ríos's metaphor, one can find John Winthrop's Boston alongside Rolando Hinojosa's Klail City, or Gloria Anzaldúa's borderlands alongside Emily Dickinson's "Tell all the Truth but tell it slant–," or even John F. Kennedy's Camelot alongside Cesar Chávez's Delano.

Afterword

When I first came to Yale to study American literature in 1973, I knew very little about America. I was nurtured in the rhetoric of the U.S.-Mexico borderlands, what Américo Paredes called the liminal spaces of "Greater Mexico." . . . Nothing in my background prepared me for my initial encounter with the other America—a secular nation living like a dream on the back of a tiger. . . . I was quickly immersed in the foundational myths of the Puritan fathers, evident everywhere around me at the Old Campus, from its neogothic buildings named after dissenters like Jonathan Edwards to the crunchy "literary criticism" practices taught me in undergraduate tutorials and seminars. Beyond the walled-in panopticon of the Old Campus was something called the "New England way." To see this New England America as a fantasmatics was to historicize my own hybrid identifications.

—José David Saldívar,
"Tracking English and American Literary Criticism"

Now at the end, I more clearly understand why Tomás Rivera's "When We Arrive" belongs alongside John Winthrop's "A Model of Christian Charity" (1630). Reading them together, one can see how Winthrop's social compact, written and delivered aboard the *Arbella* on its way to the New World, resonates for Rivera in imagining where migrant workers fit in the cultural rituals of America the beautiful. Whereas Winthrop gave liturgical and legal language to his community's future, Rivera notes by contrast how far and selectively the promise of America has traveled. Nevertheless, the plentitude of broken-down trucks, broken dreams, and lost loves does not, according to Rivera, bar his migrant workers from a better future. The future, however rocky, is still theirs, and their social compact is their faith in perseverance, courage, and love of children. Rivera, like Winthrop before him, articulates the unvoiced but much desired likelihood that this immigrant community will come into its own–it's just a matter of time.

In the preceding chapters, I have tried to shape a literary history with a binational character. I have tried to answer a question written in desire–when we arrive–a desire that is really about belonging. This belonging means different things to different people. For me, it has meant the opportunity to feel the weight of history and literature and the need to convert it into a story full of the presence of Mexican Americans, Chicanos y Chicanas. I admit having written myself into this story as well–full of "hybrid identifications" that are both product and process of having explored the divisions between and the borders of my being Mexican and American, student and scholar in this time in history.

Like José David Saldívar, I was an undergraduate at Yale University, but in the early 1980s. My experiences there were shaped by growing up, not in agricultural South Texas, but in urban Houston, and by the election of Ronald Reagan in November 1980. My own "first contact" with Puritan America occurred, coincidentally, on my first Thanksgiving in New England. My roommate's father, something of a local historian, thought I might like to visit the ancestral home of Stephen F. Austin, Sr.– the major architect of the Anglo colonization of Texas in the 1830s. Austin's home in Durham, Connecticut, was a shock to my system. I had traveled so far from home only to find myself culturally hailed as a native son by the legacy of an Anglo Puritan colonialism, albeit a Mexican Texan. This bizarre moment at nineteen years of age, and many others since then, shaped me as an intellectual and shaped the writing of this book.

I end on a personal note to make absolutely clear that this study is not just an intellectual exercise, or just an individual accomplishment. Having grown up under the shadow of Houston's skyline, I was lured away by the promises of an eastern education. For over ten years, first as an undergraduate at Yale and then as a graduate student at Brown, I sought out a cultural and intellectual fulfillment made possible only by the changes wrought by the Civil Rights Movement. While scores of teachers are responsible for shaping my education, it was in the end affirmative action that had the most telling influence on my life. It is to the countless activists, lawyers, politicians, and administrators that made affirmative action a university commitment that I express my enduring gratitude.

Notes

Introduction

1. Tomás Rivera, . . . *Y no se lo tragó la tierra/And the Earth Did Not Devour Him* (Houston, Tex.: Arte Público Press, 1992), 146.

2. Interestingly, on the dust jacket of the 1992 bilingual edition of *. . . Y no se lo tragó la tierra/And the Earth Did Not Devour Him*, the publishers quote Rivera as part of their advertising campaign. Rivera remarks: "I wanted to document the spiritual strength, the concept of justice so important for the American continents. Within those immigrants I saw that strength. They may be economically deprived, politically deprived, socially deprived, but they kept moving, never staying in one place to suffer or be subdued, but always searching for work; that's why they were 'migrant' workers. I see that same sense of movement in the Europeans who came here and that concept of spiritual justice. It was there. And the migrant workers still have that role: to be searchers. That's an important metaphor in the Americas."

3. Donald E. Pease, "National Identities, Postmodern Artifacts, and Post-national Narratives," in *National Identities and Post-Americanist Narratives*, ed. Donald E. Pease (Durham, N.C.: Duke University Press, 1994).

4. Nina Baym, "Early Histories of American Literature: A Chapter in the Institution of New England," *American Literary History* 1, 3 (1989): 459–88.

5. Sacvan Bercovitch, "The Ends of American Puritan Rhetoric," in *The Ends of Rhetoric: History, Theory, Practice*, ed. John Bender and David E. Wellbery (Stanford, Calif.: Stanford University Press, 1990), 171–91.

6. Annette Kolodny, "Letting Go Our Grand Obsessions: Notes Towards a New Literary History of the American Frontier," *American Literature* 64, 1 (1992): 1–18.

7. Paul Lauter, "The Literatures of America: A Comparative Discipline," in *Redefining American Literary History*, ed. A. LaVonne Brown Ruoff and Jerry W. Ward, Jr. (New York: Modern Language Association, 1990), 10–34.

8. Betsy Erkkila, "Ethnicity, Literary Theory, and the Grounds of Resistance," *American Quarterly* 47, 4 (1995): 563–94.

9. See Gregory Jay, "Taking Multiculturalism Personally: Ethnos and Ethos in the Classroom," *American Literary History* 6, 4 (1994): 613–32.

10. See Juan Bruce-Novoa, "Canonical and Noncanonical Texts," *Américas Review* 14, 3–4 (1986): 119–35. Also see Ramón A. Gutiérrez, "Community, Patriarchy, and Individualism: The Politics of Chicano History and the Dream of Equality," *American Quarterly* 45, 1 (1993): 44–72.

Chapter 1

1. Edward J. Escobar, "The Dialectics of Repression: The Los Angeles Police Department and the Chicano Movement, 1968–1971," *Journal of American History* 79 (1993): 1483–1514.

2. See Angie Chabram-Dernersesian, "Conceptualizing Chicano Critical Discourse," in *Criticism in the Borderlands: Studies in Chicano Literature, Culture, and Ideology,* ed. Héctor Calderón and José David Saldívar (Durham, N.C.: Duke University Press, 1991), 127–148. See also, Juan Flores, "Latino Studies: New Contexts, New Concepts," *Harvard Educational Review* 67, 2 (1997): 208–21.

3. Donald E. Pease, "New Americanist: Revisionist Interventions into the Canon," *boundary 2* 17, 1 (1990): 1–37; also Patricia Nelson Limerick, Clyde A. Milner II, and Charles E. Rankin, eds., *Trails: Toward a New Western History* (Lawrence: University of Kansas Press, 1991).

4. Lora Romero, " 'When Something Goes Queer': Familiarity, Formalism, and Minority Intellectuals in the 1980s," *Yale Journal of Criticism* 6, 1 (1993): 121–41; Juan Bruce-Novoa, "Dialogical Strategies, Monological Goals: Chicano Literature," in *An Other Tongue: Nation and Ethnicity in the Linguistic Borderlands,* ed. Alfred Artega (Durham, N.C.: Duke University Press, 1994), 225–45.

5. Homi Bhabha, "DissemiNation: Time, Narrative, and the Margins of the Modern Nation," in *Nation and Narration,* ed. Homi Bhabha (New York: Routledge, 1990), 297.

6. Luis Valdez, "Introduction: 'La Plebe,' " in *Aztlán: An Anthology of Mexican American Literature,* ed. Luis Valdez and Stan Steiner (New York: Knopf, 1972), xiii–xv.

7. Rosa Linda Fregoso and Angie Chabram, "Chicana/o Cultural Representations: Reframing Alternative Critical Discourses," *Cultural Studies* 4, 3 (1990): 205.

8. See Angie Chabram-Dernersesian, "On the Social Construction of Whiteness within Selected Chicana/o Discourses," in *Displacing Whiteness: Essays in Social and Cultural Criticism,* ed. Ruth Frankenberg (Durham, N.C.: Duke University Press, 1997), 107–64.

9. For a poignant example, see Ana Castillo, "Our Tongue Was Nahuatl," in *The Third Woman,* ed. Dexter Fisher (Boston: Houghton Mifflin, 1980), 390–92. Also, for a fine collection of Chicana writing in this period, see *Chicana Feminist Thought: The Basic Historical Writings,* ed. Alma M. García (New York: Routledge, 1997).

10. "El Plan Espiritual de Aztlán," in *Aztlán: Essays on the Chicano Homeland*, ed. Rudolfo A. Anaya and Francisco A. Lomelí (Albuquerque, N.Mex.: Academia/El Norte Publications, 1989), 1. Although generally cited as an anonymously written manifesto from the Chicano Youth Liberation Conference, organized by Rodolfo "Corky" Gonzalez's Crusade for Justice, Luis Leal identifies the poet Alurista as the author. See Luis Leal, "In Search of Aztlán," in *Aztlán: Essays on the Chicano Homeland*, 6–13.

11. Fregoso and Chabram, "Chicana/o Cultural Representations," 205–6.

12. See Estevan T. Flores, "The Mexican–Origin People in the United States and Marxist Thought in Chicano Studies," in *The Left Academy: Marxist Scholarship on American Campuses*, vol. III, ed. Bertell Ollman and Edward Vernoff (New York: Praeger, 1986), 103–63.

13. In his analysis, Raoul Contreras comes to a similar conclusion about the origins of Chicano/a studies: "On the one hand, it is a new Social Science that emerges in opposition to the academic role of dominant ('Enlightenment') Social Science. On the other hand, it is also a Chicano Movement ideology, a worldview, that counters and opposes the *ideological role* of dominant Social Science." See "What Is Latino Studies?: The Ideological Dimension of Program 'Construction' and Program Location," *Latino Studies Journal* 11, 1 (2000): 32.

14. Deluvina Hernández, "La Raza Satellite System," *Aztlán* 1, 1 (1970): 13–36.

15. For pre–1960 examples of labor strikes, see Rodolfo Acuña, *Occupied America: A History of Chicanos*, 3d ed. (New York: Harper & Row, 1988).

16. Juan Gómez–Quiñones, "Toward a Perspective on Chicano History," *Aztlán* 2, 2 (1971): 1–49.

17. In hindsight, one can appreciate the monumental political juggling of Gómez–Quiñones and the other *Aztlán* editors by comparing their efforts to the August Twenty–Ninth Movement and their militant political platform. See *Fan the Flames: Revolutionary Position on the Chicano National Question* (Los Angeles: August Twenty–Ninth Movement, 1976).

18. Juan Gómez–Quiñones, "On Culture," *Revista Chicano-Riqueña* 5, 2 (spring 1977): 29.

19. Juan Gómez–Quiñones, *Mexican Students por La Raza: The Chicano Student Movement in Southern California, 1967–1977* (Santa Barbara, Calif.: Editorial La Causa, 1978).

20. Roberta Fernández, "*Abriendo caminos* in the Brotherland: Chicana Writers Respond to the Ideology of Literary Nationalism," *Frontiers* 14, 2 (1994): 28.

21. Ignacio M. García, "Constructing the Chicano Movement: Synthesis of a Militant Ethos," in *Perspectives in Mexican American Studies*, vol. 6 (Tucson, Ariz.: Mexican American Studies and Research Center, 1997), 13.

22. See Wilson Neate, introduction to *Tolerating Ambiguity: Ethnicity and Community in Chicano/a Writing* (New York: Peter Lang, 1998), 16. Also, for a concise

and splendidly executed summary of the Chicano/a Movement as it relates to Chicano/a literature, read pages 5–25.

23. Antonio C. Márquez ponders a similar thought when he writes: "Chicana writers, lesbian and male homosexual writers (Richard Rodriguez, for example) are at the forefront of the new wave of Chicano/a literature." "Richard Rodriguez's *Hunger of Memory* and New Perspectives on Ethnic Autobiography," in *Teaching American Ethnic Literatures: Nineteen Essays*, ed. John R. Maitino and David R. Peck (Albuquerque: University of New Mexico Press, 1996), 244.

24. Monika Kaup charts a similar trajectory when she argues that writers like Sandra Cisneros and Richard Rodriguez "employ the architectural metaphor of the new and temporary dwellings to question the organic view of Chicano/a culture embodied in old houses and ancient landscapes [i.e. the myth of Aztlán as central to Chicano/a identity]." "The Architecture of Ethnicity in Chicano Literature," *American Literature* 69, 2 (1997): 366.

25. An exception to the dominant negative response is Antonio C. Márquez's view, who writes, "*Hunger of Memory* is an important work because it raises a problematic issue: *What is ethnic literature?*" "Richard Rodriguez's *Hunger of Memory* and New Perspectives on Ethnic Autobiography," 239.

26. Rosaura Sánchez, "Calculated Musing: Richard Rodriguez's Metaphysics of Difference," in *The Ethnic Canon: Histories, Institutions, and Interventions*, ed. David Palumbo–Liu (Minneapolis: University of Minnesota Press, 1995), 171.

27. Kevin R. McNamara, "A Finer Grain: Richard Rodriguez's *Days of Obligation*," *Arizona Quarterly* 53, 1 (1997): 106.

28. Richard Rodriguez, "Objects of Desire," *The News Hour with Jim Lehrer*, 22 April 1996; "New Reformation," *The News Hour with Jim Lehrer*, 29 March 1996. Online Newshour: www.pbs.org/newshour/ww.rodriguez.html

29. For more on class and social aspirations, see Henry Staten, "Ethnic Authenticity, Class, and Autobiography: The Case of *Hunger of Memory*," *PMLA* 113, 1 (1998): 103–16.

30. For an extended discussion of this process as a conversion narrative, see Raymund A. Paredes, "Autobiography and Ethnic Politics: Richard Rodriguez's *Hunger of Memory*," in *Multicultural Autobiography: American Lives*, ed. James Robert Payne (Knoxville: University of Tennessee Press, 1992), 280–96.

31. Staten, "Ethnic Authenticity, Class, and Autobiography." Staten writes: "Whatever the ambiguities of *Hunger of Memory* and in part because of them, the book presents truthful witness to the complexities facing persons of Mexican descent in the United States and provides a needed corrective to the more edifying and equally necessary truths partially brought into being by those who have invoked the Chicano–Chicana identitive" (113).

32. Lora Romero draws a similar observation: "One way to differentiate between Rodríguez's and Moraga's autobiographies would be to say that whereas

Hunger of Memory reiterates the familiar trajectory of the ethnic intellectual (away from family and community), *Loving in the War Years* reverses the paradigm by narrating instead the ethnic intellectual's return to her community of origin." "'When Something Goes Queer,'" 123.

33. Tey Diana Rebolledo, "The Politics of Poetics: Or, What Am I, a Critic, Doing in This Text Anyhow?" in *Chicana Creativity and Criticism: Charting New Frontiers in American Literature*, ed. María Herrera-Sobek and Helena María Viramontes (Houston, Tex.: Arte Público Press, 1988), 131.

34. For an extended discussion of this dilemma, see Betsy Erkkila, "Ethnicity, Literary Theory, and the Grounds of Resistance."

35. Angie Chabram-Dernersesian, "Conceptualizing Chicano Critical Discourse," 148.

36. Hector A. Torres, review of *Chicano Narrative: The Dialectics of Difference*, by Ramón Saldívar, *College Literature* (double issue), 19, 3; 20, 1 (1992/1993): 269.

37. Sonia Saldívar Hull makes a similar argument when she writes: "Though the text often has been dismissed as indulging in a quest for lost origins or criticized for appropriating an indigenous heritage that does not belong to Chicanas, I propose that even in its most mystical, spiritual moments, the text circles back to a political consciousness with a specific political agenda that identifies not with the patriarchal nation-state of Aztlán but with the feminist state, Coatlicue." See *Feminism on the Border: Chicana Gender Politics and Literature* (Berkeley: University of California Press, 2000), 64.

38. See Carl Gutiérrez-Jones, "Desiring B/orders," *diacritics* 25, 1 (1995): 99–112.

39. See respectively, María Amparo Ruiz de Burton, *Who Would Have Thought It?* (1872), ed. Rosaura Sánchez and Beatrice Pita (Houston, Tex.: Arte Público Press, 1995); Leonor Villegas de Magnón, *The Rebel*, ed. Clara Lomas (Houston, Tex.: Arte Público Press, 1994).

40. Rafael Pérez-Torres, "Refiguring Aztlán," *Aztlán* 22, 2 (1997): 16.

41. Daniel Cooper Alarcón makes a very similar argument for the retention of the myth of Aztlán; see chapter 1, "Toward a New Understanding of Aztlán and Chicano Cultural Identity, in *The Aztec Palimpsest: Mexico in the Modern Imagination* (Tucson: University of Arizona Press, 1997), 4–35.

42. Norma Alarcón, "Chicana Feminism: In the Tracks of 'The' Native Woman," and Angie Chabram-Dernersesian, "'Chicana! Rican? No, Chicana Riqueña!' Refashioning the Transnational Connection," in *Between Woman and Nation: Nationalism, Transnational Feminisms, and the State*, ed. Caren Kaplan, Norma Alarcón, and Minoo Moallem (Durham, N.C.: Duke University Press, 1999), 63–71, 264–95.

43. Robert C. Smith, "Mexicans in New York: Memberships and Incorporation in a New Immigrant Community," in *Latinos in New York: Communities in*

Transition, ed. Gabriel Haslip–Viera and Sherrie L. Baver (Notre Dame, Ind.: University of Notre Dame, Press), 57.

Chapter 2

1. See Avery F. Gordon and Christopher Newfield, eds., *Mapping Multicultural- ism* (Minneapolis: University of Minnesota Press, 1996); also, Gregory S. Jay, *Ameri- can Literature and the Culture Wars* (Ithaca, N.Y.: Cornell University Press, 1997).

2. Allan Bloom, *The Closing of the American Mind: How Higher Education Has Failed Democracy and Impoverished the Souls of Today's Students* (New York: Simon & Schuster, 1987); also, E. D. Hirsch, *Cultural Literacy: What Every American Needs to Know* (New York: Random House, 1988); and for a critique of multiculturalism as "political correctness," see Dinesh D'Souza, *Illiberal Education: The Politics of Race and Sex on Campus* (New York: Free Press, 1991).

3. See Henry A. Giroux and Peter McLaren, eds., *Between Borders: Pedagogy and the Politics of Cultural Studies* (New York: Routledge, 1994).

4. See Michael Bérubé and Cary Nelson, eds., *Higher Education under Fire: Politics, Economics, and the Crisis of the Humanities* (New York: Routledge, 1995).

5. I was first alerted to this Hughes poem by Sacvan Bercovitch; see "The Ends of American Puritan Rhetoric."

6. See "The Spanish Legacy and the Historical Imagination," in *The Spanish Frontier in North America*, David J. Weber (New Haven, Conn.: Yale University Press, 1992), 335–60.

7. Bercovitch sees this deployment as the legacy of a ritual mode of a com- munity in crisis: "therefore using crisis as a strategy of social revitalization; a settlement in peril and therefore drawing strength from adversity, transition, and flux; a company–in–covenant deprived by history of their identity and therefore using their self–declared newness to create a vision of America that reconceived history at large (including that of the Old World) as hinging on *their* failure or success" ("Ends of American Puritan Rhetoric," 186).

8. *The Puritan Origins of the American Self* (New Haven, Conn.: Yale University Press, 1975), 136.

9. For more on the concept of "cultural work," see Jane Tompkins, *Sensational Designs: The Cultural Work of American Fiction, 1790–1860* (New York: Oxford Univer- sity Press, 1985).

10. Taylor's poetry was published for the first time in 1939. Johnson's intro- duction encouraged a generation of readers to find an American poet "in the tradition of Donne and the Anglo–Catholic conceitists." *The Poetic Works of Ed- ward Taylor*, ed. Thomas H. Johnson (Princeton, N.J.: Princeton University Press, 1971), 11.

11. My thanks to Krista Comer for alerting me to this important literary and institutional link.

12. Because of feminist scholarship and the recovery of women writers and their texts, we know now that *American Renaissance* helped to distort and conceal the presence and popularity of writers that did not conform sufficiently to Matthiessen's Romantic model of a literary work.

13. See Kermit Vanderbilt, *American Literature and the Academy: The Roots, Growth, and Maturity of a Profession* (Philadelphia: University of Pennsylvania Press, 1986).

14. My analysis here is drawn from Vanderbilt's history and from Spiller's *Literary History of the United States* (New York: Macmillan, 1948), cited hereafter as *LHUS*. All subsequent references and quotations from this text come from the 1948 Macmillan edition.

15. Spiller would later convert this theory into a larger study, *The Cycle of American Literature: An Essay in Historical Criticism* (New York: Macmillan, 1955). In his preface, Spiller foregrounds the rationale for his theory of literature in the following manner: "If there is one idea that most major American authors have in common, it is the belief that life is organic; and the American literary historian can do no better than to adopt for his study an organic view of history" (xiii). Spiller's organic theory is obviously dependent on an essentialist collapsing of knowledge with the "natural," and those two with culture. In that collapse, women and/or people of color are figured out of the narrative on behalf of the hegemonic impulses of the nation.

16. Indeed, the table of authors represents a veritable who's who list of that period's scholars. It included Howard Jones, Kenneth Murdock, Thomas Johnson, Carl Van Doren, F. O. Matthiessen, Henry Nash Smith, H. L. Mencken, Carlos Baker, William Charvat, Malcolm Cowley, and Merle Curti, to name a few. The project was intended to be a substantial improvement over the 1917 *Cambridge History of American Literature* (New York: Putnam, 1917).

17. Kolodny refers to *LHUS* as "that monumental pony upon which generations of American literature graduate students, from 1948 on, rode to their Ph.D. orals." Annette Kolodny, "The Integrity of Memory: Creating a New Literary History of the United States," *American Literature* 57, 2 (1985): 291–307.

18. This is basically the scholarly perspective brought to bear early on in "Address to the Reader." The first paragraph reads: "The literary history of this nation began when the first settler from abroad of sensitive mind paused in his adventure long enough to feel that he was under a different sky, breathing new air, and that a New World was all before him with only his strength and Providence for guides. With him began a different emphasis upon an old theme in literature, the theme of cutting loose and faring forth, renewed under the powerful influence of a fresh continent for civilized man. It has provided, ever since those first days, an element in our native literature, whose other theme has come from a nostalgia for the rich culture of Europe, so much of which was perforce left behind" (xiii).

19. These writers are the subjects of single-author chapters, in a section titled "Literary Fulfillment." The title of the initial background chapter, "Democratic Vistas," is borrowed from Thoreau (x). Vanderbilt argues that David Bowers, the writer of "Democratic Vistas," "framed the period with an obvious borrowing from Matthiessen's thesis, namely, 'the reorientation of literature under the influence of New England transcendentalism'" (523).

20. Robert Spiller et al., "Postscript at Mid-Century," *Literary History of the United States*, rev. ed. (New York: Macmillan, 1953). They write: "Instead of the beginning [the 1940s], this was an end of an era. By 1952 it had become possible to demonstrate the reality of a second literary renaissance and to place its zenith at some time between 1920 and 1940" (1393).

21. Evans began the project around 1950 and finished five years later. "An Address to the Colonial Society of Massachusetts, on the Occasion of Its Centennial," *New England Quarterly* 66, 3 (1993): 359.

22. What this phenomenon says of the *Heath Anthology of American Literature*—ed. Paul Lauter et al. (Lexington, Mass.: D. C. Heath, 1990)—is a good question to ask. I cite the *Heath Anthology* here for two reasons. First, it promotes itself as the culmination of scholarship that began during the Civil Rights period, scholarship that actively questioned the presumptions of the previous generation and that sought to rectify the literary status of women and/or people of color in the United States. Second, while not claiming to be a literary history per se, the *Heath Anthology*'s collection of canonical and noncanonical authors bespeaks a desire to see a different kind of literary history enacted.

23. For a wonderful example of these writers and their academic appointments, see *El Espejo—The Mirror: Selected Chicano Literature*, ed. Octavio Ignacio Romano-V and Herminio Ríos C. (Berkeley, Calif.: Quinto Sol, 1972).

24. See Mario T. García's *Mexican Americans: Leadership, Ideology, and Identity, 1930–1960* (New Haven, Conn.: Yale University Press, 1989) and Juan Gómez-Quiñones's *Chicano Politics: Reality and Promise, 1940–1990* (Albuquerque: University of New Mexico Press, 1990). Of particular interest to this study are the activist roles Chicano/a writers and scholars played in this period, from Ernesto Galarza's leadership in the migrant farm unions to Alurista's role in the establishment of the Movimiento Estudiantil Chicano de Aztlán (MEChA).

25. Philip D. Ortego, "The Chicano Renaissance," *Social Casework* 52, 5 (1971): 294–307.

26. Ortego's assessment of Chicano/a literature as redefining American literature from the outside was later echoed by Chicano/a scholars. In addition, his vision of a reconstructed American literary history that includes the colonial histories of the Southwest anticipates the scholarship found in *Recovering the U.S. Hispanic Literary Heritage* (1993).

27. *Chicano Literature: A Reference Guide*, ed. Julio A. Martínez and Francisco A. Lomelí (Westport, Conn.: Greenwood Press, 1985), 20.

28. In "Cultural Nationalism and Chicano Literature: 1965–1975," Alurista writes: "the literary products of 1965–75 sought to affirm a nationalism founded on the most ancient and pre-colonial origins [Aztlán] available to the modern Chicano writer. . . . In the face of flagrant institutional and personal racism and ethnocentrism Chicanos sought to redefine themselves . . . in terms other than those prescribed by the Anglo-Saxon, male Protestant state to 'keep Mexicans in their place.'" In *Missions in Conflict: Essays on U.S.-Mexican Relations and Chicano Culture*, ed. Renate von Bardeleben, Dietrich Briesemeister, and Juan Bruce-Novoa (Tübingen: Gunter Narr, 1986), 41.

29. Gustavo V. Segade, "Identity and Power: An Essay on the Politics of Culture and the Culture of Politics in Chicano Thought," *Aztlán* 9 (1978): 88.

30. In "Chicano Literature: The Establishment of Community" (1982), Tomás Rivera finds a tenuous political and social organization within and an absence of care without during the 1950s and 1960s. As a result, "the impetus to document and develop the Chicano community became the essential raison d'être of the Chicano Movement itself and of the writers who tried to express that. . . . One of the most important goals was to establish a lugar or a place. Aztlán became the place in most writing. Myth or not, the urge to have, to establish, and to nurture a place of origin, of residence became the most important need to meet. This was not surprising. . . . The Chicano had to begin decolonizing the mind." Reprinted in *Tomás Rivera, The Complete Works*, ed. Julián Olivares (Houston, Tex.: Arte Público Press, 1991), 399.

31. See Luis Leal, "In Search of Aztlán," trans. Gladys Leal, in *Aztlán: Essays on the Chicano Homeland*, 8.

32. In *Chicano Criticism in the Borderlands: Studies in Chicano Literature, Culture, and Ideology*, ed. Héctor Calderón and José David Saldívar (Durham, N.C.: Duke University Press, 1991), 11. An earlier version can be found in Saldívar's *Chicano Narrative* (Madison: University of Wisconsin Press, 1990), 204–18.

33. Saldívar draws from the following works by Bercovitch: "The Rites of Assent: Rhetoric, Ritual, and the Ideology of American Consensus" (1981), "The Problem of Ideology in American History" (1986), and *Reconstructing American Literary History* (1986).

34. This is a paraphrase of Bercovitch's argument that Saldívar has quoted from "The Problem of Ideology in American History" (10).

35. Saldívar's critique is based on Bercovitch's *Reconstructing American Literary History* (1986) and Sollors's *Beyond Ethnicity* (1986).

36. Saldívar quotes from *American Renaissance* (1941, preface).

37. R. C. De Prospo, "Marginalizing Early American Literature," *New Literary History* 23, 2 (1992): 233–65.

38. Paul Lauter, "The Literatures of America: A Comparative Discipline," in *Redefining American Literary History*, 16.

39. Nicolás Kanellos, foreword to *Recovering the U.S. Hispanic Literary Heritage*,

ed. Ramón Gutiérrez and Genaro Padilla (Houston, Tex.: Arte Público Press, 1993), 13.

40. Erlinda Gonzalez-Berry, "Two Texts for a New Canon: Vicente Bernal's *Las Primicias* and Felipe Maximiliano Chacón's *Poesía y prosa*," in *Recovering the U.S. Hispanic Literary Heritage*, 129.

41. Charles Tatum, "Some Considerations on Genres and Chronology for Nineteenth-Century Hispanic Literature," in *Recovering the U.S. Hispanic Literary Heritage*, 199–200.

42. Introduction to *Recovering the U.S. Hispanic Literary Heritage*, vol. II, 14.

43. Sau-ling Cynthia Wong, *Reading Asian American Literature: From Necessity to Extravagance* (Princeton, N.J.: Princeton University Press, 1993).

Chapter 3

1. "Recollections of Early Times in San Diego." See Earl Samuel McGhee, "E. W. Morse, Pioneer Merchant and Co-Founder of San Diego" (master's thesis, San Diego State College, 1950), 257–60.

2. For a compelling reading of how to understand the social emplotments of western spaces and their relationship to narrative, see Krista Comer, *Landscapes of the New West: Gender and Geography in Contemporary Women's Writing* (Chapel Hill: University of North Carolina Press, 1999).

3. Genaro Padilla, *My History, Not Yours: The Formation of Mexican American Autobiography* (Madison: University of Wisconsin Press, 1993). See also Rosaura Sánchez, *Telling Identities: The Californio Testimonios* (Minneapolis: University of Minnesota Press, 1995).

4. David J. Weber, " 'From Hell Itself': The Americanization of Mexico's Northern Frontier," in *Myth and the History of the Hispanic Southwest: Essays by David J. Weber* (Albuquerque: University of New Mexico Press, 1988). Part of this record is also the Mexican Constitution of 1824 that was modeled on both the Spanish Constitution of 1812 and the U.S. Constitution of 1788, the latter being the more influential and indicative of the Mexican liberals in parliament who envisioned Mexico assuming in the years to come the geopolitical status of the United States in the Americas.

5. Rosaura Sánchez and Beatrice Pita, introduction to *The Squatter and the Don* (Houston, Tex.: Arte Público Press, 1992 [1885]), 5–51.

6. Major portions of this biography appear in José F. Aranda, Jr., "María Amparo Ruiz de Burton," in *American Prose Writers, 1870–1920*, vol. 2, ed. Sharon M. Harris, *Dictionary of Literary Biography* (Detroit: Gale Research, 2000), 310–16. This chapter is also informed by the biographical material presented in the introductions to Ruiz de Burton's novels by Rosaura Sánchez and Beatrice Pita. See *The Squatter and The Don* and *Who Would Have Thought It?* (Houston, Tex.: Arte Público Press, 1995), 5–51, vii–lxv.

7. The title of this ballad is also the alternative title of a famous postwar novel by Ned Buntline, *The Volunteer, or The Maid of Monterrey, A Tale of the Mexican War* (1847). Monterey in this novel is in fact Monterrey, Nuevo Leon, Mexico. See Frederick Bryant Oden, "The Maid of Monterey: The Life of María Amparo Ruiz de Burton, 1832–1895 (master's thesis, University of California, San Diego, 1992), 17–18. My eternal gratitude to Amelia María de la Luz Montes, who shared with me this crucial research material. I use Oden's findings liberally throughout this chapter.

8. See Sánchez and Pita, introduction to *The Squatter and the Don*, who quote Davidson on this point (12).

9. See William Arba Ellis, ed., *Norwich University, 1819–1911: Her History, Her Graduates, Her Roll of Honor*, vol. 2 (Montpelier, Vt.: Capital City Press, 1911), 282–83. Special thanks to Julie P. Bressor, Mack Librarian for Special Collections, Norwich University, for making available entries on Henry S. Burton and his stepfather, E. B. Williston.

10. Kathleen Crawford, "María Amparo Ruiz de Burton: The General's Lady," *Journal of San Diego History* 30, 3 (1984): 207–208.

11. See José F. Aranda, Jr., "Contradictory Impulses: María Amparo Ruiz de Burton, Resistance Theory, and the Politics of Chicano/a Studies," *American Literature* 70, 3 (1998): 560–63.

12. "Samuel L. M. Barlow," *Dictionary of American Biography*, ed. Allen Johnson, vol. I (New York: Scribner, 1928), 613–15.

13. Richard M. Garten, "The Political Activities of S. L. Barlow, 1856–1864" (master's thesis, Columbia University, 1947).

14. James Osborne Wright, *Of the American Library of the late Samuel Latham Mitchill Barlow* (New York: American Art Association, 1889); also, Joseph Rosenblum, "Two Americanists: Samuel L. M. Barlow and Henry Harrisse," *American Book Collector* 6, 2 (1985): 14–25.

15. J. B. Lippincott Company, *Centennial Reflections: J. B. Lippincott Company in the 1870s* (Philadelphia: Lippincott, 1976).

16. Geoffrey Bret Harte, ed., *The Letters of Bret Harte* (Boston: Houghton Mifflin, 1926), 170, 251, 268, 271, 274.

17. See *The Mexican War in Baja California: The Memorandum of Captain Henry W. Halleck, Concerning His Expeditions in Lower California, 1846–1848*, ed. Doyce B. Nunis, Jr. (Los Angeles: Dawson's Book Shop, 1977), 38.

18. From Secretary of the Navy George Bancroft, who on July 12, 1846, gave the only official order to invade the Californias, to Secretary of War William L. Marcy, who ordered General Stephen W. Kearny to end all disputes over an American occupation of Baja California, everyone assumed that both Californias were to be added to the United States.

19. Cecil Robinson explains that while detractors of the Mexican–American

War existed (Henry David Thoreau was one), the war's connection with westward expansion committed many to believing that Mexicans were unfit to govern anyone, much less themselves. Robinson points out, for example, the early enthusiasm of Walt Whitman: "What has miserable, inefficient Mexico with her superstition, her burlesque upon freedom, her actual tyranny by the few over the many—what has she to do with the great mission of peopling the New World with a noble race? Be it ours to achieve that mission! Be it ours to roll down all of the upstart leaven of old despotism, that comes our way!" Cecil Robinson, *Mexico and the Hispanic Southwest in American Literature*, rev. ed. (Tucson: University of Arizona Press, 1977), 26.

20. See Nicolás Kanellos, *Thirty Million Strong: Reclaiming the Hispanic Image in American Culture* (Golden, Colo.: Fulcrum, 1998); also David J. Weber, "The Spanish Legacy and the Historical Imagination," in *The Spanish Frontier in North America* (New Haven, Conn.: Yale University Press, 1992), 335–60.

21. John S. D. Eisenhower, *So Far from God: The U.S. War with Mexico, 1846–1848* (New York: Random House, 1989), 202.

22. Alex M. Saragoza, "The Significance of Recent Chicano-related Historical Writings: An Appraisal," *Ethnic Affairs* 1 (1987): 24–62.

23. Saragoza writes: "In short, the interface between Mexicans and the westward movement of American capitalism was not a simple, one dimensional process" (37).

24. Yet, even among these Chicano historians, there was then no specific consideration of the differing cultures of colonialism that existed from Texas to California. Despite their focus on the differences among Mexican communities, they continued to identify colonialism primarily as an Anglo enterprise. There was no exploration of how Mexican frontier colonialism might have actually paved the way for American expansionism, or how Anglo Americans living on the Mexican frontier might have influenced or imported into Manifest Destiny a regard for those experiences, regions, and cultural artifacts they came to identify with the Southwest.

25. John Louis O'Sullivan is credited with coining the phrase "Manifest Destiny" to explain the rationale behind the westward expansion in the United States in the 1840s. See Robert W. Johannsen, "The Meaning of Manifest Destiny," in *Manifest Destiny and Empire: American Antebellum Expansionism*, ed. Sam W. Haynes and Christopher Morris (College Station: Published for the University of Texas at Arlington by Texas A&M University Press, 1997), 7–20.

26. The writings of these overt imperialists have been cited over and over since the nineteenth century to establish the inevitable westward expansion of Anglo America.

27. Samuel J. Watson, "The Uncertain Road to Manifest Destiny: Army Of-

ficers and the Course of American Territorial Expansionism, 1815–1846," in *Manifest Destiny and Empire*, 70.

28. For the more accepted position that patriotism was a visible feature of the war by both combatants and civilians, see Robert W. Johannsen, "The True Spirit of Patriot Virtue," in *To the Halls of Montezuma: The Mexican War in the American Imagination* (New York: Oxford University Press, 1985), 45–67.

29. Michael Hogan, *The Irish Soldiers of Mexico* (Guadalajara, Mexico: Fondo Editorial Universitario, 1997), 85.

30. Between careerist American officers who served out of a nonpartisan sense of duty and volunteer segments of the army who represented at best a loose coalition of regional interests in westward expansion, this was a war fought less on ideological or nationalist grounds and more out of a broad conviction of racial and cultural superiority.

31. For this connection, I am beholden to research reported by Nancy Hernández's conference paper "The Lynching of Mexican American Identities." She writes: "The writers involved in *El Nuevo Mundo* were firm believers in the universal ideals of democracy, freedom and separation from monarchy. These writers were firmly convinced that all people in the Americas could get along because they all wanted one thing—freedom from the crown. It made perfect sense to the writers of *El Nuevo Mundo* that the Americas would become one land full of people who held the same ideals" (2). Delivered at the fourth conference of Recovering the U.S. Hispanic Literary Heritage Project, "Interpreting and Contextualizing the Recovered Text," University of Houston, November 1996.

32. Oden writes: "Captain Burton also helped organize the 'New England Society,' a club for San Diegans from New England or of New England parentage. He won a seat as Vice President of the society, which was formed in November 1854" (29).

33. Morse himself was a New Englander from Massachusetts. He left for the gold fields of California in the late winter of 1849, along with a hundred or so friends and neighbors. The gold rush had a similar appeal in many New England communities. Eventually, with fellow New Englander Levi Slack, Morse headed for San Diego. Both men had read about the region in Dana's *Two Years before the Mast*. They opened Boston House in 1850 (McGhee, 1–4).

34. Ruiz de Burton, *Who Would Have Thought It?* ed. Rosaura Sánchez and Beatrice Pita (Houston: Arte Público Press, 1995), 62. All quotations come from this edition.

35. Jane Hatch, ed., *The American Book of Days*, 3d ed. (New York: H. W. Wilson, 1978), 1055.

36. "Asa Burton," *Dictionary of American Biography*, ed. Allen Johnson, vol. 3 (New York: Scribner, 1929), 340–41.

37. "Alden Partridge," in *The National Cyclopaedia of American Biography* (Clifton, N.J.: James T. White, 1922), 322.

38. "Fort Monroe," in *Encyclopedia of Historic Forts: The Military, Pioneer, and Trading Posts of the United States,* by Robert B. Roberts (New York: Collier Macmillan, 1988), 815–18.

39. Ellis, ed., *Norwich University, 1819–1911,* 257–58; also, James Grant Wilson and John Fiske, eds., *Appletons' Cyclopaedia of American Biography* (New York: D. Appleton, 1889), 541.

40. Wilson and Fiske, eds., *Appletons' Cyclopaedia of American Biography,* 154–56.

41. Nina Baym, "Early Histories of American Literature," 460.

42. For this information, I rely on his correspondence with Colonel W. Hoffman; see Brigadier General Fred C. Ainsworth, ed., *The War of the Rebellion: A Compilation of the Official Orders of Union and Confederate Armies,* series II, vol. V (Washington, D.C.: Government Printing Office, 1899), 629–30.

43. My special thanks to Rosaura Sánchez and Beatrice Pita for having shared this information. Their conversations with me about their ongoing research on Ruiz de Burton have been inspirational.

44. Antoinette May, *Haunted Houses of California* (San Carlos, Calif.: Wide World Publishing/Tetra, 1993 [1990]), 196–98.

45. "National Conservation Group Buys 4,800 Acres for SD's Newest Wildlife Refuge," *The Press Box,* 14 August 1997, www.co.san–diego.ca.us/cnty/bos/sup2/news/rchjamul.html

Chapter 4

1. Alan Knight, *The Mexican Revolution,* vol. 2, *Counter-Revolution and Reconstruction* (Cambridge: Cambridge University Press, 1986), 523.

2. Acuña, *Occupied America,* 188.

3. See Leonard Pitt, *The Decline of the Californio: A Social History of the Spanish-Speaking Californians, 1846–1890* (Berkeley: University of California Press, 1966); Robert F. Heizer and Alan F. Almquist, *The Other Californians: Prejudice and Discrimination under Spain, Mexico, and the United States to 1920* (Berkeley: University of California Press, 1971); David Montejano, *Anglos and Mexicans in the Making of Texas, 1836–1986* (Austin: University of Texas Press, 1987); and Acuña, *Occupied America.*

4. Camille Guerin–Gonzales, *Mexican Workers and American Dreams: Immigration, Repatriation, and California Farm Labor, 1900–1939* (New Brunswick, N.J.: Rutgers University Press, 1994), 2.

5. See introduction to David Gutiérrez, *Walls and Mirrors: Mexican Americans, Mexican Immigrants, and the Politics of Ethnicity* (Berkeley: University of California Press, 1995), 1–11.

6. For more on the divergent meanings of the Statue of Liberty, see Juan F.

Perea, "The Statue of Liberty: Notes from Behind the Gilded Door," in *Immigrants Out!: The New Nativism and the Anti-Immigrant Impulse in the United States,* ed. Juan F. Perea (New York: New York University Press, 1997), 44–58.

7. See Juan Gómez-Quiñones, "Labor Conflict and Attempts at Organization," ch. 3 of *Mexican American Labor, 1790–1990* (Albuquerque: University of New Mexico Press, 1994), 65–96.

8. Richard Hofstadter, *Social Darwinism in American Thought,* rev. ed. (New York: George Braziller, 1959 [1944]); John Higham, *Strangers in the Land: Patterns of American Nativism, 1860–1925,* 2d ed. (New Brunswick, N.J.: Rutgers University Press, 1988 [1955]); Edward G. Hartmann, *The Movement to Americanize the Immigrant* (New York: AMS Press, 1967 [1948]).

9. Nina Baym, "Early Histories of American Literature."

10. Russell J. Reising, "The Problem of Puritan Origins in Literary History and Theory," ch. 2 of *The Unusable Past: Theory and the Study of American Literature* (New York: Methuen, 1986), 49–91. For a good example of the lament, see Perry Miller's preface to *Orthodoxy in Massachusetts, 1630–1650* (New York: Harper, 1970 [1933]), xxxii.

11. Virginia D. Anderson, *New England's Generation: The Great Migration and the Formation of Society and Culture in the Seventeenth Century* (New York: Cambridge University Press, 1991), 16.

12. Moses Coit Tyler, *A History of American Literature during the Colonial Period, 1607–1765* (New York: Putnam, 1878), 94–95.

13. For another way of connecting modern nativism to the Puritans, see Joe R. Feagin, "Old Poison in New Bottles: The Deep Roots of Modern Nativism," in *Immigrants Out!* ed. Juan F. Perea.

14. See Perry Miller, *Errand into the Wilderness* (Cambridge, Mass.: Harvard University Press, Belknap Press, 1956).

15. Kenneth Ballard Murdock, *Increase Mather: The Foremost American Puritan* (Cambridge: Harvard University Press, 1926), 24; see also Samuel Eliot Morison, *Builders of the Bay Colony,* 2d ed. (Boston: Houghton Mifflin, 1958 [1930]), 71–75.

16. Gómez-Quiñones, *Mexican American Labor, 1790–1990,* 94; also, Mary Kidder Rak, *Border Patrol* (Boston: Houghton Mifflin, 1938) and *They Guard the Gates: The Way of Life on the American Border* (Evanston, Ill.: Row, Peterson, 1941), 8.

17. For an alternative use of the term "Great Migration," see Joe William Trotter, Jr., "Introduction: Black Migration in Historical Perspective, A Review of the Literature," in *The Great Migration in Historical Perspective: New Dimensions of Race, Class, and Gender* (Bloomington: Indiana University Press, 1991), 1–21.

18. Vanderbilt, *American Literature and the Academy,* 461.

19. David Levin, "Perry Miller at Harvard," *Southern Review* 19, 4 (October 1983): 802–803.

20. Rodolfo Acuña, *Occupied America; The Chicano Struggle Toward Liberation* (San Francisco: Canfield Press, 1972), 199. Also Juan Gómez–Quiñones's *Chicano Politics*, 33–41.

21. Lest we should underestimate the function of a Puritan identity in American scholarship at this period, Edmund Morgan remembers needing to fulfill a genealogical prerequisite before being admitted into the Colonial Society of Massachusetts. See "An Address to the Colonial Society of Massachusetts, on the Occasion of Its Centennial," 356.

22. Edmund S. Morgan, *The Puritan Dilemma: The Story of John Winthrop* (Boston: Little, Brown, 1958), xii.

23. Nicolás Kanellos, *A History of Hispanic Theatre in the United States: Origins to 1940* (Austin: University of Texas Press, 1990); A. Gabriel Meléndez, *So All Is Not Lost: The Poetics of Print in Nuevomexicano Communities, 1834–1958* (Albuquerque: University of New Mexico Press, 1997); Genaro M. Padilla, *My History, Not Yours: The Formation of Mexican American Autobiography*; Rosaura Sánchez, *Telling Identities: The Californio Testimonios*; Tey Diana Rebolledo, *Women Singing in the Snow: A Cultural Analysis of Chicana Literature* (Tucson: University of Arizona Press, 1995).

24. Américo Paredes, *With His Pistol in His Hand: A Border Ballad and Its Hero* (Austin: University of Texas Press, 1958).

25. María Herrera–Sobek, *The Mexican Corrido* (Bloomington: Indiana University Press, 1990); José E. Limón, *Mexican Ballads, Chicano Poems: History and Influence in Mexican American Social Poetry* (Austin: University of Texas Press, 1992); Teresa McKenna, *Migrant Song: Politics and Process in Contemporary Chicano Literature* (Austin: University of Texas Press, 1997).

26. Kitty Calavita, *Inside the State: The Bracero Program, Immigration, and I.N.S.* (New York: Routledge, 1992).

27. J. Frank Dobie, ed., *Puro Mexicano* (Austin: Texas Folklore Society, 1935), 222–24.

28. This section is wholly beholden to the biographical and historical matter found in Amy Doherty's recovery of Mena's short stories. See *The Collected Stories of María Cristina Mena*, ed. Amy Doherty (Houston, Tex.: Arte Público Press, 1997).

29. See Daniel Venegas, *The Adventures of Don Chipote, or, When Parrots Breast Feed*, trans. Ethriam Cash Brammer (Houston, Tex.: Arte Público Press, 2000).

30. See Carol Nackenoff, *The Fictional Republic: Horatio Alger and American Political Discourse* (New York: Oxford University Press, 1994).

31. See Américo Paredes, *George Washington Gómez: A Mexicotexan Novel* (Houston, Tex.: Arte Público Press, 1990).

32. For the established reading of Guálinto Gómez as native, not immigrant, see Ramón Saldívar, "The Borderlands of Culture: Américo Paredes's *George Washington Gómez* and Chicano Literature at the End of the Twentieth Century," *American Literary History* 5, 2 (1993): 272–93.

33. See Américo Paredes, *The Shadow* (Houston, Tex.: Arte Público Press, 1998).

34. For a recent translation, see Juan Rulfo, *Pedro Páramo*, trans. Margaret Sayers Peden (New York: Grove Press, 1994).

35. For this section I am wholly beholden to the recovery work of José E. Limón and María Cotera. See Jovita González and Eve Raleigh, *Caballero: A Historical Novel*, ed. José E. Limón and María Cotera (College Station: Texas A&M University Press, 1996); Jovita González, *Dew on the Thorn*, ed. José E. Limón (Houston, Tex.: Arte Público Press, 1997).

36. This comparison to *Gone With the Wind* is made on the dust jacket of the novel; also see Thomas H. Kreneck, "Recovering the 'Lost' Manuscripts of Jovita González: The Production of South Texas Mexican–American Literature," *Texas Library Journal* 74, 2 (1998): 76–79.

37. See introduction to *Caballero*, xix.

38. See Jovita González, "Social Life in Cameron, Starr, and Zapata Counties" (master's thesis University of Texas at Austin, 1930).

39. María Cotera, *"Hombres Necios*: A Critical Epilogue," in *Caballero*, 339.

40. See Fabiola Cabeza de Baca, *We Fed Them Cactus*, 2d ed. (Albuquerque: University of New Mexico Press, 1994 [1954]); Nina Otero, *Old Spain in Our Southwest* (New York: Harcourt, Brace, 1936); Cleofas Jaramillo, *Romance of a Little Village Girl* (Albuquerque: University of New Mexico Press, 1995 [1955]).

41. For a very similar argument based on González's short story "Shades of the Tenth Muse," see María Eugenia Cotera, "Engendering a 'Dialectics of Our America': Jovita González's Pluralist Dialogue as Feminist Testimonio," in *Las Obreras: Chicana Politics of Work and Family*, Aztlán Anthology Series 1, vol. ed. Vicki L. Ruiz (Los Angeles: UCLA Chicano Studies Research Center, 2000), 237–48. My eternal thanks to María for sharing her research and criticism on this short story with me. For a new collection of González's short works, see Jovita González, *The Woman Who Lost Her Soul and Other Stories*, ed. Sergio Reyna (Houston, Tex.: Arte Público Press, 2000), 108–15.

42. For this section I am wholly beholden to the recovery work of Lauro Flores. See Luis Perez, *El Coyote, The Rebel*, intro. Lauro Flores (Houston, Tex.: Arte Público, 2000 [1947]).

43. See Ramón Saldívar, *Chicano Narrative*, 60–73.

44. For more on this postwar generation and their influence on the Chicano/a Movement, see Mario T. García, *Mexican Americans: Leadership, Ideology, and Identity, 1930–1960*; Juan Gómez–Quiñones, *Chicano Politics*; Benjamin Márquez, *LULAC: The Evolution of a Mexican American Political Organization* (Austin: University of Texas Press, 1993); George J. Sánchez, *Becoming Mexican American: Ethnicity, Culture, and Identity in Chicano Los Angeles, 1900–1945* (New York: Oxford University Press, 1993).

45. See Miguel Antonio Otero, Jr., *My Life on the Frontier* (New York: Press of the

Pioneers, 1939 [1936]); *The Real Billy the Kid* (Houston, Tex.: Arte Público Press, 1998); Leonor Villegas de Magnón, *The Rebel*; for the works of Fray Angelico Chavez, see Phyllis S. Morales, *Fray Angelico Chavez: A Bibliography of His Published Writings, 1925–1978* (Santa Fe, N.Mex.: Lightning Tree Press, 1980); Josephina Niggli, *Mexican Village* (Albuquerque: University of New Mexico Press, 1994 [1945]); Luis Perez, *El Coyote, The Rebel* (New York: Henry Holt, 1947).

Chapter 5

1. Juan Gómez–Quiñones, "The Promise and the Reality from 1941 to the 1960s," in *Chicano Politics*, 89. See also Mario T. García, *Mexican Americans*.

2. For an extensive exploration of this topic, see Ignacio M. García, *Viva Kennedy: Mexican Americans in Search of Camelot* (College Station: Texas A&M University Press, 2000).

3. Julie Leininger Pycior, "From Hope to Frustration: Mexican Americans and Lyndon Johnson in 1967," *Western Historical Quarterly* 24, 4 (1993): 470–94.

4. Genaro Padilla, "Myth and Comparative Cultural Nationalism: The Ideological Uses of Aztlán," in *Aztlán: Essays on the Chicano Homeland*, 111–34.

5. Taken from *Chicano Authors: Inquiry by Interview*, ed. Juan Bruce–Novoa (Austin: University of Texas Press, 1980), 152–53.

6. Alberto Ríos, "Chicano/a Borderlands Literature and Poetry," in *Contemporary Latin American Culture: Unity and Diversity*, ed. C. Gail Guntermann (Tempe, Ariz.: Center for Latin American Studies, Arizona State University, 1984), 81.

7. Pat Mora, *Nepantla: Essays from the Land in the Middle* (Albuquerque: University of New Mexico Press, 1993), 16.

8. There is another interesting connection between Cotton Mather and Latin America. According to Raymund A. Paredes, New England clergy made "Spanish America" a convenient target of the larger diatribes against Catholicism and the Pope. Like his grandfather before him, John Cotton, Mather combined his anti-Catholicism with anti–Spanish colonial anxieties. These two concerns led Mather to learn to read and write in Spanish. The product of this endeavor was his 1699 treatise *La Fe del Christiano (The Christian's Faith)*. Apparently, Mather thought his book would inspire the "reconversion of Spanish America." Raymund A. Paredes, "The Image of the Mexican in American Literature" (Ph.D. diss., University of Texas, 1973), 40–42.

9. This poem appears in her second volume of poetry, *Borders* (Houston, Tex.: Arte Público Press, 1986), 15. The poem's point of view is shared between Mexican and Polish immigrants in the United States. The crux of the poem appears at the end: "Will they like / our boy, our girl, our fine american / boy, our fine american girl?"

10. Scholars, from Ramón Saldívar to Houston Baker, Jr., have made much of Cuban theorist Robert Fernández Retamar's thesis that the figure of Caliban in *The Tempest* represents the prototypical colonial enslavement of the Native Amer-

ican through language and books. Mora's poem, I argue, offers an alternative to recurring rituals of male vengeance and violence by relinquishing her compromised "native" voice to the desert. Though the site of imperial designs, the land remains in some "essential" category apart from all languages; it can bequeath its blessings precisely because it is immune to human history. See Robert Fernández Retamar, "Caliban: Notes Towards a Discussion of Culture in Our America," *Massachusetts Review* 15, 1–2 (1974): 7–72; Houston Baker, Jr., "Caliban's Triple Play," in *"Race," Writing and Difference*, ed. Henry Louis Gates, Jr. (Chicago: University of Chicago Press, 1985), 381–95; Ramón Saldívar, "Ideologies of the Self: Chicano Autobiography," ch. 7 of *Chicano Narrative*, 154–70.

11. Part of Mather's acceptance of the term "American" resides in his implicit understanding that all peoples in the Americas arrived, at some point, as immigrants. In his view, there is no indigenous population. In chapter 1 of *Magnalia Christi Americana*, he relates the conjectures of Hornius's *Discourses* and Dr. Woodward's *Natural History of the Earth* that the first immigrants to the Americas came by way of the Bering Strait—a hypothesis still in currency today (44–46).

12. From Mora's second volume of poetry, *Borders*, 86.

13. Rudolfo A. Anaya "An American Chicano in King Arthur's Court," in *Old Southwest/New Southwest: Essays on a Region and Its Literature*, ed. Judy Nolte Lensink (Tucson, Ariz.: Tucson Public Library, 1987), 116.

14. Winner of the Pittsburgh Press Award, *Emplumada* (1981) established Cervantes as one of several second-generation Chicano/a poets to combine Chicano/a Movement politics and aesthetic qualities to critical acclaim. Other poets include Bernice Zamora (*Restless Serpents*, 1976), Gary Soto (*The Elements of San Joaquín*, 1977), and Orlando Ramírez (*Speedway*, 1979).

15. From *The Puritans*, ed. Perry Miller and Thomas H. Johnson (New York: American Book Company, 1938), 587. All quotations of this poem come from this anthology, though the lines have been broken in the standard 4/3 stress pattern.

16. Jeffrey A. Hammond, " 'Ladders of Your Own': The Day of Doom and the Repudiation of 'Carnal Reason,' " *Early American Literature* 19, 1 (1984): 59.

17. Walter Hughes " 'Meat Out of the Eater': Panic and Desire in American Puritan Poetry," in *Engendering Men: The Question of Male Feminist Criticism*, ed. Joseph A. Boone and Michael Cadden (New York: Routledge, 1990), 107.

18. Kathleen Verduin " 'Our Cursed Natures': Sexuality and the Puritan Conscience," *New England Quarterly* 56, 2 (1983): 226.

19. Here I am indebted to Verduin's argument that the Puritan clergy resolved their association of idolatry, paganism, and apocalyptic judgement with "sins of the flesh" by advocating more patriarchal control through all facets of society (231).

20. Ann Kibbey, *The Interpretation of Material Shape in Puritanism: A Study of Rhetoric, Prejudice, and Violence* (New York: Cambridge University Press, 1986).

21. Jonathan Boyarin, "Reading Exodus into History," *New Literary History* 23,

3 (summer 1992): 523–54. Boyarin discusses several historic discourses that have depended on biblical scripture, especially Exodus, in either arguing for liberation of an oppressed people or justifying conquest in search of the promised land.

22. Sacvan Bercovitch, *The American Jeremiad* (Madison: University of Wisconsin Press, 1978), 10–11.

23. Bruce-Novoa, biographical note for Lorna Dee Cervantes, in *Heath Anthology of American Literature,* vol. 2 (Lexington, Mass.: D. C. Heath, 1994), 3097.

24. John F. Crawford, "Toward a New Multicultural Criticism: Three Works by Women of Color," in *A Gift of Tongues: Critical Challenges in Contemporary American Poetry,* ed. Marie Harris and Kathleen Aguero (Athens, Ga.: University of Georgia Press, 1987), 170.

25. Marta Sánchez, "The Chicana as Scribe: Harmonizing Gender and Culture in Lorna Dee Cervantes's 'Beneath the Shadow of the Freeway,' " in *Contemporary Chicana Poetry: A Critical Approach to an Emerging Literature* (Berkeley: University of California Press, 1985), 85.

26. The text is taken from Lorna Dee Cervantes's *Emplumada,* 3–5. All subsequent quotations will come from this edition.

27. Cervantes chose an epigraph to this effect: "Consider the power of wrestling / your ally. His will is to kill you. / He has nothing against you" (1).

28. For a comparison that insists Soto seeks a more absolute break with a Puritan literary legacy, see Michael Tomasek Manson, "Poetry and Masculinity on the Anglo/Chicano Border," in *The Calvinist Roots of the Modern Era,* ed. Aliki Barnstone, Michael Tomasek Manson, and Carol J. Singley (Hanover, N.H.: University Press of New England, 1997), 263–80.

29. Gary Soto, interview by Jean W. Ross, in *Contemporary Authors,* vol. 125, ed. Hal May and Susan M. Trosky (Detroit: Gale Research, 1989), 424–27.

30. "Why I'm the Poet I've Become: Berryman and the Lucky 13," *New York Times Book Review,* 26 December 1993, 3.

31. For more, see Philip Levine, interview by J. M. Spalding and Guy Shahar, *Cortland Review,* issue 7 (May 1999). www.cortlandreview.com.

32. *The New American Poetry: 1945–1960,* ed. Donald M. Allen (New York: Grove Press, 1960), xi.

33. Patricia de la Fuente, "Ambiguity in the Poetry of Gary Soto," *Revista Chicano-Riqueña* 11, 2 (1983): 35.

34. Mutlu Konuk Blasing, *American Poetry: The Rhetoric of Its Forms* (New Haven, Conn.: Yale University Press, 1987), 17.

35. Laurel Ulrich, *Good Wives: Image and Reality in the Lives of Women in Northern New England, 1650–1750* (New York: Oxford University Press, 1983), 9.

36. *The Poetical Works of Edward Taylor,* ed. Thomas H. Johnson (Princeton, N.J.: Princeton University Press, 1971).

37. Gary Soto, *Black Hair* (Pittsburgh, Pa.: University of Pittsburgh Press, 1985).

38. See Phyllis M. Jones and Nicholas R. Jones, *Salvation in New England* (Austin: University of Texas Press, 1977), 6.

Afterword

Epigraph: José David Saldívar, "Tracking English and American Literary Criticism," *Daedalus* 126, 1 (1997): 155–56.

Bibliography

Acuña, Rodolfo. *Occupied America: The Chicano Struggle Toward Liberation.* San Francisco: Canfield Press, 1972.

—. *Occupied America: A History of Chicanos.* 3d ed. New York: Harper & Row, 1988.

Ainsworth, Brigadier General Fred C., Jr., ed. *The War of the Rebellion: A Compilation of the Official Orders of Union and Confederate Armies.* Series II, vol. V. Washington, D.C.: Government Printing Office, 1899.

Alarcón, Daniel Cooper. *The Aztec Palimpsest: Mexico in the Modern Imagination* (Tucson: University of Arizona Press, 1997).

Alarcón, Norma. "Chicana Feminism: In the Tracks of 'The' Native Woman." In *Between Woman and Nation: Nationalism, Transnational Feminisms, and the State,* edited by Caren Kaplan, Norma Alarcón, and Minoo Moallem, 63–71. Durham, N.C.: Duke University Press, 1999.

—. "Tropology of Hunger: The 'Miseducation' of Richard Rodriguez." In *The Ethnic Canon: Histories, Institutions, and Interventions,* edited by David Palumbo-Liu, 140–52. Minneapolis: University of Minnesota Press, 1995.

"Alden Partridge." In *The National Cyclopaedia of American Biography.* Clifton, N.J.: James T. White, 1922.

Allen, Donald M., ed. *The New American Poetry: 1945–1960.* New York: Grove Press, 1960.

Almaguer, Tomás. *Racial Fault Lines: The Historical Origins of White Supremacy in California.* Berkeley: University of California Press, 1994.

Alurista. "Cultural Nationalism and Chicano Literature: 1965–1975." In *Missions in Conflict: Essays on U.S.-Mexican Relations and Chicano Culture,* edited by Renate von Bardeleben, Dietrich Briesemeister, and Juan Bruce-Novoa, 41–52. Tübingen: Gunter Narr, 1986.

Anaya, Rudolfo A. "An American Chicano in King Arthur's Court." In *Old Southwest/New Southwest: Essays on a Region and Its Literature,* edited by Judy Nolte Lensink, 113–18. Tucson: Tucson Public Library, 1987.

Anaya, Rudolfo A., and Francisco A. Lomelí, eds. *Aztlán: Essays on the Chicano Homeland.* Albuquerque, N.Mex.: Academia/El Norte Publications, 1989.

Anderson, Virginia D. *New England's Generation: The Great Migration and the Formation of Society and Culture in the Seventeenth Century*. New York: Cambridge University Press, 1991.

Anna, Timothy E. *The Mexican Empire*. Lincoln: University of Nebraska Press, 1990.

Anzaldúa, Gloria. *Borderlands/La Frontera: The New Mestiza*. San Francisco: Spinsters/Aunt Lute, 1987.

Aranda, José F., Jr. "Contradictory Impulses: María Amparo Ruiz de Burton, Resistance Theory, and the Politics of Chicano/a Studies." *American Literature* 70, 3 (1998): 551–79.

—. "María Amparo Ruiz de Burton." *American Prose Writers, 1870–1920*. Vol. 2, edited by Sharon M. Harris. *Dictionary of Literary Biography*. Detroit: Gale Research, 2000.

"Asa Burton." In *Dictionary of American Biography*, edited by Allen Johnson. Vol. 3. New York: Scribner, 1929.

Asbaugh, Carolyn. *Lucy Parsons: American Revolutionary*. Chicago: Herr, 1976.

Baker, Houston, Jr. "Caliban's Triple Play." In *"Race," Writing, and Difference*, edited by Henry Louis Gates, Jr., 381–95. Chicago: University of Chicago Press, 1985.

Bancroft, George. *The History of the United States: From the Discovery of the Continent*. New York: D. Appleton, 1882.

Barnstone, Aliki, Michael Tomasek Manson, and Carol J. Singley, eds. *The Calvinist Roots of the Modern Era*. Hanover, N.H.: University Press of New England, 1997.

Baym, Nina. "Early Histories of American Literature: A Chapter in the Institution of New England." *American Literary History* 1, 3 (1989): 459–88.

Bercovitch, Sacvan. *The American Jeremiad*. Madison: University of Wisconsin Press, 1978.

—. "The Ends of American Puritan Rhetoric." In *The Ends of Rhetoric: History, Theory, Practice*, edited by John Bender and David E. Wellbery, 171–91. Stanford, Calif.: Stanford University Press, 1990.

—. *The Puritan Origins of the American Self*. New Haven, Conn.: Yale University Press, 1975.

—, ed. *Reconstructing American Literary History*. Cambridge: Harvard University Press, 1986.

Berryman, John. *Homage to Mistress Bradstreet*. New York: Farrar, Straus & Giroux, 1967 [1956].

Bérubé, Michael, and Cary Nelson, eds. *Higher Education under Fire: Politics, Economics, and the Crisis of the Humanities*. New York: Routledge, 1995.

Bhabha, Homi. "DissemiNation: Time, Narrative, and the Margins of the Modern Nation." In *Nation and Narration*, edited by Homi Bhabha, 291–321. New York: Routledge, 1990.

Blasing, Mutlu Konuk. *American Poetry: The Rhetoric of Its Forms*. New Haven, Conn.: Yale University Press, 1987.

Bloom, Allan. *The Closing of the American Mind: How Higher Education Has Failed Democracy and Impoverished the Souls of Today's Students*. New York: Simon & Schuster, 1987.

Boyarin, Jonathan. "Reading Exodus into History." *New Literary History* 23, 3 (summer 1992): 523–54.

Bruce-Novoa, Juan. Biographical note for Lorna Dee Cervantes. In *Heath Anthology of American Literature*, vol. 2, 3097. Lexington, Mass.: D. C. Heath, 1994.

—. "Canonical and Noncanonical Texts." *Américas Review* 14, 3–4 (1986): 119–35.

—. *Chicano Authors: Inquiry by Interview*. Austin: University of Texas Press, 1980.

—. "Dialogical Strategies, Monological Goals: Chicano Literature." In *An Other Tongue: Nation and Ethnicity in the Linguistic Borderlands*, edited by Alfred Artega, 225–45. Durham, N.C.: Duke University Press, 1994.

Buntline, Ned. *The Volunteer, or The Maid of Monterrey, A Tale of the Mexican War*. Boston: F. Gleason, 1847.

Cabeza de Baca, Fabiola *We Fed Them Cactus*. 2d ed. Albuquerque: University of New Mexico Press, 1994 [1954].

Cain, William E. *F. O. Matthiessen and the Politics of Criticism*. Madison: University of Wisconsin Press, 1988.

Calavita, Kitty. *Inside the State: The Bracero Program, Immigration, and I.N.S.* New York: Routledge, 1992.

Calderón, Héctor, and José David Saldívar, eds. *Criticism in the Borderlands: Studies in Chicano Literature, Culture, and Ideology*. Durham, N.C.: Duke University Press, 1991.

Cannon, Lou. "Latinos Leading Boom in Southern California." *Houston Chronicle*, 20 July 1997, p. 10A.

Cárdenas de Dwyer, Carlota. "The Development of Chicano Drama and Luis Valdez's *Actos*." In *Modern Chicano Writers: A Collection of Critical Essays*, edited by Joseph Sommers and Tomás Ybarra-Frausto, 160–66. Englewood Cliffs, N.J.: Prentice-Hall, 1979.

Castillo, Ana. "Our Tongue Was Nahuatl." In *The Third Woman*, edited by Dexter Fisher, 390–92. Boston: Houghton Mifflin, 1980.

Cather, Willa. *My Ántonia*. New York: Viking Penguin, 1999 [1918].

Cervantes, Lorna Dee. *Emplumada*. Pittsburgh: University of Pittsburgh Press, 1981.

Chabram-Dernersesian, Angie. "'Chicana! Rican? No, Chicana Riqueña!': Refashioning the Transnational Connection." In *Between Woman and Nation: Nationalism, Transnational Feminisms, and the State*, edited by Caren Kaplan, Norma Alarcón, and Minoo Moallem, 264–95. Durham, N.C.: Duke University Press, 1999.

—. "Conceptualizing Chicano Critical Discourse." In *Criticism in the Borderlands: Studies in Chicano Literature, Culture, and Ideology*, edited by Héctor Calderón and José David Saldívar, 127–48. Durham, N.C.: Duke University Press, 1991.

—. "I Throw Punches for My Race, but I Don't Wanna Be a Man: Writing Us–Chica–nos (Girl, Us)/Chicanas–into the Movement Script." In *Cultural Studies*, edited by Lawrence Grossberg, Cary Nelson, and Paul A. Treichler, 81–95. New York: Routledge, 1992.

—. "On the Social Construction of Whiteness within Selected Chicana/o Discourses." In *Displacing Whiteness: Essays in Social and Cultural Criticism*, edited by Ruth Frankenberg, 107–64. Durham, N.C.: Duke University Press, 1997.

Cisneros, Sandra. *The House on Mango Street*. New York: Vintage, 1989 [1984].

Colton, Walter. *Three Years in California*. New York: A. S. Barnes, 1851.

Comer, Krista. *Landscapes of the New West: Gender and Geography in Contemporary Women's Writing*. Chapel Hill: University of North Carolina Press, 1999.

Contreras, Raoul. "What Is Latino Studies?: The Ideological Dimension of Program 'Construction' and Program Location." *Latino Studies Journal* 11, 1 (2000): 25–49.

Cook, Eleanor. "Reading Typologically, For Example, Faulkner." *American Literature* 63, 4 (1991): 693–711.

Corona, Bert. "Chicano Scholars and Public Issues in the United States in the Eighties." In *History, Culture and Society: Chicano Studies in the 1980s*, edited by Mario T. Garcia et al., 11–18. Ypsilanti, Mich.: National Association of Chicano Studies, Bilingual Press, 1983.

Cotera, María Eugenia. "Engendering a 'Dialectics of Our America': Jovita González's Pluralist Dialogue as Feminist Testimonio." In *Las Obreras: Chicana Politics of Work and Family*. Aztlán Anthology Series 1, vol. ed. Vicki L. Ruiz (Los Angeles: UCLA Chicano Studies Research Center Publications, 2000).

—. "*Hombres Necios*: A Critical Epilogue." In *Caballero: A Historical Novel*, by Jovita González and Eve Raleigh, 339–46. College Station: Texas A&M University Press, 1996.

Crawford, John. "Notes Toward a New Multicultural Criticism: Three Works by Women of Color." In *A Gift of Tongues: Critical Challenges in Contemporary American Poetry*, edited by Marie Harris and Kathleen Aguero, 155–95. Athens Ga.: University of Georgia Press, 1987.

Crawford, Kathleen. "María Amparo Ruiz de Burton: The General's Lady." *Journal of San Diego History* 30, 3 (1984): 207–208.

Dana, Richard Henry. *Two Years before the Mast and Twenty-Four Years After*, edited by Charles W. Eliot. New York: Collier, 1909 [1840].

Davidson, Cathy. *Revolution and the Word: The Rise of the Novel in America*. New York: Oxford University Press, 1986.

Davis, Lennard J., and M. Bella Mirabella, eds. *Left Politics and the Literary Profession*. New York: Columbia University Press, 1990.

De la Fuente, Patricia. "Ambiguity in the Poetry of Gary Soto." *Revista Chicano-Riqueña* 11, 2 (1983): 34–39.

De Prospo, R. C. "Marginalizing Early American Literature." *New Literary History* 23, 2 (1992): 233–65.

De Zavala, Adina. *History and Legends of the Alamo and Other Missions*, edited by Richard Flores. Houston, Tex.: Arte Público Press, 1996.

Dobie, J. Frank. *Puro Mexicano*. Austin: Texas Folklore Society, 1935.

D'Souza, Dinesh. *Illiberal Education: The Politics of Race and Sex on Campus*. New York: Free Press, 1991.

Dubelier, Eric Alan. "Charles F. Smith: The Forgotten Soldier." B.A. honors thesis, Tulane University, 1977.

Eisenhower, John S. D. *So Far from God: The U.S. War with Mexico, 1846–1848*. New York: Random House, 1989.

Ellis, William Arba, ed. *Norwich University, 1819–1911: Her History, Her Graduates, Her Roll of Honor*. Vol. 2. Montpelier Vt.: Capital City Press, 1911.

"El Plan Espiritual de Aztlán." In *Aztlán: Essays on the Chicano Homeland*, edited by Rudolfo A. Anaya and Francisco A Lomelí, 1. Albuquerque: Academia/El Norte Publications, 1989.

Erkkila, Betsy. "Ethnicity, Literary Theory, and the Grounds of Resistance." *American Quarterly* 47, 4 (1995): 563–94.

Escobar, Edward J. "The Dialectics of Repression: The Los Angeles Police Department and the Chicano Movement, 1968–1971." *Journal of American History* 79 (1993): 1483–1514.

Feagin, Joe R. "Old Poison in New Bottles: The Deep Roots of Modern Nativism. In *Immigrants Out!: The New Nativism and the Anti-Immigrant Impulse in the United States*, edited by Juan F. Perea, 13–43. New York: New York University Press, 1997.

Fernández, Roberta. "*Abriendo caminos* in the Brotherland: Chicana Writers Respond to the Ideology of Literary Nationalism." *Frontiers: A Journal of Women Studies* 14, 2 (1994): 23–50.

Flores, Estevan T. "The Mexican–Origin People in the United States and Marxist Thought in Chicano Studies." In *The Left Academy: Marxist Scholarship on American Campuses*. Vol. III, edited by Bertell Ollman and Edward Vernoff, 103–63. New York: Praeger, 1986.

Flores, Juan. "Latino Studies: New Contexts, New Concepts." *Harvard Educational Review* 67, 2 (1997): 208–21.

Foerster, Norman. *The Reinterpretation of American Literature*. New York: Harcourt, Brace, 1928.

Fregoso, Rosa Linda, and Angie Chabram. "Chicana/o Cultural Representations: Reframing Alternative Critical Discourses." *Cultural Studies* 4, 3 (1990): 203–12.

García, Alma M., ed. *Chicana Feminist Thought: The Basic Historical Writings*. New York: Routledge, 1997.

García, Ignacio M. "Constructing the Chicano Movement: Synthesis of a Militant

Ethos." In *Perspectives of Mexican American Studies*. Vol. 6, 1–19. Tucson, Ariz.: Mexican American Studies and Research Center, 1997.

——. *Viva Kennedy: Mexican Americans in Search of Camelot*. College Station: Texas A&M University Press, 2000.

García, Mario T. "La Frontera: The Border as Symbol and Reality in Mexican-American Thought." *Mexican Studies/Estudios Mexicanos* 1, 2 (summer 1985): 195–225.

——. *Mexican Americans: Leadership, Ideology, and Identity, 1930–1960*. New Haven, Conn.: Yale University Press, 1989.

Garten, Richard M. "The Political Activities of S. L. Barlow, 1856–1864." Master's thesis, Columbia University, 1947.

Giroux, Henry A., and Peter McLaren, eds. *Between Borders: Pedagogy and the Politics of Cultural Studies*. New York: Routledge, 1994.

Goldman, Anne. Review of *The Squatter and the Don*, by María Amparo Ruiz de Burton. *MELUS* 19, 3 (1994): 129–31.

Gómez-Quiñones, Juan. *Chicano Politics: Reality and Promise, 1940–1990*. Albuquerque: University of New Mexico Press, 1990.

——. *Mexican American Labor, 1790–1990*. Albuquerque: University of New Mexico Press, 1994.

——. *Mexican Students Por La Raza: The Chicano Student Movement in Southern California, 1967–1977*. Santa Barbara, Calif.: Editorial La Causa, 1978.

——. "On Culture." *Revista Chicano-Riqueña* 5, 2 (spring 1977): 29.

——. "Toward a Perspective on Chicano History." *Aztlán* 2, 2 (1971): 1–49.

González, Deena J. *Refusing the Favor: The Spanish-Mexican Women of Santa Fe, 1820–1880*. New York: Oxford University Press, 1999.

González, Henry B. "Response to Chicano Militancy." In *Readings on La Raza, the Twentieth Century*, edited by Matt S. Meier and Feliciano Rivera, 258–63. New York: Hill & Wang, 1974.

González, Jovita. *Dew on the Thorn*. Edited by José E. Limón. Houston, Tex.: Arte Público Press, 1997.

——. "Social Life in Cameron, Starr, and Zapata Counties." Master's thesis, University of Texas at Austin, 1930.

——. *The Woman Who Lost Her Soul and Other Stories*. Edited by Sergio Reyna. Houston: Arte Público Press, 2000.

González, Jovita, and Eve Raleigh. *Caballero: A Historical Novel*. Edited by José E. Limón and María Cotera. College Station: Texas A&M University Press, 1996.

Gonzales-Berry, Erlinda. "Two Texts for a New Canon: Vicente Bernal's *Las Primicias* and Felipe Maximiliano Chacón's *Poesía y prosa*." In *Recovering the U.S. Hispanic Literary Heritage*, edited by Ramón Gutiérrez and Genaro Padilla, 129–51. Houston, Tex.: Arte Público Press, 1993.

Gonzales-Berry, Erlinda, and Chuck Tatum, eds. *Recovering the U.S. Hispanic Literary Heritage*. Vol. II. Houston, Tex.: Arte Público Press, 1996.

Gordon, Avery F., and Christopher Newfield, eds. *Mapping Multiculturalism.* Minneapolis: University of Minnesota Press, 1996.

Griswold del Castillo, Richard. *The Treaty of Guadalupe Hidalgo: A Legacy of Conflict.* Norman: University of Oklahoma Press, 1990.

Guerin-Gonzáles, Camille. *Mexican Workers and American Dreams: Immigration, Repatriation, and California Farm Labor, 1900–1939.* New Brunswick, N.J.: Rutgers University Press, 1994.

Gura, Philip. *The Crossroads of American History and Literature.* University Park, Pa.: Pennsylvania State University Press, 1996.

—. "Turning Our World Upside Down: Reconceiving Early American Literature." *American Literature* 63, 1 (1991): 104–12.

Gutiérrez, David. *Walls and Mirrors: Mexican Americans, Mexican Immigrants, and the Politics of Ethnicity.* Berkeley: University of California Press, 1995.

Gutiérrez, Ramón A. "Community, Patriarchy, and Individualism: The Politics of Chicano History and the Dream of Equality." *American Quarterly* 45, 1 (1993). 44–72.

—. *When Jesus Came, the Corn Mothers Went Away: Marriage, Sexuality and Power in New Mexico 1500–1846.* Palo Alto, Calif.: Stanford University Press, 1991.

Gutiérrez-Jones, Carl. "Desiring B/orders." *diacritics* 25, 1 (1995): 99–112.

—. *Rethinking the Borderlands: Between Chicano Culture and Legal Discourse.* Berkeley: University of California Press, 1995.

Haas, Lisbeth. *Conquests and Historical Identities in California, 1769–1936.* Berkeley: University of California Press, 1995.

Halleck, Henry W. *The Mexican War in Baja California: The Memorandum of Captain Henry W. Halleck, Concerning His Expeditions in Lower California, 1846–1848.* Edited with an introduction by Doyce B. Nunis, Jr. Los Angeles: Dawson's Book Shop, 1977.

Hammond, Jeffrey A. " 'Ladders of Your Own': The Day of Doom and the Repudiation of 'Carnal Reason.' " *Early American Literature* 19, 1 (1984): 42–67.

Handlin, Oscar. *The Uprooted: The Epic Story of the Great Migrations That Made the American People.* New York: Grosset & Dunlap, 1951.

Harden, Blaine. "52 Deaf Mexicans Rescued from Abusive Work." *Houston Chronicle,* 20 July 1997, p. 10A.

Harlow, Neal. *California Conquered: War and Peace on the Pacific, 1846–1850.* Berkeley: University of California Press, 1982.

Harper, Michael S. "History as Apple Tree." In *The Heath Anthology of American Literature,* edited by Paul Lauter, et al. Vol. 2, 2487–89. Lexington, Mass.: D. C. Heath, 1990.

Harte, Geoffrey Bret, ed. *The Letters of Bret Harte.* Boston: Houghton Mifflin, 1926.

Hartmann, Edward G. *The Movement to Americanize the Immigrant.* New York: AMS Press, 1967 [1948].

Hatch, Jane, ed. *The American Book of Days.* 3d ed. New York: H. W. Wilson, 1978.

Heizer, Robert F., and Alan F. Almquist. *The Other Californians: Prejudice and Discrimination under Spain, Mexico, and the United States to 1920*. Berkeley: University of California Press, 1971.

Hernández, Deluvina. "La Raza Satellite System." *Aztlán* 1, 1 (1970): 13–36.

Hernández, Nancy. "The Lynching of Mexican American Identities." Paper delivered at the fourth conference of Recovering the U.S. Hispanic Literary Heritage Project, "Interpreting and Contextualizing the Recovered Text," University of Houston, Houston, Texas, November 1996.

Herrera-Sobek, María. *The Mexican Corrido*. Bloomington: Indiana University Press, 1990.

Higham, John. *Strangers in the Land: Patterns of American Nativism, 1860–1925*. 2d ed. New Brunswick, N.J.: Rutgers University Press, 1988 [1955].

Hirsch, E. D. *Cultural Literacy: What Every American Needs to Know*. New York: Random House, 1988.

Hofstadter, Richard. *Social Darwinism in American Thought*. Rev. ed. New York: George Braziller, 1959 [1944].

Hogan, Michael. *The Irish Soldiers of Mexico*. Guadalajara, Mexico: Fondo Editorial Universitario, 1997.

Howard, David A. *Conquistador in Chains: Cabeza de Vaca and the Indians of the Americas*. Tuscaloosa: University of Alabama Press, 1997.

Hughes, Walter. "'Meat Out of the Eater': Panic and Desire in American Puritan Poetry." *Engendering Men: The Question of Male Feminist Criticism*, edited by Joseph A. Boone and Michael Cadden, 102–21. New York: Routledge, 1990.

Hurtado, Albert L. *Intimate Frontiers: Sex, Gender, and Culture in Old California*. Albuquerque: University of New Mexico Press, 1999.

Jaramillo, Cleofas. *Romance of a Little Village Girl*. Albuquerque: University of New Mexico Press, 1995 [1955].

Jay, Gregory. *American Literature and the Culture Wars*. Ithaca, N.Y.: Cornell University Press, 1997.

—. "Taking Multiculturalism Personally: Ethnos and Ethos in the Classroom." *American Literary History* 6, 4 (1994): 613–32.

Johannsen, Robert W. "The Meaning of Manifest Destiny." In *Manifest Destiny and Empire: American Antebellum Expansionism*, edited by Sam W. Haynes and Christopher Morris, 7–20. College Station: Published for the University of Texas at Arlington by Texas A & M University Press, 1997.

—. "The True Spirit of Patriot Virtue." *To the Halls of Montezuma: The Mexican War in the American Imagination*. New York: Oxford University Press, 1985.

Jones, Phyllis M., and Nicholas R. Jones. *Salvation in New England*. Austin: University of Texas Press, 1977.

Kanellos, Nicolás. Foreword to *Recovering the U.S. Hispanic Literary Heritage*, edited by Ramón Gutiérrez and Genaro Padilla, 13–15. Houston, Tex.: Arte Público Press, 1993.

—. *A History of Hispanic Theatre in the United States: Origins to 1940*. Austin: University of Texas Press, 1990.

—. *Thirty Million Strong: Reclaiming the Hispanic Image in American Culture*. Golden, Colo.: Fulcrum, 1998.

Kaplan, Amy, and Donald E. Pease, eds. *Cultures of United States Imperialism*. Durham, N.C.: Duke University Press, 1993.

Karlson, Carol F. *The Devil in the Shape of a Woman: Witchcraft in Colonial New England*. New York: Norton, 1987.

Kaup, Monika. "The Architecture of Ethnicity in Chicano Literature." *American Literature* 69, 2 (1997): 361–97.

—. *Thirty Million Strong: Reclaiming the Hispanic Image in American Culture*. Golden, Colo.: Fulcrum, 1998.

Kibbey, Ann. *The Interpretation of Material Shape in Puritanism: A Study of Rhetoric, Prejudice, and Violence*. New York: Cambridge University Press, 1986.

Knight, Alan. *The Mexican Revolution*. Vol. 2, *Counter-Revolution and Reconstruction*. Cambridge: Cambridge University Press, 1986.

Kolodny, Annette. "The Integrity of Memory: Creating a New Literary History of the United States." *American Literature* 57, 2 (1985): 291–307.

—. *The Land before Her: Fantasy and Experience of the American Frontiers, 1630–1860*. Chapel Hill: University of North Carolina Press, 1984.

—. *The Lay of the Land: Metaphor as Experience and History in American Life and Letters*. Chapel Hill: University of North Carolina Press, 1975.

—. "Letting Go Our Grand Obsessions: Notes Towards a New Literary History of the American Frontier." *American Literature* 64, 1 (1992): 1–18.

Kreneck, Thomas J. "Recovering the 'Lost' Manuscripts of Jovita González: The Production of South Texas Mexican-American Literature." *Texas Library Journal* 74, 2 (1998): 76–79.

Lauter, Paul. "The Literatures of America: A Comparative Discipline." In *Redefining American Literary History*, edited by A. LaVonne Brown Ruoff and Jerry W. Ward, Jr., 10–34. New York: Modern Language Association, 1990.

Lauter, Paul, et al., eds. *The Heath Anthology of American Literature*. Lexington, Mass.: D. C. Heath, 1990.

Leal, Luis. "In Search of Aztlán." In *Aztlán: Essays on the Chicano Homeland*, edited by Rudolfo A. Anaya and Francisco A. Lomelí, 6–13. Albuquerque: Academia/El Norte Publications, 1989.

Levin, David. "Perry Miller at Harvard." *Southern Review* 19, 4 (1983): 802–16.

Levine, Philip. Interview by J. M. Spalding and Guy Shahar. *Cortland Review*, issue 7 (May 1999). www.cortlandreview.com.

—. "Why I'm the Poet I've Become: Berryman and the Lucky 13." *New York Times Book Review*, 26 December 1993, p. 3.

Limerick, Patricia Nelson, Clyde A. Milner II, and Charles E. Rankin. *Trails: Toward a New Western Literary History*. Lawrence: University of Kansas Press, 1991.

Limón, José E. *Dancing with the Devil: Society and Cultural Politics in Mexican-American South Texas.* Madison: University of Wisconsin Press, 1994.

—. "The Folk Performance of 'Chicano' and the Cultural Limits of Political Ideology." In *"And Other Neighborly Names": Social Process and Cultural Image in Texas Folklore,* edited by Richard Bauman and Roger D. Abrahams, 197–225. Austin: University of Texas Press, 1981.

—. Introduction to *Caballero: A Historical Novel,* by Jovita González and Eve Raleigh, xii–xxvi. College Station: Texas A&M University Press, 1996.

—. Introduction to *Dew on the Thorn,* xv–xxviii. Houston: Arte Público Press, 1997.

—. *Mexican Ballads, Chicano Poems: History and Influence in Mexican American Social Poetry.* Austin: University of Texas Press, 1992.

Lippincott Company, J. B. *Centennial Reflections: J. B. Lippincott Company in the 1870s.* Philadelphia: J. B. Lippincott, 1976.

Lucero–Trujillo, Christine. "Machismo Is Part of Our Culture." In *The Third Woman,* edited by Dexter Fisher, 401–402. Boston: Houghton Mifflin, 1980.

Lum, Lydia. "Minority Enrollment: How to Stop the Hemorrhaging?" *Houston Chronicle,* 14 August 1997, p. 19A.

Manson, Michael Tomasek. "Poetry and Masculinity on the Anglo/Chicano Border." In *The Calvinist Roots of the Modern Era,* edited by Aliki Barnstone, Michael Tomasek Manson, and Carol J. Singley, 263–80. Hanover, N.H.: University Press of New England, 1997.

Márquez, Antonio C. "Richard Rodriguez's *Hunger of Memory* and New Perspectives on Ethnic Autobiography." In *Teaching American Ethnic Literatures: Nineteen Essays,* edited by John R. Maitino and David R. Peck, 237–54. Albuquerque: University of New Mexico Press, 1996.

Márquez, Benjamin. *LULAC: The Evolution of a Mexican American Political Organization.* Austin: University of Texas Press, 1993.

Martínez, Julio A., and Francisco A. Lomelí. *Chicano Literature: A Reference Guide.* Westport, Conn.: Greenwood Press, 1985.

Mather, Cotton. *Magnalia Christi Americana, or The Ecclesiastical History of New England.* Hartford, Conn.: Silas Andrus & Son, 1885 [1702].

Matthiessen, F. O. *American Renaissance: Art and Expression in the Age of Emerson and Whitman.* New York: Oxford University Press, 1941.

May, Antoinette. *Haunted Houses of California.* San Carlos, Calif.: Wide World Publishing/Tetra, 1993 [1990].

Mayo–Smith, Richard. *Emigration and Immigration: A Study in Social Science.* New York: Scribner, 1890.

McDonnell, Patrick J. "Mexicans Settle in Every Region of the U.S./Their Numbers May Be Redefining American Immigrant experiences." *Houston Chronicle,* 2 January 1998, pp. 1A, 16A.

McGhee, Earl Samuel. "E. W. Morse, Pioneer Merchant and Co–Founder of San Diego." Master's thesis, San Diego State College, 1950.

McKenna, Teresa. *Migrant Song: Politics and Process in Contemporary Chicano Literature.* Austin: University of Texas Press, 1997.

McNamara, Kevin R. "A Finer Grain: Richard Rodriguez's *Days of Obligation.*" *Arizona Quarterly* 53, 1 (1997): 103–22.

Meléndez, A. Gabriel. *So All Is Not Lost: The Poetics of Print in Nuevomexicano Communities, 1834–1958.* Albuquerque: University of New Mexico Press, 1997.

Mena, María Cristina. *The Collected Short Stories of María Cristina Mena,* edited by Amy Doherty. Houston, Tex.: Arte Público Press, 1997.

Menchaca, Martha. "Chicano Indianism: A Historical Account of Racial Oppression in the United States." *American Ethnologist* 20, 3 (1993): 583–603.

—. *The Mexican Outsiders: A Community History of Marginalization and Discrimination in California.* Austin: University of Texas Press, 1995.

Miller, Arthur. *The Crucible.* New York: Viking Press, 1953.

Miller, Perry. *Errand into the Wilderness.* Cambridge, Mass.: Harvard University Press, Belknap Press, 1956.

—. Foreword to *A History of American Literature, 1607–1765,* by Moses Coit Tyler, 10–11. New York: Collier Books, 1962 [1878].

—. *The New England Mind, The Seventeenth Century.* Cambridge: Harvard University Press, Belknap Press, 1939.

—. *Orthodoxy in Massachusetts, 1630–1650.* New York: Harper, 1970 [1933].

Miller, Perry, and Thomas H. Johnson. *The Puritans.* New York: American Book Company, 1938.

Mocho, Jill. *Murder and Justice in Frontier New Mexico, 1821–1846.* Albuquerque: University of New Mexico Press, 1997.

Montejano, David. *Anglos and Mexicans in the Making of Texas, 1836–1986.* Austin: University of Texas Press, 1987.

Mora, Pat. *Borders.* Houston, Tex.: Arte Público Press, 1986.

—. *Nepantla: Essays from the Land in the Middle.* Albuquerque: University of New Mexico Press, 1993.

Moraga, Cherríe. *Loving in the War Years: Lo que nunca pasó por sus labios.* Boston: South End Press, 1983.

Morales, Phyllis S. *Fray Angelico Chavez: A Bibliography of His Published Writings, 1925–1978.* Santa Fe, N.Mex.: Lightning Tree Press, 1980.

Morgan, Edmund. "An Address to the Colonial Society of Massachusetts, on the Occasion of Its Centennial. *New England Quarterly* 66, 3 (1993): 355–65.

—. *The Puritan Dilemma: The Story of John Winthrop.* Boston: Little, Brown, 1958.

Morison, Samuel Eliot. *Builders of the Bay Colony.* 2d ed. Boston: Houghton Mifflin, 1958.

Mount, Graeme S. "Nuevo Mexicanos and the War of 1898." *New Mexico Historical Review* 58, 4 (1993): 381–96.

Murdock, Kenneth Ballard. *Increase Mather: The Foremost American Puritan.* Cambridge: Harvard University Press, 1926.

Nackenoff, Carol. *The Fictional Republic: Horatio Alger and American Political Discourse.* New York: Oxford University Press, 1994.

"The National Conservation Group Buys 4,800 Acres for SD's Newest Wildlife Refuge." *The Press Box*, 14 August 1997, www.co.san–diego.ca.us/cnty/bos/sup2/news/rchjamul.html

Neate, Wilson. *Tolerating Ambiguity: Ethnicity and Community in Chicano/a Writing.* New York: Peter Lang, 1998.

Niggli, Josephina. *Mexican Village.* Albuquerque: University of New Mexico Press, 1994 [1945].

Nunis, Doyce B., Jr., ed. *The Mexican War in Baja California: The Memorandum of Captain Henry W. Halleck, Concerning His Expedition in Lower California, 1846–1848.* Los Angeles: Dawson's Book Shop, 1977.

Oden, Frederick Bryant. "The Maid of Monterey: The Life of María Amparo Ruiz de Burton, 1832–1895." Master's thesis, University of San Diego, 1992.

Ortego, Philip D. "The Chicano Renaissance." *Social Casework* 52, 5 (1971): 294–307.

Osio, Antonio María. *The History of Alta California: A Memoir of Mexican California.* Translated and edited by Rose Marie Beebe and Robert M. Senkewicz. Madison: University of Wisconsin Press, 1996 [1851].

Otero, Miguel Antonio, Jr. *My Life on the Frontier.* New York: Press of the Pioneers, 1939 [1936].

—. *The Real Billy the Kid.* Houston, Tex.: Arte Público Press, 1998.

Otero, Nina. *Old Spain in Our Southwest.* New York: Harcourt, Brace, 1936.

Padilla, Genaro. *My History, Not Yours: The Formation of Mexican American Autobiography.* Madison: University of Wisconsin Press, 1993.

—. "Myth and Comparative Cultural Nationalism: The Ideological Uses of Aztlán." In *Aztlán: Essays on the Chicano Homeland*, edited by Rudolfo A. Anaya and Francisco A. Lomelí, 111–34. Albuquerque, N.Mex.: Academia/El Norte Publications, 1989.

—. "Recovering Mexican–American Autobiography." In *Recovering the U.S. Hispanic Literary Heritage.* Vol. 1, edited by Ramón Gutiérrez and Genaro Padilla, 153–78. Houston, Tex.: Arte Público Press, 1993.

Palumbo–Liu, David. *The Ethnic Canon: Histories, Institutions, and Interventions.* Minneapolis: University of Minnesota Press, 1995.

Paredes, Américo. *George Washington Gómez: A Mexicotexan Novel.* Houston, Tex.: Arte Público Press, 1990.

—. *The Shadow.* Houston, Tex.: Arte Público Press, 1998.

—. *With His Pistol in His Hand: A Border Ballad and Its Hero.* Austin: University of Texas Press, 1958.

Paredes, Raymund A. "Autobiography and Ethnic Politics: Richard Rodriguez's *Hunger of Memory*." In *Multicultural Autobiography: American Lives*, edited by James Robert Payne, 280–96. Knoxville: University of Tennessee Press, 1992.

—. "The Image of the Mexican in American Literature." Ph.D. diss., University of Texas, 1973.

Pease, Donald E. "New Americanist: Revisionist Interventions into the Canon." *boundary 2* 17, 1 (spring 1990): 1–37.

—. "National Identities, Postmodern Artifacts, and Postnational Narratives." In *National Identities and Post-Americanist Narratives,* edited by Donald E. Pease, 1–13. Durham, N.C.: Duke University Press, 1994.

Perea, Juan F. "The Statue of Liberty: Notes from Behind the Gilded Door." In *Immigrants Out!: The New Nativism and the Anti-Immigrant Impulse in the United States,* edited by Juan F. Perea. New York: New York University Press, 1997.

Perez, Luis. *El Coyote, The Rebel.* Houston: Arte Público Press, 2000 [New York: Henry Holt, 1947].

Pérez-Torres. Rafael. *Movements in Chicano Poetry: Against Myths, against Margins.* New York: Cambridge University Press, 1995.

—. "Refiguring Aztlán." *Aztlán* 22, 2 (1997): 15–41.

Pitt, Leonard. *The Decline of the Californio: A Social History of the Spanish-Speaking Californians, 1846–1890.* Berkeley: University of California Press, 1966.

Pope, Robert G. *The Half-Way Covenant: Church Membership in Puritan New England.* Princeton, N.J.: Princeton University Press, 1969.

Pycior, Julie Leininger. "From Hope to Frustration: Mexican Americans and Lyndon Johnson in 1967." *Western Historical Quarterly* 24, 4 (1993): 470–93.

Quintana, Alvina E. *Home Girls: Chicana Literary Voices.* Philadelphia: Temple University Press, 1996.

Rak, Mary Kidder. *Border Patrol.* Boston: Houghton Mifflin, 1938.

—. *They Guard the Gates: The Way of Life on the American Border.* Evanston. Ill.: Row, Peterson, 1941.

Ramírez, Orlando. *Speedway.* San Jose, Calif.: Mango, 1979.

Rebolledo, Tey Diana. "The Politics of Poetics: Or, What Am I, A Critic, Doing in This Text Anyhow?" In *Chicana Creativity and Criticism: Charting New Frontiers in American Literature,* edited by María Herrera-Sobek and Helena María Viramontes, 129–38. Houston, Tex.: Arte Público Press, 1988.

—. *Women Singing in the Snow: A Cultural Analysis of Chicana Literature.* Tucson: University of Arizona Press, 1995.

Reising, Russell J. *The Unusable Past: Theory and the Study of American Literature.* London: Methuen, 1986.

Retamar, Robert Fernández. "Caliban: Notes Towards a Discussion of Culture in Our America." *Massachusetts Review* 15, 1–2 (1974): 7–72.

Ríos, Alberto, "Chicano/a Borderlands Literature and Poetry." In *Contemporary Latin American Culture: Unity and Diversity,* edited by C. Gail Guntermann, 79–91. Tempe: Center for Latin American Studies, Arizona State University, 1984.

Rivera, Tomás. "Chicano Literature: The Establishment of Community." In *Tomás*

Rivera, *The Complete Works*, edited by Julián Olivares, 348–405. Houston, Tex.: Arte Público Press, 1991.

—. *. . . Y no se lo tragó la tierra/And the Earth Did Not Devour Him*. Houston, Tex.: Arte Público Press, 1992.

Roberts, Robert B. "Fort Monroe." In *Encyclopedia of Historic Forts: The Military, Pioneer, and Trading Posts of the United States*, by Robert B. Roberts, 815–18. New York: Collier Macmillan, 1988.

Robinson, Cecil. *Mexico and the Hispanic Southwest in American Literature*. Rev. ed. Tucson: University of Arizona Press, 1977.

Rodriguez, Richard. *Hunger of Memory: The Education of Richard Rodriguez*. New York: Bantam Books, 1982.

—. "New Reformation." *The News Hour with Jim Lehrer*, 29 March 1996, Online Newshour: www.pbs.org/newshour/ww.rodriguez.html

—. "Objects of Desire." *The News Hour with Jim Lehrer*, 22 April 1996, Online Newshour: www.pbs.org/newshour/ww.rodriguez.html

Romano-V, Octavio Ignacio, and Herminio Ríos C., eds. *El Espejo—The Mirror: Selected Chicano Literature*. Berkeley: Quinto Sol, 1972.

Romero, Lora. " 'When Something Goes Queer': Familiarity, Formalism, and Minority Intellectuals in the 1980s." *Yale Journal of Criticism* 6, 1 (1993): 121–41.

Rosenblum, Joseph. "Two Americanists: Samuel L. M. Barlow and Henry Harrisse." *American Book Collector* 6, 2 (1985): 14–25.

Ross, Edward Alsworth. *The Old World in the New: The Significance of Past and Present Immigration to the American People*. New York: Century, 1914.

Ruiz de Burton, María Amparo. *The Squatter and the Don*. Edited by Rosaura Sánchez and Beatrice Pita. Houston, Tex.: Arte Público Press, 1992 [1885].

—. *Who Would Have Thought It?* Edited with introduction by Rosaura Sánchez and Beatrice Pita. Houston, Tex.: Arte Público Press, 1995 [1872].

Rulfo, Juan. *Pedro Páramo*. Translated by Margaret Sayers Peden. New York: Grove Press, 1994.

Saldívar, José David. *Border Matters: Remapping American Cultural Studies*. Berkeley: University of California Press, 1997.

—. *The Dialectics of Our America: Genealogy, Cultural Critique, and Literary History*. Durham, N.C.: Duke University Press, 1991.

—. "Tracking English and American Literary Criticism." *Daedalus* 126, 1 (1997): 155–74.

Saldívar, Ramón. "The Borderlands of Culture: Américo Paredes's *George Washington Gómez* and Chicano Literature at the End of the Twentieth Century." *American Literary History* 5, 2 (1993): 272–93.

—. *Chicano Narrative: The Dialectics of Difference*. Madison: University of Wisconsin Press, 1990.

—. "Narrative, Ideology, and the Reconstruction of American Literary History." In *Chicano Criticism in the Borderlands: Studies in Chicano Literature, Culture, and Ideology*, edited by Héctor Calderón and José David Saldívar, 11–20. Durham, N.C.: Duke University Press, 1991.

Saldívar-Hull, Sonia. *Feminism on the Border: Chicana Gender Politics and Literature*. Berkeley: University of California Press, 2000.

"Samuel L. M. Barlow." In *Dictionary of American Biography*, edited by Allen Johnson. Vol. 1. New York: Scribner, 1928.

Sánchez, George. *Becoming Mexican American: Ethnicity, Culture, and Identity in Chicano Los Angeles, 1900–1945*. New York: Oxford University Press, 1993.

Sánchez, Marta. "The Chicana as Scribe: Harmonizing Gender and Culture in Lorna Dee Cervantes's 'Beneath the Shadow of the Freeway.'" In *Contemporary Chicana Poetry: A Critical Approach to an Emerging Literature*, 85–138. Berkeley: University of California Press, 1985.

Sánchez, Rosaura. "Calculated Musings: Richard Rodriguez's Metaphysics of Difference." In *The Ethnic Canon: Histories, Institutions, and Interventions*, edited by David Palumbo-Liu, 153–73. Minneapolis: University of Minnesota Press, 1995.

—. *Telling Identities: The Californio Testimonios*. Minneapolis: University of Minneapolis Press, 1995.

Sánchez, Rosaura, and Beatrice Pita. Introduction to *The Squatter and the Don*, by María Amparo Ruiz de Burton, 5–51. Houston, Tex.: Arte Público Press, 1992 [1885].

Santoni, Pedro. *Mexicans at Arms: Puro Federalists and the Politics of War, 1845–1848*. Fort Worth: Texas Christian University Press, 1996.

Saragoza, Alex M. "The Significance of Recent Chicano-related Historical Writings: An Appraisal." *Ethnic Affairs* 1 (1987): 24–62.

Segade, Gustavo V. "Identity and Power: An Essay on the Politics of Culture and the Culture of Politics in Chicano Thought." *Aztlán* 9 (1978): 88.

Smith, Henry Nash. *Virgin Land: The American West as Symbol and Myth*. Cambridge: Harvard University Press, 1950.

Smith, Macklin. *Prudentius' Psychomachia: A Reexamination*. Princeton, N.J.: Princeton University Press, 1976.

Smith, Robert C. "Mexicans in New York: Memberships and Incorporation in a New Immigrant Community." In *Latinos in New York: Communities in Transition*, edited by Gabriel Haslip-Viera and Sherrie L. Baver, 57–103. Notre Dame, Ind.: University of Notre Dame Press, 1996.

Sollors, Werner. *Beyond Ethnicity: Consent and Descent*. New York: Oxford University Press, 1986.

Soto, Gary. *Black Hair*. Pittsburgh: University of Pittsburgh Press, 1985.

—. *The Elements of San Joaquín*. Pittsburgh, Pa.: University of Pittsburgh Press, 1977.

—. Interview by Jean W. Ross. In *Contemporary Authors*. Vol. 125, edited by Hal May and Susan M. Trosky, 424–27. Detroit: Gale Research, 1989.

Spiller, Robert Ernest. *The Cycle of American Literature: An Essay in Historical Criticism*. New York: Macmillan, 1955.

Spiller, Robert Ernest, et al., eds. *Literary History of the United States*. New York: Macmillan, 1948.

Sprague, Claire. *Van Wyck Brooks: The Early Years, A Selection from His Works, 1908–1925*. Boston: Northeastern University Press, 1993.

Staten, Henry. "Ethnic Authenticity, Class, and Autobiography: The Case of *Hunger of Memory*." *PMLA* 113, 1 (1998): 103–16.

Strong, Josiah. *Our Country: Its Possible Future and Its Present Crisis*. New York: Baker & Taylor, for the American Home Missionary Society, 1885.

Tatum, Charles. "Some Considerations on Genres and Chronology for Nineteenth-Century Hispanic Literature." In *Recovering the U.S. Hispanic Literary Heritage*, edited by Ramón Gutiérrez and Genaro Padilla, 199–208. Houston, Tex.: Arte Público Press, 1993.

Taylor, Edward. *The Poetical Works of Edward Taylor*. Edited by Thomas H. Johnson. Princeton, N.J.: Princeton University Press, 1971.

Tompkins, Jane. *Sensational Designs: The Cultural Work of American Fiction, 1790–1860*. New York: Oxford University Press, 1985.

Torres, Hector A. Review of *Chicano Narrative: The Dialectics of Difference*, by Ramón Saldívar. *College Literature* (double issue), 19, 3; 20, 1 (1992/1993): 265–69.

Trent, William P., et al., eds. *Cambridge History of American Literature*. New York: Putnam, 1917.

Trotter, Joe William, Jr. *The Great Migration in Historical Perspective: New Dimensions of Race, Class, and Gender*. Bloomington: Indiana University Press, 1991.

Tyler, Moses Coit. *A History of American Literature during the Colonial Period, 1607–1765*. New York: Putnam, 1878.

Valdez, Luis. "Introduction: 'La Plebe.'" In *Aztlán: An Anthology of Mexican American Literature*, edited by Luis Valdez and Stan Steiner, xiii–xv. New York: Knopf, 1972.

Vanderbilt, Kermit. *American Literature and the Academy: The Roots, Growth, and Maturity of a Profession*. Philadelphia: University of Pennsylvania Press, 1986.

Venegas, Daniel. *The Adventures of Don Chipote, or, When Parrots Breast Feed*. Translated by Ethriam Cash Brammer. Recovering the U.S. Hispanic Literary Heritage. Houston, Tex.: Arte Público Press, 2000.

—. *Las aventuras de Don Chipote o, cuando los pericos mamen*. Houston, Tex.: Arte Público Press, 1999.

Verduin, Kathleen. "'Our Cursed Natures': Sexuality and the Puritan Conscience." *New England Quarterly* 56, 2 (1983): 220–37.

Villegas de Magnón, Leonor. *The Rebel.* Edited by Clara Lomas. Houston, Tex.: Arte Público Press, 1994.

Watson, Samuel J. "The Uncertain Road to Manifest Destiny: Army Officers and the Course of American Territorial Expansionism, 1815–1846. In *Manifest Destiny and Empire,* edited by Sam W. Haynes and Christopher Morris, 68–114. College Station: Published for the University of Texas at Arlington by Texas A&M University Press, 1997.

Weber, David J. "'From Hell Itself': The Americanization of Mexico's Northern Frontier." In *Myth and the History of the Hispanic Southwest: Essays by David J. Weber.* Albuquerque: University of New Mexico Press, 1988.

—. "The Spanish Legacy and the Historical Imagination." In *The Spanish Frontier in North America.* New Haven, Conn.: Yale University Press, 1992.

Wigglesworth, Michael. *Day of Doom.* In *The Puritans,* edited by Perry Miller and Thomas H. Johnson, 585–606. New York: American Book Company, 1938.

Williams, William Carlos. *In the American Grain.* New York: New Directions Books, 1956 [1925].

Wilson, James Grant, and John Fiske, eds. *Appletons' Cyclopaedia of American Biography.* New York: D. Appleton, 1889.

Wong, Sau-ling Cynthia. *Reading Asian American Literature: From Necessity to Extravagance.* Princeton, N.J.: Princeton University Press, 1993.

Wright, James Osborne. *Of the American Library of the Late Samuel Latham Mitchill Barlow.* New York: American Art Association, 1889.

Yezierska, Anzia. *Bread Givers.* New York: Persea Books, 1975 [1925].

Zamora, Bernice. *Restless Serpents.* Menlo Park, Calif.: Diseños Literarios, 1976.

Zavella, Patricia. "Feminist Insider Dilemmas: Constructing Ethnic Identity with 'Chicana' Informants." *Frontiers* 13, 3 (1993): 53–76.

Credits

Index

Acuña, Rodolfo F., 102, 138

affirmative action, 206

African American writers, xx, xxi, 46–47, 88. *See also* Douglass, Frederick; DuBois, W. E. B.; Hughes, Langston; Hurston, Zora Neale; Jacobs, Harriet

Alarcón, Daniel Cooper, 38

Alarcón, Norma, 5, 40–41

Allen, Donald M., 192

Alta California, 89, 90–91, 99–100, 104, 108

Alurista, 21, 61, 163

American Dream, 124–26, 128, 148–51, 156–58, 170, 178, 198, 199, 205

American Indian Movement, 18. *See also* Native Americans

American literary history, xvii, 54–55, 59, 67–71, 87, 131, 138, 163, 167, 206

American literary nationalism, xix, xx, 47, 57, 67, 68, 70

American literature, xvi, 44, 67, 161, 165; approaches to, xix–xxii, 46–48, 68–70, 73, 78, 80; canon of, xvii, xix, xvi, xxiv, xxvii, 59, 62–64, 66–68, 71–76, 135, 138–39, 163, 164, 166, 167; and dissent, xvii, xxvi, 53, 65, 68, 127, 139, 163, 165, 205; organic metaphor of, 51, 54, 55. *See also* Puritan myth of origins

American Studies, xvi, xx, 6, 51, 56, 134, 135. *See also* New American Studies

Anaya, Rudolfo, 176–77

Anzaldúa, Gloria, xxi, 28, 150, 203; *Borderlands/La Frontera: The New Mestiza*, 24–25, 30–31, 32–36

Asian American literature, 77–78

Asian Americans, 159

Asian American Studies, 77–79

Austin, Stephen F., Jr., 103, 106, 206

"auto–American–biography," 49, 57, 169–70, 171, 172

autobiography. *See* "auto–American–biography"; Chicano/a literature: autobiography; fictional autobiography

Aztecs, 11, 61–62. *See also* indios

Aztlán: Chicano Journal of the Social Sciences and the Arts, 13–15

Aztlán, myth of, xix, xxiv, xxvi, 11–25, 30, 34–38, 40–41, 61–62, 86, 164–66, 177. *See also* "El Plan Espiritual de Aztlán"

Baja California, 90–91, 98–100, 104

Barlow, Samuel L. M., 95–97, 115

baseball, 136–37, 195–96, 198, 199, 200

Baym, Nina, 113, 131

Bercovitch, Sacvan, 48, 63, 169, 170, 171, 173, 182, 184

Bhabha, Homi, 7, 9, 10, 12

biculturalism, 34, 159

binational identity, xviii, xix, 166, 206

Blasing, Mutlu, 193

Bloom, Allan, 45, 191

body, 185, 197–98, 202; Christian, 178, 180–81, 184; mestiza, 179. *See also* skin color

border. *See* United States–Mexico border

borderlands, 4–5, 33, 205; as a metaphor, 32, 33, 40. *See also* borderlands studies

borderlands studies, 5, 24, 30, 34, 36–37

Border Patrol. *See* United States Border Patrol

Bracero Program, 144

Bruce-Novoa, Juan, 6, 185, 186, 192

Buchanan, President James, 115

Burdock, Kenneth, 133

Burton, Almira (née Partridge), 109, 110

Burton, Asa, 110

Burton, Henry Halleck, 92, 94, 95, 118, 119

Burton, Captain Henry S., 89, 91, 92, 94, 104, 107, 109, 110, 111, 112

Burton, Nellie, 92, 94, 118

Burton, Oliver G., 109, 110

Cabeza de Baca, Fabiola, 154

California. *See* Alta California; Baja California

Californios, 83, 85, 87, 88, 92, 98–102, 104, 106, 117

Camarillo, Albert, 102

canon. *See* American literature, canon of

Catholicism, 109, 111, 113, 165, 166, 202

Century Magazine, 145, 146

Cervantes, Lorna Dee, 166, 178, 179, 185–91; *Emplumada*, 178, 179, 185; "Lots: I," 191; "Uncle's First Rabbit," 178, 179, 185, 186–91

Chabram-Dernersesian, Angie, 5, 9, 12, 30, 40–41, 76

Chávez, Cesar, xxii, 8, 162, 163, 203. *See also* United Farm Workers

Chavez, Fray Angelico, 160

Chicana feminism, 5, 11, 20–21, 28, 39, 170, 177–78, 179, 186–91

"Chicano," 37, 162

Chicano/a cultural nationalism, 13, 14, 16–17, 22, 23, 58–59, 152, 153, 166

Chicano/a historiography, 98–99, 102, 105, 142

Chicano/a history, 16–18, 21–22, 31, 86, 98, 102

Chicano/a literature, xvii, 31, 60, 63–64, 79, 142, 147, 150, 163–64, 166; autobiography, 24–25, 43; binational character of, 169; and the Chicano/a Movement, 21, 58–59; history of, xvi, xvii, xix, xxii–xxiii, 62; poetry, protest, xviii, 8, 10, 61, 166, 177, 188, 191; and the Puritan myth of origins, xxvi, 62. *See also* Chicano/a Renaissance; Mexican American literature

Chicano/a Movement, xv, xxii, xxiii, 3–4, 6–8, 16, 44, 85, 102, 140, 160, 166, 177; and Chicano/a Studies, 18–22, 29–30, 36, 38, 41; and a myth of origins, 58, 164

Chicano/a Renaissance, 58–60, 79, 141, 147, 160, 161, 162, 192. *See also* Chicano/a literature

Chicano/a Studies, xv–xvi, xxii–xxiv, 4, 5, 7, 16, 23, 34–37, 38, 41, 122; divisions within, 6, 13, 14; and Marxist scholarship, 14–15; and *mestizaje*, 24, 36, 40; New, 36, 38–40, 41, 87; and a "usable past," 13

Chicano/a writers, 31, 43, 163–64, 166, 203; compared to Puritan writers, xvi, 58, 163–64, 165; and the "orphan complex," 164–65; and Puritan history, xvii, xxvii, 63. *See also* Mexican American writers

Chicanos/as: and cultural identity, 7, 9, 61, 176–77; and working-class experience, xxii, 122, 128, 144–45, 162

Christianity, 173–75, 179–82, 196

Cisneros, Sandra, xxi, 28, 80; *House on Mango Street*, 43, 44

citizenship, 121, 123, 126, 127, 131, 158, 188; Anglo Puritan model of, xviii; and education, 157, 158

"City on a Hill," 43, 50, 62

Civil Rights Movement, 7, 44, 58, 59, 60, 139, 162, 167, 206

Civil War. *See* United States Civil War

colonialism, xvi, xvii, xxiv–xxv, 5, 58, 70–71, 106, 108, 117, 194; cultures of, 99, 102, 105; Mexican, 10, 35, 87, 153, 154–55; Spanish, 10, 153, 154–55

comparative approach. *See* American literature: approaches to

Cooper, James Fenimore, 44

Corpi, Lucha, 3; *Eulogy for a Brown Angel*, 3, 4, 41

corrido, 141–42, 144

Cortés, Hernando, 176

Cortez, Gregorio, 163

Cotera, María, 154

Crawford, John F., 185

cultural nationalism. *See* Chicano/a cultural nationalism

culture wars, xviii, 45–46

cummings, e. e., 192

curriculum. *See* education, higher: curriculum of

Dana, Richard Henry, 103

Davis, Jefferson, 93, 109, 110

Davis, Varina (Mrs. Jefferson Davis), 93, 109

De la Fuente, Patricia, 193

Delano, California. *See* United Farm Workers

De Prospo, R. C., 66–69, 70, 168

De Voto, Bernard, 138

Díaz, Porfirio, 145, 146

Dickinson, Emily, 203

displacement, poetics of, xv, 191, 194, 195

Dobie, J. Frank, 154

Douglass, Frederick, xx

DuBois, W. E. B., 46, 49

Early Americanists, xix, 168

Early American literature, xxii–xxiii, 66–67, 69, 71, 168

education, higher, 69, 134, 135, 156, 157, 158, 165, 166, 206; at Brown University, 206; at Harvard University, 46, 134, 135, 138; at Yale University, 205, 206; curriculum of, xvi, xxvii, 44, 57, 70–71; demonization of, 35, 45

Edwards, Jonathan, 44, 169, 205

Eliot, T. S., 50, 145, 193–94

Elliot, William Yandall, 137

"El Plan Espiritual de Aztlán," 12, 14, 20, 34. *See also* Aztlán, myth of

Emerson, Ralph Waldo, 51, 55, 127, 131–32, 168, 169

Erkkila, Betsy, xix–xx

Escobar, Edward J., 3

ethnic studies, xx, xxiv, 60

feminism. *See* Chicana feminism
Fernández, Roberta, 20, 21
fictional autobiography, 156, 158
Fiedler, Leslie, 138
Fitzhugh, Claggett D., 115–16
Fourth of July, xv, 143
Fregoso, Rosa Linda, 5, 9, 12, 76

García, Ignacio M., 20–21
Garcia, Mario T., 102
gender, 155, 182, 186, 188, 189, 195, 196,
    197, 200–201
genre, 167–68. *See also* "auto-
    American-biography"; Chicano/a
    literature: autobiography; fictional
    autobiography; jeremiad
Gómez-Quiñones, Juan, 14, 17–20, 21,
    22, 102, 161
Gone with the Wind (Mitchell), 153
Gonzales-Berry, Erlinda, 75–76, 79
González, Jovita, 153–56; *Caballero*,
    153–56; *Dew on the Thorn*, 153. *See also*
    Raleigh, Eve
Gonzalez, Rodolfo "Corky," 14, 61
grape boycott. *See* United Farm
    Workers
Great Depression, xviii, 50, 122, 134,
    158, 161
Great Migration, 132, 133, 140. *See also*
    immigration
Griswold del Castillo, Richard, 102
Guerin-Gonzales, Camille, 123, 124–
    26, 127, 128, 148, 156, 157
Gutiérrez, David, 5, 123, 127–29, 142,
    143, 150
Gutiérrez, Ramón, 5; *When Jesus Came,
    the Corn Mothers Went Away*, 105
Gutiérrez-Jones, Carl, 5

H.D., 192
Halleck, Henry Wager, 92–93

Hammond, Jeffrey, 180, 182
Handlin, Oscar, 139
Harte, Bret, 97, 132
Hawthorne, Nathaniel, 44, 51, 127, 132,
    165
Heath Anthology of American Literature, 67
Hemingway, Ernest, 165
Hernández, Deluvina, 14–16, 22
Hinojosa, Rolando, 150, 203
Horton, Alonzo E., 84
Huerta, Dolores, 163
Hughes, Langston, 46–47, 49
Hughes, Walter, 181
Hurston, Zora Neale, xxi
Hutchinson, Anne, 182, 201

immigrants: Asian, 134; ideal, 112, 124,
    131, 134, 140; Mexican, 134, 142, 146,
    147, 148, 149, 150, 153, 158
immigration, 121, 122, 127, 129, 133–
    34, 140, 142–43, 206. *See also* Great
    Migration
immigration laws, 133, 140
indios, 145. *See also* Aztecs; Mayans;
    Native Americans
Iowa Writers' Workshop, 192
Irving, Washington, 44

Jacobs, Harriet, xx
Jamul Ranch, 93, 94–95, 97
Jaramillo, Cleofas, 154
Jeffers, Robinson, 163
Jefferson, Thomas, 184
jeremiad, 168, 178, 179, 180, 184–85,
    186, 189, 191
Johnson, Lyndon B., 162

Kanellos, Nicolás, 5, 74–75, 114, 147,
    148
Kennedy, President John F., 161–62,
    163, 203

Kibbey, Anne, 184
King, Martin Luther, Jr., 184
Kolodny, Annette, xix, 52, 70, 75, 80

L.A.P.D. *See* Los Angeles Police Department
labor, 121, 122, 128
landscape, 11, 172–73, 174
La Raza Unida Party, 7
Lauter, Paul, xix, xx, 72, 80
Levin, David, "Perry Miller at Harvard," 135–37, 138
Levine, Philip, 163, 192
Limerick, Patricia, 6
Limón, José, 5
Lincoln, President Abraham, 93, 96, 109, 114–15
Lincoln, First Lady Mary Todd, 93, 109, 115
Lippincott, J. B., 96, 115
literary binationalism, xxiii, 167, 203
literary history, 69–70. *See also* American literary history; Chicano/a literature: history of
Literary History of the United States (LHUS), 51, 52, 53–57, 135
literary nationalism. *See* American literary nationalism
literary origins. *See* origins myths
Los Angeles Police Department, 3, 4
Lowell, Robert, 163, 192
Luna de Rodríguez, Celia, 163

MacLeish, Archibald, 135
Maid of Monterey, 88–89, 104. *See also* Ruiz de Burton, María Amparo
Manifest Destiny, xviii, xxii, xxiv, 99, 106, 108, 111, 117, 172
Marx, Leo, 138
Marxist scholarship, 13, 14–15, 22
masculinity, 186, 191, 200

Mather, Cotton, 44, 48, 173–74, 176; *Magnalia Christi Americana*, 169, 170, 174–75
Mather, Increase, 133
Mather, Richard, 133
Matthiessen, F. O., xviii, 65, 135, 137, 138; *American Renaissance*, 50–51
Mayans, 61. *See also* indios
Melendez, A. Gabriel, 141
Melville, Herman, 51, 55, 127, 165
Mena, María Cristina, 145–47, 156
Menchaca, Martha, 5
Mencken, H. L., 132
mestiza consciousness, 33, 34, 35
mestizo/a, 24, 29, 83, 85, 145, 170, 177, 179
Mexican American literature, xvi, xxii–xxiii; by women, 141, 166. *See also* Chicano/a literature
Mexican Americans, voting power of, 161–62
Mexican American soldiers, 104, 123. *See also* soldiers of color
Mexican–American War, xxv, 12, 84, 85, 88, 98–99, 104, 108, 153, 171
Mexican American writers, xvi, 58, 87–88, 160, 167. *See also* Chicano/a writers
Mexican characters, 145, 147
Mexican–Indian characters, 145, 147
Mexican Revolution, 121, 122, 145, 146, 157, 158
migrant workers, xv, 148, 157, 165, 192, 205–6
Miller, Perry, 52, 133, 135–38, 170; *The New England Mind: The Seventeenth Century*, 50
modernism, xviii; aesthetics of, 50
modernists, 192, 193–94
Monterey, California, 89, 99, 100, 103, 109, 141

Moore, Marianne, 192

Mora, Pat, 166–67, 170–73; *Chants*, 171, 172–73, 175–78, 179

Moraga, Cherríe, 28, 32, 37–38; *Loving in the War Years: Lo que nunca pasó por sus labios*, 24–25, 29

Moreno, Hector, 198, 200, 201

Morgan, Edmund S., 56–57; *The Puritan Dilemma: The Story of John Winthrop*, 139, 140. *See also* Winthrop, John

Morison, Samuel Eliot, 136, 137

Morse, E. W., 84, 107

Morse, Mary C. *See* Walker, Mary C.

multiculturalism: and the curriculum, 44, 70–71; debates, xx, xxvii, 45; discourse of, xvi; presentist concerns of, 67

Muñoz, Rosalío, 163

Murdock, Kenneth, 138

National Chicano Moratorium, xxii, 3, 9

Native Americans, 83, 84, 119, 159, 173, 176. *See also* American Indian Movement; indios

Neate, Wilson, 32–33

New American Studies, 6. *See also* American Studies

New England, xix, 50, 71, 111, 117, 120, 169, 192, 205; canonical stature of, xviii; history of, xvii; moral authority, 112–13; power of, 107, 108. *See also* Puritan myth of origins

New Historicism, 70, 78

New Western History, 6, 86, 98

Niggli, Josephina, 160

Nunis, Doyce B., Jr., 99

origins myths, xvi, xix, 45, 47, 58, 69, 107. *See also* Aztlán, myth of; Puritan myth of origins

"orphan complex," 164–65

Ortego, Philip D., 59–60

Otero, Miguel Antonio, Jr., 13, 160

Otero Warren, Nina, 154

Overland Monthly, 97

Padilla, Genaro, 5, 85, 141, 164–65

Paredes, Américo, xxi, 141, 150–53, 156, 163, 205; *George Washington Gomez: A Mexicotexan Novel*, 151–53; *The Shadow*, 152–53

Partridge, Alden, 110

Partridge, Almira. *See* Burton, Almira

patriarchal violence. *See* violence, patriarchal

Paz, Octavio, 164

Pease, Donald, xvi, 6

Pedrorena, Miguel, 118

Pérez, Emma, 5

Perez, Luis, 156; *El Coyote: The Rebel*, 156–58

Pérez-Torres, Rafael, 36, 38

Pico, Pío, 93, 95, 119

Pita, Beatrice, 87, 90

Poe, Edgar Allen, 44, 132

poetry. *See* Chicano/a literature: poetry, protest

Polk, President James K., 91, 99

Puritan culture, xviii, 57, 123, 178, 184, 191, 192, 200

Puritan history, xvi, xviii, 113, 139, 140, 200

Puritan myth of origins, xxvi–xxvii, 46–50, 52–53, 55–56, 58–60, 80, 86, 124, 132, 167, 203, 205; as hegemonic discourse, 55, 170; resistance to, xix, 62, 64–65, 66–69

Puritan Studies, 50, 68, 122, 133, 167

Puritan writers, xvii, xviii, 46, 51; compared to Chicano/a writers, xvi, 58, 163–64, 165

Raleigh, Eve, 153. *See also* González, Jovita
Rebolledo, Tey Diana, 30, 141
Recovering the U.S. Hispanic Literary Heritage, 35, 73–77, 79, 80, 88, 98, 105, 106
refugees, Mexican, 98–101, 102–5, 121
"resistance theory" paradigm. *See* American literature: approaches to
Ríos, Alberto, 166, 203
Rivera, Tomás, xv, xvi, 150, 164, 165–66, 205–6
Rodriguez, Richard, 32; and Chicano/a Studies, 25–28; *Hunger of Memory*, 24
Rosaldo, Renato, 5
Ruiz, Federico, 92, 118
Ruiz, Doña Isabel, 91, 118
Ruiz, Don José Manuel, 90
Ruiz, Manuela, 92, 118
Ruiz de Burton, María Amparo, xxv, 84–85, 87, 88–99, 104, 105, 107–9, 110–11, 113, 116–18, 120; *The Squatter and the Don*, 84, 97, 185; *Who Would Have Thought It?*, xxv, 85, 96, 107–9, 111–15

St. Patrick's Battalion, 104
Salazar, Rubén, 3
Saldívar, José David, xvi, 5, 205
Saldívar, Ramón, 5, 63, 65, 158, 159; *Chicano Narrative: The Dialectics of Difference*, 24, 31–32, 33
Sánchez, Rosaura, 5, 25, 76, 85, 86, 87, 90, 141
San Diego, California, 83–84, 92, 93, 107, 119, 120
Sandoval, Chela, 5
Saragoza, Alex M., 102
separatism, xviii, xix, xxi, 29, 64, 77, 79, 102
Shipton, Ted, 56–57

skin color, 10, 27, 28, 144, 200. *See also* body
slavery, xx, 107, 108, 116
Smith, Elizabeth Ferguson, 109
soldiers of color, 138. *See also* Mexican American soldiers
Soto, Gary, xxi, 163, 166, 168, 191–93, 194–96, 198, 199–200, 201–3; "Black Hair," 195–96, 197, 199–200
Southwest United States, xviii, 11, 40, 159
Spanish–American War, 83, 123
Spiller, Robert. *See Literary History of the United States (LHUS)*
stereotypes, 146, 147
Stevens, Wallace, 192
Stowe, Harriet Beecher, xx, 107
subaltern, 85, 86, 87, 108

Tatum, Charles, 75–76, 79
Taylor, Edward, 168, 169, 191, 193, 194–95, 196–97, 199–201, 203; "Huswifery," 196, 199
Teatro Campesino, 8. *See also* theater, Spanish language
Thanksgiving, xvi, 45, 107, 108–9, 116
theater, Spanish language, 141. *See also* Teatro Campesino
Thoreau, Henry David, 55, 127, 184
Torres, Hector A., 32
Tortilla Curtain, 172
Treaty of Cordoba, 90
Treaty of Guadalupe Hidalgo, xxiv, 6, 32, 85, 90, 91, 96, 98, 100, 123, 155
Twain, Mark, 132
Tyler, Moses Coit, 131, 132

Ulrich, Laurel, 196
United Farm Workers (UFW), xxii, 7, 58, 162, 192. *See also* Chávez, Cesar
United States Border Patrol, 134, 149

United States Civil War, 107, 108, 110, 111, 114–15, 117, 123

United States–Mexico border, xvi, 33–34, 128, 144, 152

"usable past," xxiv, xxvi, 13, 36, 40, 86, 154

Valdez, Luis, 8, 9, 163

Vallejo, Guadalupe, 105

Vanderbilt, Kermit, 52–54, 55–56, 135

Venegas, Daniel, 147–49, 152; *Las Aventuras de Don Chipote: O, cuando los pericos mamen*, 147, 148–49, 157

Verduin, Kathleen, 181, 182

Vietnam War, 3, 9, 58, 167

Villareal, José Antonio, 158–60; *Pocho*, 158

Villegas de Magnón, Leonor, 160

violence, patriarchal, 178, 179, 186–88

Viva Kennedy Clubs, 161, 162

voting power. *See* Mexican Americans, voting power of

Walker, Mary C. (Mrs. E. W. Morse), 83–85, 119

Watson, Samuel J., 103, 104

Weber, David, 102

white ethnics, 126, 127, 129, 130–31, 137–38, 144, 162, 172

"whiteness," 5, 137

Whitman, Walt, 55, 127, 165, 166, 194

Whittier, John Greenleaf, 112

Wigglesworth, Michael, 178, 185, 189, 191; *Day of Doom*, 178–84; *God's Controversy with New England*, 180–81

Williams, William Carlos, 192, 194

Williston, E[benezer] B[ancroft], 110, 111

Winthrop, John, 139, 173–74, 176, 203, 205, 206; *A Model of Christian Charity*, 43, 50. *See also* Morgan, Edmund S.

Wong, Sau-ling Cynthia, 77–79, 80, 168

Yezierska, Anzia, 146

Zamora, Bernice, 163

Zapata, Emiliano, 13

Zavella, Patricia, 5

Zoot Suit Riots, 159

Zukofsky, Louis, 192

About the Author

José F. Aranda, Jr., is an associate professor of Chicano/a and American literature in the Department of English at Rice University. He received his Ph.D. from Brown University. Professor Aranda has written articles on early U.S. criticism, nineteenth-century Mexican American literature, and the future of Chicano/a studies, and most recently he investigated the relationship between modernism and Mexican American literature. He has also begun work on his next book, tentatively entitled *Why I Dreamed of Jeannie but Became a Chicano Instead.* This book is a critical exploration of television, popular culture, the Vietnam War, and the news media and the roles they played in shaping the political and cultural identities of the first generation of Mexican American children to be hailed by the Chicano Movement. Finally, he is also at work on a long-term project to write the cultural biography of nineteenth-century Californio writer María Amparo Ruiz de Burton. He teaches courses in Chicano/a literature, Asian American fiction, and nineteenth- and twentieth-century U.S. literature.

Nationally, he sits on the board of Recovering the U.S. Hispanic Literary Heritage Project. He has been appointed by the MLA Executive Council to the Committee on the Literatures of People of Color for a three-year term. He is also an active member of the MLA Chicana and Chicano Literature Division. In Houston, he is a board member of three literary arts organizations, Inprint, Nuestra, and Nuestra Palabra. He is married to Krista Comer, professor of American and Women's Studies in the Rice English department. They have two boys, Benito and Jesse Aranda-Comer.